CLIFFS

VERBAL REVIEW

for

STANDARDIZED TESTS

by

William A. Covino, Ph.D.
Peter Z Orton, M.Ed.

WILEY
Wiley Publishing, Inc.

Author's Acknowledgements

My loving thanks to my wife Camille, for her encouragement, and for putting up with the clutter and lost weekends. To my sons Christopher and Nicholas, I'm grateful for the delightful interruptions.

     Bill Covino

My sincerest thanks to my parents, William and Esta Orton, for their continued love and support through the years.

     Peter Z Orton

The authors would also like to thank Michele Spence of Cliffs Notes for final editing and careful attention to the production process.

Cliffs Verbal Review for Standardized Tests

Published by:
Wiley Publishing, Inc.
909 Third Avenue
New York, NY 10022
www.wiley.com

Copyright © 1986 by Wiley Publishing, Inc.

Published by Wiley Publishing, Inc., New York, NY
Published simultaneously in Canada

ISBN: 0-8220-2034-3

Printed in the United States of America

10 9 8 7

1O/RZ/QV/QT/IN

CONTENTS

PART I: INTRODUCTION

PART II: GRAMMAR AND USAGE

PART III: WRITING TIMED ESSAYS

PART IV: VERBAL ABILITY

PART V: READING COMPREHENSION

Part I: Introduction

WHY YOU NEED THIS GUIDE

Are you planning to take the . . .

GMAT   GRE   SAT   ACT   NTE

LSAT   CBEST   PSAT   PPST

State Teacher Competency and Credentialing Exam

Education Program Entry Exam

College Entrance or Advance Placement Exam

If one of these tests is in your future, then this guide will be invaluable to you. **Verbal Review for Standardized Tests** is designed specifically to review, refresh, and reintroduce essential grammar and verbal abilities skills. It focuses directly on test-oriented question types.

This guide is much more than simply a grammar or verbal review book. It is clear, concise, and easy to use, and its focus by test preparation experts gives insight into the types of questions you'll face on your exam. It demonstrates how to avoid the common and costly errors that will trap those unprepared for the kinds of questions that the test makers ask. Our unique approach will not only review the essential basic skills but also show you how to apply them EFFECTIVELY AND SPECIFICALLY ON STANDARDIZED TESTS. Throughout the guide, the language will be nontechnical but consistent with the terminology and conventions you need to know for standardized verbal-skills tests.

WHAT THIS GUIDE CONTAINS

Verbal Review for Standardized Tests provides an excellent and extensive overview of the areas of concern for most test takers:

- Grammar and Usage Review
- English Usage and Sentence Correction Questions
- Timed Essay Writing
- Verbal Ability Questions—Antonyms, Analogies, and Sentence Completion

- Reading Comprehension Questions
- Strategies for Each Question Type
- Practice Exercises with Hundreds of Questions and Complete Explanations

If you're taking the GMAT, GRE, SAT, ACT, CBEST, NTE, LSAT, PPST, PSAT, or any other exam with a grammar or verbal section, this book was designed for YOU!

TYPES OF QUESTIONS

The following chart will indicate the types of questions that appear on some of the most widely used exams.

	Sentence Correction	Usage	Usage*	Essay	Verbal Ability**	Reading Comprehension
GMAT	✓					✓
GRE					✓	✓
SAT	✓***	✓***			✓	✓
ACT			✓			✓
LSAT			✓			✓
CBEST			✓			✓
PPST	✓	✓	✓			✓
PSAT					✓	✓
NTE	✓	✓				✓

*ACT Type
**Antonyms, Analogies, and Sentence Completion
***Appear on Test of Standard Written English given with the SAT

NOTE: Most state-produced teacher entry, competency, and credentialing exams have verbal sections that include timed essay writing, reading comprehension, and a type of grammar and verbal skills question. See the bulletin for your exam to determine the specific grammar/verbal skills question type.

RANGE OF DIFFICULTY

The range of difficulty of question types varies significantly for each of the grammar, essay, verbal, and reading comprehension areas of the various tests. Typically, all questions on the LSAT, GMAT, and GRE will be more difficult than the similar questions on the NTE, CBEST, SAT, ACT, teacher exams, etc.

A GENERAL GUIDELINE

Before you start Part II of this book, use the following chart to note the chapters containing material specific to certain exams.

PART II: Grammar and Usage Review—Use for ALL exams containing verbal sections (with the exception of the GRE and PSAT). You will also find this material very helpful for all essay writing.

Usage and Sentence Correction—GMAT, SAT, ACT, NTE, CBEST, PPST, and other grammar exams.

PART III: Writing Timed Essays—LSAT, CBEST, PPST and other essay exams.

PART IV: Verbal Ability—GRE, SAT, PSAT and other verbal ability exams.

PART V: Reading Comprehension—GMAT, LSAT, GRE, SAT, ACT, PSAT, CBEST, NTE, PPST and other reading comprehension exams.

NOTE: As mentioned above, the Grammar and Usage Review should be thoroughly studied by candidates for ALL verbal-skills exam sections (except GRE and PSAT). Regardless of the specific question type in your exam, practice in all question types is very beneficial because many question types test for precisely the same knowledge, but in varying formats. Reviewing all the verbal skills presented here will enhance your performance on any verbal-skills exam by sharpening your overall basic verbal ability.

HOW TO USE THIS GUIDE

1. Review the materials concerning your test provided by the testing company. This information is usually available at no charge and will detail the areas and question types for your particular exam.
2. Take the diagnostic test at the beginning of Part II: Grammar and Usage. Note any area of particular difficulty.
3. Study the Grammar and Usage Review in its entirety, concentrating particularly on those areas that gave you difficulty in the Diagnostic Test. Complete each of the exercises in this section to be sure that you've thoroughly understood each concept.
4. Based on the information in your test bulletin and on the chart of question types on page 4 of this book, determine which sections pertain to your specific exam.
5. Thoroughly study the strategy sections for each of those question types.
6. Work all the practice sections for your question types, breaking the work into shorter timed study sessions. The test bulletin will tell you how many questions you will be expected to answer in a given time period. Base the length of your work sessions on these requirements. You will find it helpful to allow yourself slightly *less* time than you will have on the actual exam.
7. If time permits, be sure to work through those strategy and practice sessions that are not specific to your exam as well. You will find that this practice will "fine-tune" your verbal skills.

Part II: Grammar and Usage

- English Usage and Sentence Correction Question Types
- Diagnostic Test
- Grammar and Usage Review
- English Usage and Sentence Correction Practice

GRAMMAR AND USAGE

This section deals with questions of grammar and usage that are likely to be tested on most standardized exams. A brief description of the three major English usage and sentence correction question types you will encounter in these tests follows. Even if a specific question type does not appear on your exam, you should review *all* of this section thoroughly, as it *deals with material that is tested in virtually every standardized test containing verbal sections,* though the form of a question may vary. (Note that the GRE and PSAT are exceptions.)

After reading the following section, be sure to take the Diagnostic Test to find those areas which are difficult for you. To be sure of the best test preparation possible, you should read the entire Grammar and Usage Review which follows and do all of the exercises. This review focuses on areas that are most commonly tested. The results of the Diagnostic Test will guide you in choosing which areas to concentrate on.

Finish your review by working the practice sections and by reading the answers carefully.

ENGLISH USAGE AND SENTENCE CORRECTION QUESTION TYPES

ENGLISH USAGE—TYPE 1

Directions

English usage questions test your ability to identify errors of standard written English as they appear in sentences. Each sentence may contain one error in grammar, usage, idiom, or diction (word choice). You are to mark the letter (A, B, C, or D) of the part of the sentence which is incorrect. If no part of the sentence is incorrect, mark letter (E). This type of question appears on exams such as the Graduate Management Admissions Test (GMAT) and the Test of Standard Written English on the Scholastic Aptitude Test (SAT).

9

Analysis

It is important to remember that you are looking for errors in standard *written* English, not conversational English, and that the parts not underlined in the sentence are correct. *Thus you must use the nonunderlined parts to help you determine which underlined part may be wrong.* For example:

1. Each boy in the third and <u>fourth</u> sections <u>of the class</u>
                                  A   B

    gave <u>their</u> reasons <u>for liking</u> sports. <u>No error.</u>
           C   D   E

Note that *Each boy* is not underlined, so the subject of the sentence is singular. Therefore, *their* is incorrect. It should be *his* to agree with the singular subject. The incorrect part of the sentence is (C).

Other agreement errors in standard written English may include *subject–verb errors* such as:

2. The <u>wandering</u> pack of dogs, first <u>seen</u> by the citizens many
         A   B

    years ago, <u>were</u> feared by all <u>who</u> lived in the town. <u>No error.</u>
                 C   D   E

Here, since the subject of the sentence is *pack* (singular), the verb must also be singular, *was*. The incorrect part of this sentence is (C).

Other errors may include *faulty parallelism:*

3. Ernie's diligence <u>in studying every night</u> allowed him to
                        A

    score <u>high grades,</u> to gain the respect <u>of his peers,</u>
            B   C

    and <u>admission</u> to college. <u>No error.</u>
          D   E

The final part of the series is not in the same form as the first two parts. It should be something like *to earn admission* or *to win admission,* so that it parallels the form of the other items—*to score* and *to gain.* Choice (D) should be chosen.

You may also find an error in *idiom* (nonstandard usage):

4. <u>Compromising over</u> a number of delicate issues, the members
         A

   <u>of the school board</u> <u>successfully</u> resolved <u>their</u> problems.
        B   C   D

   <u>No error.</u>
     E

The expression *compromising over* is unidiomatic. It should be *compromising on*. Part (A) is not correct standard written English and therefore is the correct answer.

Many other types of usage errors will appear in this question type. You will find them explained in the Grammar and Usage Review which follows the Diagnostic Test.

ENGLISH USAGE–TYPE 2

Directions

Another sort of English usage question appears on tests such as the American College Testing exam (ACT). This type prints complete paragraphs and requires you to determine if part of a sentence is incorrect and then to correct it, if necessary, by choosing from among several choices. If the underlined part is correct and makes sense with the rest of the passage, choose the answer that says "NO CHANGE."

Analysis

You should assume that any part of the passage not underlined is correct and that the requirements are of *standard written English, not conversational English*. For example:

Furthering one's goals may require
more effort than one had originally
intended. However, a man may underestimate <u>their</u> capacity for work when
  1
setting out to accomplish some task.

    1.A. NO CHANGE
      B. its
      C. ones'
      D. his

Since the subject of the second sentence is *a man* (singular), *their* (plural) is incorrect. The pronoun must be singular to agree with *man*. Choice (D) properly corrects the error.

Punctuation may also need to be corrected. For example:

When packing for a hiking trip, you should insure that the following items are included in your <u>backpack; insect</u> <center>2</center>spray, a good compass, a map, and a bottle of water.	2.F. NO CHANGE G. backpack, insect H. backpack: insect J. backpack. Insect

The correct punctuation preceeding a list is a colon. Therefore choice (H) is correct.

Many other kinds of usage errors will appear in this question type, and they are included in the Grammar and Usage Review.

SENTENCE CORRECTION

Directions

This is a third form of question testing your knowledge of standard written English. In this question type, you must choose the best of five different versions of a sentence. If the original sentence most fully meets the requirements of correct and effective English, choice (A), which repeats the underlined portion exactly, is correct. If the underlined part is incorrect, awkward, or ambiguous, you must pick the version that best corrects it and retains the meaning of the originally underlined phrase. Again, you must assume that any part of the sentence not underlined is correct and cannot be changed.

Analysis

An example:

1. The rigors of high office often demand <u>stamina, persistence, and having great patience.</u>
   (A) stamina, persistence, and having great patience.
   (B) stamina, persistence, and great patience.
   (C) that a person has stamina, persistence, and patience.
   (D) having stamina, persistence, and having great patience.
   (E) having stamina, being persistent, and having patience.

The correct answer is (B). The underlined part contains *faulty parallelism*. The last item in the series should not be preceeded by *having* but should be in the same form as *stamina* and *persistence*. By omitting the word *great,* choices (C) and (E) slightly change the meaning of the original and also have errors of parallelism.

Another example:

2. Rushing to avoid being late, <u>Bill's head collided with the cabinet door which was open.</u>
   (A) Bill's head collided with the cabinet door which was open.
   (B) Bill's head hit the open cabinet door.
   (C) Bill's head collided with the open cabinet door.
   (D) Bill hit his head on the open cabinet door.
   (E) Bill hit the cabinet door, having been opened.

The correct answer is choice (D). The sentence begins with an *-ing* phrase, which modifies what immediately follows the comma. In the original, *Bill's head* follows the modifying phrase. Was Bill's head doing the rushing? Certainly not. The sentence should read, *Rushing to avoid being late, Bill hit his head ... Bill* should follow the modifying phrase because he, not his head, was doing the rushing.

In the Grammar and Usage Review following the Diagnostic Test, you will find other kinds of errors of grammar, sentence structure, usage, or diction that appear in the sentence correction tests.

ANSWER SHEET FOR THE DIAGNOSTIC TEST
(Remove This Sheet and Use It to Mark Your Answers)

PART I: ENGLISH USAGE	PART II: SENTENCE CORRECTION	PART III: ENGLISH USAGE

PART III: ENGLISH USAGE
Passage I

PART I: ENGLISH USAGE

1 Ⓐ Ⓑ Ⓒ Ⓓ Ⓔ
2 Ⓐ Ⓑ Ⓒ Ⓓ Ⓔ
3 Ⓐ Ⓑ Ⓒ Ⓓ Ⓔ
4 Ⓐ Ⓑ Ⓒ Ⓓ Ⓔ
5 Ⓐ Ⓑ Ⓒ Ⓓ Ⓔ

6 Ⓐ Ⓑ Ⓒ Ⓓ Ⓔ
7 Ⓐ Ⓑ Ⓒ Ⓓ Ⓔ
8 Ⓐ Ⓑ Ⓒ Ⓓ Ⓔ
9 Ⓐ Ⓑ Ⓒ Ⓓ Ⓔ
10 Ⓐ Ⓑ Ⓒ Ⓓ Ⓔ

11 Ⓐ Ⓑ Ⓒ Ⓓ Ⓔ
12 Ⓐ Ⓑ Ⓒ Ⓓ Ⓔ
13 Ⓐ Ⓑ Ⓒ Ⓓ Ⓔ
14 Ⓐ Ⓑ Ⓒ Ⓓ Ⓔ
15 Ⓐ Ⓑ Ⓒ Ⓓ Ⓔ

16 Ⓐ Ⓑ Ⓒ Ⓓ Ⓔ
17 Ⓐ Ⓑ Ⓒ Ⓓ Ⓔ
18 Ⓐ Ⓑ Ⓒ Ⓓ Ⓔ
19 Ⓐ Ⓑ Ⓒ Ⓓ Ⓔ
20 Ⓐ Ⓑ Ⓒ Ⓓ Ⓔ

PART II: SENTENCE CORRECTION

1 Ⓐ Ⓑ Ⓒ Ⓓ Ⓔ
2 Ⓐ Ⓑ Ⓒ Ⓓ Ⓔ
3 Ⓐ Ⓑ Ⓒ Ⓓ Ⓔ
4 Ⓐ Ⓑ Ⓒ Ⓓ Ⓔ
5 Ⓐ Ⓑ Ⓒ Ⓓ Ⓔ

6 Ⓐ Ⓑ Ⓒ Ⓓ Ⓔ
7 Ⓐ Ⓑ Ⓒ Ⓓ Ⓔ
8 Ⓐ Ⓑ Ⓒ Ⓓ Ⓔ
9 Ⓐ Ⓑ Ⓒ Ⓓ Ⓔ
10 Ⓐ Ⓑ Ⓒ Ⓓ Ⓔ

11 Ⓐ Ⓑ Ⓒ Ⓓ Ⓔ
12 Ⓐ Ⓑ Ⓒ Ⓓ Ⓔ
13 Ⓐ Ⓑ Ⓒ Ⓓ Ⓔ
14 Ⓐ Ⓑ Ⓒ Ⓓ Ⓔ
15 Ⓐ Ⓑ Ⓒ Ⓓ Ⓔ

16 Ⓐ Ⓑ Ⓒ Ⓓ Ⓔ
17 Ⓐ Ⓑ Ⓒ Ⓓ Ⓔ
18 Ⓐ Ⓑ Ⓒ Ⓓ Ⓔ
19 Ⓐ Ⓑ Ⓒ Ⓓ Ⓔ
20 Ⓐ Ⓑ Ⓒ Ⓓ Ⓔ

Passage I

1 Ⓐ Ⓑ Ⓒ Ⓓ
2 Ⓕ Ⓖ Ⓗ Ⓙ
3 Ⓐ Ⓑ Ⓒ Ⓓ
4 Ⓕ Ⓖ Ⓗ Ⓙ
5 Ⓐ Ⓑ Ⓒ Ⓓ
6 Ⓕ Ⓖ Ⓗ Ⓙ
7 Ⓐ Ⓑ Ⓒ Ⓓ
8 Ⓕ Ⓖ Ⓗ Ⓙ
9 Ⓐ Ⓑ Ⓒ Ⓓ

Passage II

10 Ⓐ Ⓑ Ⓒ Ⓓ
11 Ⓕ Ⓖ Ⓗ Ⓙ
12 Ⓐ Ⓑ Ⓒ Ⓓ
13 Ⓕ Ⓖ Ⓗ Ⓙ
14 Ⓐ Ⓑ Ⓒ Ⓓ
15 Ⓕ Ⓖ Ⓗ Ⓙ
16 Ⓐ Ⓑ Ⓒ Ⓓ
17 Ⓕ Ⓖ Ⓗ Ⓙ

Passage III

18 Ⓐ Ⓑ Ⓒ Ⓓ
19 Ⓕ Ⓖ Ⓗ Ⓙ
20 Ⓐ Ⓑ Ⓒ Ⓓ
21 Ⓕ Ⓖ Ⓗ Ⓙ
22 Ⓐ Ⓑ Ⓒ Ⓓ
23 Ⓕ Ⓖ Ⓗ Ⓙ
24 Ⓐ Ⓑ Ⓒ Ⓓ
25 Ⓕ Ⓖ Ⓗ Ⓙ

CUT HERE

15

DIAGNOSTIC TEST

PART I: ENGLISH USAGE

DIRECTIONS

Some of the following sentences are correct. Others contain problems in grammar, usage, idiom, or diction (word choice). There is not more than one error in any sentence.

If there is an error, it will be underlined and lettered. Find the one underlined part that must be changed to make the sentence correct, and choose the corresponding letter on your answer sheet. Mark (E) if the sentence contains no error.

1. The mayor <u>continually</u> asserted that one of the crucial strengths

              A

of the political system <u>is</u> each <u>individual</u> having the right to

                   B   C

determine which way <u>he or she</u> will vote. <u>No error.</u>

                D   E

2. The concept of hypocrisy <u>applies</u> to morals; a person should

                  A

be good and <u>not merely</u> seem <u>so</u>, and a bad person

            B   C

<u>is little mended</u> by pretense of goodness. <u>No error.</u>

      D   E

3. We should support those proposals for increasing

or <u>redistributing</u> tax money <u>that</u> <u>will raise</u> the per pupil

    A   B   C

expenditure in our cities and <u>equalize them</u> throughout the

                              D

public school system. <u>No error.</u>

                    E

4. <u>Like Faulkner,</u> Porter's short stories <u>give</u> the reader a vivid

   A   B

sense of what life in New Orleans <u>must have been</u> <u>like</u> in the

                             C   D

twenties and thirties. <u>No error.</u>

                    E

5. His intention was not to establish a new sect or in any way
                                                        A
   to decrease the power of Canterbury but in hope of making
        B   C
   the bishops cut back their lavish outlay of church funds.
                                      D
   No error.
     E

6. Despite his poor start, Williams is the player whom I think
      A   B
   is most likely to win the batting crown. No error.
   C   D   E

7. Most all the instruments in the orchestra are tuned just
      A   B   C
   before the concert begins; the piano, of course, is an
                                          D
   exception. No error.
               E

8. The fall in wheat prices, together with a decline in the demands
        A
   for beef, have effected a significant drop in the value of
             B   C   D
   Swenson Company stock. No error.
                           E

9. The number of Irish immigrants in Boston was larger
       A   B
   than Italian or Scottish, but it was not until 1900 that
        C
   Boston's first Irish mayor was elected. No error.
                              D   E

10. The trustees of the fund which determine the awarding of the
                              A   B
    grants are expected to meet in New York, not Washington.
           C   D
    No error.
      E

11. The increasing number of predators that carry infectious
                          A   B
    diseases to the herds of zebra and gnu are a serious concern
             C   D
    of park rangers. No error.
                      E

12. The humor of the fable on which these questions are based
                          A   B
    derive from a logical problem relating to the drawing of
    C   D
    conclusions from evidence. No error.
                               E

13. Everybody stationed at the American embassy in Moscow
    have been affected in some way by the radio waves, but there is
     A   B
    not yet any certainty about just what the effects have been.
                              C   D
    No error.
    E

14. The speaker discussed the difficulty of finding a single job
                                                    A
    that combines financial security, creativity, personal growth,
    B
    and opportunities to help others and effect social change.
            C   D
    No error.
    E

15. Unaffected by neither hunger nor cold, Scott covered up to
                  A
    twenty miles on each of the days that the weather
                                      B
    permitted him to travel at all. No error.
    C   D   E

16. Among the pleasures of the film is the subtle performance by
                       A   B
    W. C. Fields and the more boisterous antics of the youthful
                        C   D
    Mae West. No error.
              E

17. I had no sooner picked up my spoon <u>to begin my soup</u> <u>when</u> the
                                              A   B
waiter <u>descended on</u> me with <u>my</u> salad, main course, and coffee.
              C   D
<u>No error.</u>
    E

18. Hoping <u>to lie</u> as close <u>to</u> the water as possible, I <u>laid</u> my
                A   B   C
towel on the sand, unpacked my sun lotion, and <u>settled down for</u>
                                                        D
the afternoon. <u>No error.</u>
                    E

19. <u>Seen from above,</u> the island and the mainland together are
         A
shaped <u>something</u> <u>like</u> a droopy, spreading oak tree <u>as</u> a child
            B   C   D
might draw it. <u>No error.</u>
                    E

20. The altitude, temperature, and wind conditions of the plain
<u>make</u> cattle raising impossible, and <u>this is why</u> protein
    A   B
deficiency <u>is</u> <u>so</u> common among the villagers. <u>No error.</u>
              C   D   E

PART II: SENTENCE CORRECTION

DIRECTIONS

Some part of each sentence below is underlined; sometimes the whole sentence is underlined. Five choices for rephrasing the underlined part follow each sentence; the first choice (A) repeats the original, and the other four are different. If choice (A) seems better than the alternatives, choose answer (A); if not, choose one of the others.

For each sentence, consider the requirements of standard written English. Your choice should be a correct and effective expression, not awkward or ambiguous. Focus on grammar, word choice, sentence construction, and punctuation. If a choice changes the meaning of the original sentence, do not select it.

1. The reason the cat won't eat is because he likes only liver-flavored cat food.
   (A) because he likes only liver-flavored cat food.
   (B) that he liked cat liver-flavored food only.
   (C) on account of he only likes liver-flavored cat food.
   (D) that he likes only liver-flavored cat food.
   (E) because of liking only liver-flavored cat food.

2. No sooner had the mayor announced that she would run for president than the governor threw her hat into the ring.
   (A) than the governor threw her hat
   (B) when the governor threw her hat
   (C) than the governor throws her hat
   (D) then the governor would throw her hat
   (E) but the governor threw her hat

3. If you would have been more careful, you would have broken fewer plates.
   (A) If you would have been more careful
   (B) If you had been more careful
   (C) If you would be more careful
   (D) Were you more careful
   (E) If you would have taken more care

4. Madame Arnot insisted on me speaking only in French.
   (A) on me speaking only
   (B) on me only speaking
   (C) on my speaking only
   (D) upon me speaking only
   (E) that only I speak

5. There are considerations of passenger safety which prevent the crew from drinking while they are working.
   (A) There are considerations of passenger safety which prevent
   (B) There are considerations of passenger safety which prevents
   (C) There are considerations of passenger safety that prevent
   (D) Considerations of passenger safety prevent
   (E) Considerations of passenger safety prevents

6. One of the characteristics of the earliest settlers of Massachu-
setts <u>consisted in their willingness to endure hardships.</u>
   (A) consisted in their willingness to endure hardships.
   (B) were their willingness to endure hardships.
   (C) consisted of their willingness to endure hardships.
   (D) was their willingness to endure hardships.
   (E) was in their being willing to endure hardships.

7. <u>Like many groups</u>, the aims of the Signet Society have changed
in the last ten years.
   (A) Like many groups
   (B) Like those of many groups
   (C) Like many group's
   (D) Like those of many other groups
   (E) Like those of many other group's

8. <u>When she was only five, Janet's mother married for the third
time.</u>
   (A) When she was only five, Janet's mother married for the
third time.
   (B) When only five, Janet's mother married for the third time.
   (C) When Janet was only five, her mother married for the third
time.
   (D) When Janet's mother married for the third time, she was
only five.
   (E) Janet's mother married, when Janet was only five, for the
third time.

9. We asked him about not only <u>how he expected to reduce taxes,
but his plans to increase employment.</u>
   (A) how he expected to reduce taxes, but his plans to increase
employment.
   (B) how he expected to reduce taxes, but also how he planned to
increase employment.
   (C) how he expects to reduce taxes, but also his plans to increase
employment.
   (D) how he plans to reduce taxes, but also about his plans to
increase employment.
   (E) how he expected to reduce taxes, but also about his plans to
increase employment.

10. Although England and France believe the Concorde is the plane of the future, other countries, like the United States, <u>is beginning to become concerned about the Concorde's effect upon</u> the environment.

    (A) is beginning to become concerned about the Concorde's effect upon

    (B) are beginning to become concerned about the Concorde's affect upon

    (C) are beginning to be concerned about the Concorde's affect on

    (D) are beginning to become concerned about the Concorde's effect on

    (E) is beginning to be concerned about the Concorde's effect upon

11. <u>After he graduated from college, his parents gave him a new car, ten thousand dollars, and sent him on a trip around the world.</u>

    (A) After he graduated from college, his parents gave him a new car, ten thousand dollars, and sent him on a trip around the world.

    (B) After graduating from college, his parents gave him a new car, ten thousand dollars, and sent him on a trip around the world.

    (C) After he had graduated from college, his parents gave him a new car, ten thousand dollars, and a trip around the world.

    (D) After he had graduated from college, his parents gave him a new car, ten thousand dollars, and sent him on a trip around the world.

    (E) After graduating from college, his parents gave him a new car, ten thousand dollars, and a trip around the world.

12. The difficulty with an inflated grading system is that everyone believes he or she is as good or better than everyone else as a student.
    (A) believes he or she is as good or better than everyone else as a student.
    (B) believes he or she is as good as or better than every other student.
    (C) believes he or she is as good as or better than every student.
    (D) believes they are as good as or better than every other student.
    (E) believes they are as good as or better than everyone else as a student.

13. To learn to write well is more difficult than learning to read well.
    (A) To learn to write well is more difficult than learning to read well.
    (B) Learning to write well is more difficult than learning to read well.
    (C) It is more difficult to learn to write well than it is to learn to read well.
    (D) Learning to write well is more difficult than it is to learn to read well.
    (E) To learn to write well is more difficult than it is to learn to read well.

14. When a halfback for the New York Jets, the records he set lasted fifteen years.
    (A) the records he set lasted fifteen years.
    (B) his records lasted fifteen years.
    (C) he set records that lasted fifteen years.
    (D) the records that he set lasted fifteen years.
    (E) he set records, and they lasted fifteen years.

15. The shortstop threw late to the second baseman and missed the runner, which allowed the batter to reach first base safely.

    (A) The shortstop threw late to the second baseman and missed the runner, which
    (B) The shortstop's throwing late to the second baseman and missing the runner
    (C) By throwing late to the second baseman, the shortstop missed the runner which
    (D) The shortstop throwing late to the second baseman missed the runner, and it
    (E) The shortstop threw late to the second baseman and missed the runner, and this

16. His ability to work steadily, to accept criticism, and to retain his sense of humor made O'Hara the most valued man in Sherman's army and, when the war was over, made him the obvious choice for governor.

    (A) made him
    (B) it made him
    (C) it also made him
    (D) this made him
    (E) this also made him

17. The group of composers who were in Vienna in the 1790s includes Mozart, Gramm, and Hummel, and though the younger, Mozart wrote the lasting works.

    (A) includes Mozart, Gramm, and Hummel, and though the younger
    (B) include Mozart, Gramm, and Hummel, and though the youngest
    (C) included Mozart, Gramm, and Hummel, and though the youngest
    (D) included Mozart, Gramm, and Hummel, and though he was the youngest in the group
    (E) included Mozart;

18. When you pass the first two tests, it does not guarantee that you
    will pass the course.
    (A) When you pass the first two tests, it
    (B) Because you pass the first two tests, it
    (C) You passing the first two tests
    (D) That you have passed the first two tests
    (E) Passing the tests

19. How a girl like her, who had every advantage money can buy, can
    marry a man as unsavory as him is beyond my understanding.
    (A) How a girl like her, who had every advantage money can
        buy, can marry a man as unsavory as him
    (B) How can a girl like her, who has had every advantage money
        can buy, can marry a man as unsavory as he
    (C) How can she, who has had every advantage money can buy,
        marry a man as unsavory as he
    (D) How a girl like her, who has had every advantage money can
        buy, can marry a man as unsavory as he
    (E) How can a girl who has had, like her, every advantage that
        can be bought by money can marry a man as unsavory as
        he

20. The new innovations at Shoppers' Mall are a children's theater
    and live musical entertainment.
    (A) The new innovations at Shoppers' Mall are
    (B) The new innovation at Shoppers' Mall is
    (C) The innovation at Shoppers' Mall is
    (D) The innovations at Shoppers' Mall are
    (E) Shoppers' Mall has two new innovations,

PART III: ENGLISH USAGE

DIRECTIONS

In the left-hand column, you will find passages in a "spread-out"
format with various words and phrases underlined. In the right-hand
column, you will find a set of responses corresponding to each
underlined portion. If the underlined portion is correct as it stands,

mark the letter indicating "NO CHANGE." If the underlined portion is incorrect, decide which of the choices best corrects it. Consider only underlined portions; assume that the rest of the passage is correct as written.

Passage I

Theodore Roosevelt was vice president when McKinley was assassinated in 1901. As the Republican candidate, he was elected to be the president in
1

1. A. NO CHANGE
   B. to be president
   C. to the presidency
   D. to president

1904, and he declined to run
2
for a third term. He supported Taft, the Republican nominee

2. F. NO CHANGE
   G. 1904 and
   H. 1904, and then
   J. 1904, but

in 1908, and he was elected
3
by a wide margin. By 1912,

3. A. NO CHANGE
   B. in 1908; who
   C. in 1908 who
   D. in 1908, he

Roosevelt became dissatisfied
4

4. F. NO CHANGE
   G. had become dissatisfied
   H. dissatisfied
   J. was unsatisfied

with Taft, and ran in
5
opposition to Taft and Wilson
5
as the candidate of a third party, the Progressives.

5. A. NO CHANGE
   B. ran opposed to
   C. ran as opposition of
   D. opposed to

Wilson, the Democratic
_____
6
candidate, was the winner of the
_____
6
election of 1912, and he was
to win again in the election of

6. F. NO CHANGE
   G. (DO NOT begin new
      paragraph) The
      Democratic candidate,
      Wilson,
   H. (DO NOT begin new
      paragraph) The
      Democratic candidate,
      Wilson
   J. Wilson, the
      Democratic candidate

1916. Known best, perhaps, for
      _____
      7
his failure to persuade the
Senate to join the League of
Nations, Wilson's first term as
president was marked by reform.
Wilson's management of the war
was efficient and tactful, and he
won the backing both of business
                  _____
                  8
and labor. He suffered the third
_____
8
of three strokes in 1919, and

7. A. NO CHANGE
   B. Perhaps known best
   C. Though he is,
      perhaps,
      best known
   D. Best known, perhaps,

8. F. NO CHANGE
   G. both of labor
      as well as business.
   H. of both business
      and labor.
   J. both of business
      as well as of labor.

thereafter he is without any
            _____
            9
significant political influence.
_____
9

9. A. NO CHANGE
   B. was of no significant
   C. had no significant
   D. was without
      any significant

Passage II

   For two years—ever since
a Turkish sponge diver first
spotted it—a joint Turkish-
American team has been

excavating a shipwreck 150 feet
below the surface <u>off the</u>
                    10
<u>southern coast</u> of Turkey. The
      10

10. A. NO CHANGE
    B. of the southern coast
    C. off of the
       southern coast
    D. off of the south coast

wrecked <u>ship, its</u> salvagers
           11
surmise, was Greek. It probably
set sail from Syria with a cargo
of tin and glass from farther
east and stopped in Cyprus to
load three tons of copper ingots
and several crates of pottery.
It was headed for Greece <u>when</u>
                           12
<u>it was driven on the rocks and</u>
              12
<u>sank.</u> The cargo wasn't salvaged
  12
at the time because the ship's
owners didn't have the tech-

11. F. NO CHANGE
    G. ship, so its
    H. ship, it's
    J. ship, so it's

12. A. NO CHANGE
    B. when it was driven
       on the rocks and
       was sunk.
    C. when it was driven
       on the rocks and
       was sunken.
    D. sinking, when it was
       driven on the rocks.

nology <u>to do it.</u> That was about
           13
3,400 years ago.

13. F. NO CHANGE
    G. to do that.
    H. to do so.
    J. to do this.

14. A. NO CHANGE
    B. So far
    C. So far,
    D. Up to this time,

<u>Up to the present point in</u>
              14
<u>time,</u> the salvagers have brought
   14

15. F. NO CHANGE
    G. many cargo and
       artifacts
    H. much of the artifacts
       and cargo
    J. much of the cargo
       and many artifacts

up <u>much of the cargo and of</u>
                15
<u>the artifacts,</u> as well as
       15
part of the keel and some

planking from the vessel itself. "These bones of the wreck push back our knowledge of Mediterranean ship-building by nearly a millenium," an archeologist writes. He believes the copper and tin brought west for
<u>16</u>
the express purpose of manufacturing bronze weapons and tools. His team is salvaging

16. A. NO CHANGE
    B. were brought west
    C. were being brought west
    D. was being brought west

history itself. The evidence of a
<u>17</u>
flourishing international trade; the mystery of eight stone anchors each weighing 600 to 800 pounds, somehow loaded on board before the invention of block and tackle; the artifacts of the maritime industry that was at the heart of ancient Greek civilization. They will keep scholars and onlookers enthralled for years.

17. F. NO CHANGE
    G. itself; the
    H. itself: the
    J. itself, the

Passage III

Demands for reform of the electoral process have diminished because Mr. Reagan has won two elections easily. The Electoral College comes most into question after such close presidential elections as 1960 between
<u>18</u>
John Kennedy and

18. A. NO CHANGE
    B. like 1960
    C. as that of 1960
    D. like that of 1960

Richard Nixon, in which the
19

alternation of a few votes would
19
of changed the outcome. The
19
system works as the Founding
Fathers intended, but what they
intended was a buffer against
the popular vote.
That, in fact, remains the
problem. The Electoral College
system doesn't reflect the
popular vote. Fifteen presidents
who had not received a majority
20
of the popular votes have been
elected, and the list includes
three presidents who actually
trailed their nearest opponent
in the popular vote. Some of
these were chosen not by the
Electoral College but the House
21
of Representatives, which
21
decides when no candidate wins
an electoral majority—and does
so by giving one vote to each

state regardless of their
22
population.
22

19. F. NO CHANGE
    G. in which the
       alternation
       of a few votes would
       have changed
    H. in which the changing
       of a few votes would
       have altered
    J. in which changing a
       few votes would
       of altered

20. A. NO CHANGE
    B. that have not
       received
    C. not receiving
    D. who have not
       received

21. F. NO CHANGE
    G. but chosen by the
       House of
       Representatives
    H. but instead, by
       the House of
       Representatives
    J. but by the House of
       Representatives

22. A. NO CHANGE
    B. irregardless of
       population.
    C. irregardless of
       their population.
    D. regardless of
       population.

The major cause of this
disparity is the unit system
that count all of a state's
    23
electoral votes as blocs,
ignoring second-party votes.
The procedure is far less than
representative. In 1969, following
a close contest between Richard
Nixon and Hubert Humphrey, the
House voted overwhelmingly for a
    24
constitutional amendment in
favor of direct popular election
of presidents, and a runoff
election if no candidate received
at least 40 percent of the total
vote. The proposal was done in
by the Senate filibuster of some
southerners and small-state
senators, but the time will
undoubtedly come again when the
risk of defeating the will of the
people rises new voices for
    25
reform.

23. F. NO CHANGE
    G. which count
    H. that counts
    J. counting

24. A. NO CHANGE
    B. decided by an
       overwhelming vote
    C. overwhelmingly votes
    D. voted overwhelming

25. F. NO CHANGE
    G. arises
    H. raised
    J. raises

ANSWER KEY FOR THE DIAGNOSTIC TEST

Part I English Usage	Part II Sentence Correction	Part III English Usage
1. C	1. D	1. C
2. E	2. A	2. J
3. D	3. B	3. A
4. A	4. C	4. G
5. C	5. D	5. A
6. B	6. D	6. F
7. A	7. D	7. C
8. B	8. C	8. H
9. C	9. B	9. C
10. A	10. D	10. A
11. D	11. C	11. F
12. C	12. B	12. A
13. A	13. B	13. H
14. E	14. C	14. C
15. A	15. B	15. J
16. A	16. A	16. C
17. B	17. C	17. H
18. E	18. D	18. C
19. E	19. D	19. H
20. D	20. D	20. A
		21. J
		22. D
		23. H
		24. A
		25. J

ANSWERS FOR THE DIAGNOSTIC TEST

PART I: ENGLISH USAGE

1. (C) The gerund *having* should be preceded by the possessive *individual's*.

2. (E) The sentence is correct as given.

3. (D) The singular *expenditure* should be followed by the singular *it*, not *them*.

4. (A) The sentence should begin *Like Faulkner's* or *Like those of Faulkner* to parallel the possessive *Porter's*.

5. (C) With the correlatives *not . . . but*, an infinitive must follow *but* to be parallel to the infinitive after *not* (*to establish . . . to make*).

6. (B) The *whom* should be *who*, subject of the clause *who is most likely to win*. The *I think* is parenthetical.

7. (A) The adverb *almost* should be used to modify the adjective *all*.

8. (B) The subject *fall* is singular. The correct verb is *has effected*.

9. (C) The comparison should be between *the number of Irish* and *the number of Italian or Scottish*.

10. (A) Since the trustees are humans, the pronoun *who*, not *which*, should be used. You might be tempted to choose (B), reasoning that the sentence should read . . . *the fund which determines . . . ;* however, this choice would not use appropriate diction, suggesting that a *fund* (an inanimate thing) could *determine*.

11. (D) The singular *number* is the subject; the verb should be the singular *is*.

12. (C) The subject is the singular *humor;* the verb should be the singular *derives*.

13. (A) The singular *Everybody* should be followed by the singular verb *has been.*

14. (E) The sentence is correct as given.

15. (A) With the negative *unaffected*, the correlatives should be *either . . . or.*

16. (A) The compound subject (*performance* and *antics*) requires the plural verb *are.*

17. (B) The idiom is *sooner . . . than.*

18. (E) The sentence contains no error.

19. (E) The sentence is correct as given.

20. (B) The pronoun *this* has no specific antecedent. A phrase like *and it is for this reason that* would correct the sentence.

PART II: SENTENCE CORRECTION

1. (D) With the phrase *The reason is*, you must use the pronoun *that*, not the conjunction *because.* Choice (D) is preferable to choice (B) because of the two present tenses. Choice (B) shifts from present to past tense.

2. (A) The correct idiom is *sooner . . . than.* The past perfect tense in the first clause requires a past tense in the second.

3. (B) The sentence is a contrary-to-fact construction requiring a past subjunctive (*had been*) in the *if* clause.

4. (C) The possessive *my* must be used with the gerund *speaking.*

5. (D) The use of *There are* is verbose. The plural *prevent* agrees with the plural subject *Considerations.*

6. (D) Since the subject of the sentence is the singular *one*, *was* is preferable to *consist of*, which means *to be made up of parts.* Choice (D) is the most concise version of the sentence, and the singular *was* agrees with the singular subject.

7. (D) The sentence must include both *those* and *other*, since the parallel is between aims and since the Society is a group. With *of* the possessive in choice (E) is unnecessary.

8. (C) In all but choices (C) and (E) the pronoun *she* seems to apply to Janet's mother. Choice (E) awkwardly separates elements of the sentence.

9. (B) With the correlatives *not only . . . but also,* the structure *how he expected to* should be followed by the same structure, *how he planned to.*

10. (D) The plural *countries* requires the plural verb *are.* The noun *effect* is correct here.

11. (C) In choices (B) and (E), the participle dangles and seems to suggest that the *parents* have graduated from college. In choices (A) and (D), the three parts of the series are not parallel.

12. (B) The singular *everyone* requires the singular *believes he or she is.* Choice (A) omits the necessary *as* after *good.* Choice (C) omits the necessary *other.*

13. (B) Choices (C), (D), and (E) are wordy. Choice (B) is preferable to choice (A) because it parallels *Learning* and *learning.*

14. (C) In choices (A), (B), and (D), the initial phrase dangles and seems to refer to the *records.* Choice (E) is grammatically correct but wordier than choice (C).

15. (B) The pronouns (*which, it, this*) are all ambiguous. Choice (B) eliminates the ambiguous pronoun.

16. (A) Choice (A) avoids the ambiguous pronouns and is the most concise version of the sentence.

17. (C) With the past tense *wrote,* the first verb should also be in the past tense (*included*). The comparison with three requires *youngest.* Choice (D) is wordy, and (E) is incomplete.

18. (D) Choices (A) and (B) have ambiguous pronouns. Choice (C) should use *your* before the gerund *passing.* Choice (E) leaves out an important part of the sentence (*the first two*).

19. (D) Choices (B), (C), and (E) place the verb before the subject, an error in an indirect question. The correct case of *he* is subjective, not objective as in choice (A).

20. (D) Since *innovation* means *something newly introduced,* the use of *new* is unnecessary. The plural *innovations* and *are* are necessary to agree with the plural *theater* and *entertainment.*

PART III: ENGLISH USAGE

Passage 1

1. (C) The more concise and more idiomatic phrase with *elected* is *to the presidency.*

2. (J) The *but* signals the change of direction in meaning more clearly than *and.*

3. (A) Only choice (A) has no punctuation error.

4. (G) The past perfect tense is necessary to indicate an action which took place before the past tense of *ran.*

5. (A) Only choice (A) is idiomatic.

6. (F) A new paragraph is necessary. The subject of the second paragraph is Wilson, not Roosevelt. The appositive after *Wilson* (*the Democratic candidate*) requires two commas to set it off.

7. (C) Only choice (C) avoids the dangling participle. The subject of the sentence is *Wilson's first term,* not *Wilson.* The sentence as given suggests that the *term* was *known best.*

8. (H) The *both . . . and* correlatives are used correctly and concisely in choice (H).

9. (C) Choice (C) provides the most concise expression.

Passage 2

10. (A) Choice (A) is both idiomatic and more concise than choices (C) and (D). Choice (B) distorts the meaning.

11. (F) Choice (F) is correct and concise. With the apostrophe, *it's* means *it is.*

12. (A) Choice (A) uses the verb tenses correctly.

13. (H) None of the pronouns—*it, that,* or *this*—can be used here, since there is no specific antecedent for them to refer to.

14. (C) The phrase *So far* is more concise. It should be followed by a comma.

15. (J) The phrase *much of the* or *much* should precede *cargo; many* should precede *artifacts.*

16. (C) The plural subject (*copper* and *tin*) requires a plural verb (*were*). Since the action was incomplete, the correct tense is as given in choice (C).

17. (H) The series should be introduced by a colon.

Passage 3

18. (C) With *such, as* rather than *like* must be used. The pronoun *that* is necessary to make both terms of the comparison (*elections . . . that*) similar. Without *that, elections* are compared to a date.

19. (H) The passage confuses *alternate* (*to take turns*) and *alter* (*to change*). The verb should be *would have.* The use of the preposition *of* as part of the verb is an error arising from the similar sound of *would've,* the contraction of *would have.*

20. (A) The past perfect tense is correct.

21. (J) With the correlatives *not . . . but,* the *by* after *not* should be repeated after *but.*

22. (D) The English word is *regardless.* Since *state* is a singular, the plural *their* is an agreement error.

23. (H) Since *system* is singular, the verb should be the singular *counts.*

24. (A) A past tense (*voted*) and an adverb (*overwhelmingly*) are needed here. Choice (B) is wordy.

25. (J) The present tense of the transitive verb *raise* is required. Its object is *voices.*

GRAMMAR AND USAGE REVIEW

1. PARTS OF SPEECH, ADJECTIVES AND ADVERBS, LINKING VERBS, COMPARATIVES AND SUPERLATIVES

PARTS OF SPEECH

None of the widely used tests of English grammar will ask a student to explain a dangling participle or to pick out the adjectives and adverbs in a sentence. But to make the best use of this book, you must know the meaning of several of the important grammatical terms, and you must be able to tell a noun from a verb and an adverb from an adjective.

All of the tests ask you either to find an error in a sentence or to recognize that a sentence is correct. For example, the most common type of question will ask if the following sentence is correct and, if not, which underlined part has an error.

<u>Freshened</u> by rain that <u>fell</u> during the night, the garden
   A   B
smelled <u>fragrantly</u> and <u>glistened brightly</u>. <u>No error.</u>
     C   D   E

Faced with this question, most students will see that the problem is in the word *fragrantly*. Should it be *fragrantly* or *fragrant*? (In fact, it should be *fragrant*.) When you ask even those who rightly select choice (C) as the error why they picked choice (C) instead of choice (D), the usual answer is *(C) sounds wrong, and (D) sounds right.* Sometimes, we have to depend on the *it-sounds-right/it-sounds-wrong* approach. But most of the time, this method will not work. To perform well on tests of standard written English, you must be able to see what grammatical question the test is really asking. In the example, the real issue is not which sounds better, *smells fragrant* or *smells fragrantly*, but whether we use an adverb or an adjective with the verb *smells*. And so we have to begin at the beginning—with a review of the parts of speech on which questions will be based.

39

Noun: a word used as a person, a place, a thing.
Examples: *woman, boy, hope, Boston, car, noun.*

Pronoun: a word used as a substitute for a noun.
Examples: *I, you, he, she, it, me, him, her, we, they, who, whom, which, what, this, that, one, none, someone, somebody, myself, anything, nothing.*

Verb: a word used to assert action or state of being.
Examples: *kill, eat, is, are, remain, think, study, become.*

Adjective: a word used to modify a noun or pronoun. To modify is to describe, to qualify, to limit or restrict in meaning. In the phrase *a large, red barn*, both *large* and *red* are adjectives which modify the noun *barn*.
Examples: *fat, thin, hot, cold, old, new, red.*

Adverb: a word used to modify a verb, an adjective, or another adverb. In the phrase *to eat a very large meal very slowly,* the two *very*'s and *slowly* are adverbs. The first *very* modifies an adjective (*large*), the second modifies an adverb (*slowly*), and *slowly* modifies the verb (*eat*).
Examples: *very, rather, quickly, quite, easily, hopelessly.*

ADJECTIVES AND ADVERBS

A common error in the sentences on the exams is the misuse of an adjective or an adverb. Adjectives modify nouns and pronouns; adverbs modify verbs, adjectives, and other adverbs. Errors occur when an adjective is used to do an adverb's job or an adverb to do an adjective's.

Which of the following sentences have adjective or adverb errors?

1. As the debate progressed, the defenders of tax reform grew more and more excited.
2. As the debate progressed, the defenders of tax reform spoke more and more excited.
3. Asleep awkwardly on his side, the man snored loud enough to shake the bedroom.
4. Lying awkward on his side, the sleeper snored loudly enough to shake the bedroom.

Sentence 1 is correct. Sentences 2, 3, and 4 have adjective/adverb errors. In sentence 2, the adjective *excited* modifies the verb *spoke,* describing how they spoke. But we need an adverb to modify a verb, so the correct word here is *excitedly.* The adjective *excited* is correct in the first sentence because it modifies the noun *defenders,* not the verb *grew.* In sentence 3, the adverb *awkwardly* is properly used to modify the adjective *asleep,* but the adjective *loud* should not be used to modify the verb *snored.* Sentence 4 correctly uses the adverb *loudly* but mistakenly uses the adjective *awkward* to modify the verbal adjective *lying.*

Be careful not to confuse *most* and *almost. Most* is an adjective, the superlative of *much* or *many,* as in *most children like ice cream,* but *most* may be used as an adverb to form the superlative of another adjective or adverb as in *most beautiful* or *most quickly. Almost* is an adverb meaning *nearly.* You can say *most people* or *most men,* but you must say *almost every person* or *almost all men.* A phrase like *most every person* or *most all men* is incorrect because the adjective *most* cannot modify the adjectives *every* or *all.*

LINKING VERBS

It is easy enough to remember that adjectives modify nouns and adverbs modify adjectives, verbs, and other adverbs. The hard part is deciding what word the adjective or adverb modifies. Why must we say *the defenders grew more and more excited* when we also must say *the defenders spoke more and more excitedly?* We do so because there are a number of verbs, called *linking verbs,* which express a state of being rather than an action. These verbs are followed by an adjective, not an adverb. The most common linking verb is the verb *to be* in all its forms (*am, is, are, was, were,* for example), and many other linking verbs are equivalent in meaning to the verb *to be.* They include the following:

to seem   to become   to remain   to appear

In addition, the verbs *to feel, to taste, to smell, to look* are usually linking verbs and will be followed by an adjective rather than an adverb: *I am sad. She became sad. They remain happy. He appears happy. The cloth feels soft. The food tastes bad. The garden smells sweet.* In each of these sentences, the adjective modifies the noun or pronoun subject of the sentence.

When you see a linking verb in a sentence on an exam, be alert to the possibility of an adverb-for-adjective error. But do not assume that the verbs on this list will never have adverbial modifiers.

The detective looks *carefully* at the footprints.
The butler looks *suspicious.*
The detective looks *suspiciously* at the butler.

As these sentences illustrate, *looks* may or may not be a linking verb. If the verb expresses an action rather than describes a state, and the modifier describes that action, use an adverb.

COMPARATIVES AND SUPERLATIVES

Adjectives and adverbs have three forms: positive (*quick, quickly*), comparative (*quicker, more quickly*), and superlative (*quickest, most quickly*). Many of the comparatives and superlatives are formed by adding -er and -est to the adjective stem, though some words (*good, better, best; well, better, best*) change altogether, and some simply add *more* or *most* (*eager, more eager, most eager; quickly, more quickly, most quickly*).

When it is clear that only two are compared, use a comparative not a superlative. When the comparison involves more than two, use a superlative.

Compared to Smith, Jones is *richer.*
Of all the oil-producing countries, Saudi Arabia is the *richest.*
Of the two finalists, Smith hits *harder.*
Of the eight boxers, Jones hits *hardest.*
Of the eight boxers, Jones hits *harder* than Smith, but
Williams hits *hardest* of all.

EXERCISE 1: PARTS OF SPEECH, ADJECTIVES AND ADVERBS, LINKING VERBS, COMPARATIVES AND SUPERLATIVES

Choose the correct form in each of the following sentences. Answers are on page 110.

1. (Most, Almost) every person in the stadium was wearing an orange cap.

2. After $2,500 worth of cosmetic surgery, she appears quite (different, differently) from the woman we had known.

3. The ship appeared (sudden, suddenly) out of the fog.

4. Of all the players in the tournament, Smith has the (better, best) volley.

5. Of the two finalists, Jones has the (better, best) serve.

6. The pie tasted so (bad, badly) that he left the piece uneaten.

7. Dickens has a (noticeable, noticeably) more inventive imagination than Gaskell.

8. I feel (sad, sadly) about his losing so much money on the lottery.

9. It is impossible to take his claims (serious, seriously).

10. The forest smells most (aromatic, aromatically) when the wind is from the south.

11. I don't believe him (most, almost) any time he talks about money.

12. If you look very (careful, carefully), the scratches on the car are (clear, clearly) visible.

13. The eland is the (larger, largest) of all of the antelopes but not the (slower, slowest).

14. Early in the century, the supply of bison (sure, surely) seemed (inexhaustible, inexhaustibly).

15. From a distance, the hill appears to rise (steep, steeply), but it does not look (steep, steeply) from here.

2. CASE

SUBJECT AND OBJECT ERRORS

Nouns and pronouns in English may be used as *subjects* (The *garden* is large. *I* am tired.), as *objects* (David weeded the *garden*. David hit *him*.), and as *possessors* (*David*'s garden is large. *His* arm is broken.). Nouns and pronouns, then, have a subjective case, an objective case, and a possessive case.

Since the form of a noun in the subjective case is no different from the form of the same noun in the objective case (The *bat* hit the *ball*. The *ball* hit the *bat*.), errors of case are not a problem with nouns. But several pronouns have different forms as subjects and objects.

Subject	Object
I	me
he	him
she	her
we	us
they	them
who	whom
whoever	whomever

Where are the errors of case (confusions of the subjective and objective form of the pronoun) in the following sentences?

1. I am going to the play with her.
2. Me and her are going to the games.
3. The committee gave prizes to my brother, my sister, and I.
4. For we Americans, July fourth is a special day.
5. Mary invited my cousin, her sister, a friend from New York, and I to the party.

Sentence 1 is correct, but there are case errors in sentences 2, 3, 4, and 5. In sentence 2, *me* and *her,* the subjects of the sentence, should be *I* and *she* (or better, *She* and *I*). In sentence 3, *I* should be *me,* the object of the preposition *to,* and in sentence 4, the *we* should be *us,* the object of the preposition *for*. In sentence 5, *I* should be *me,* the object of the verb *invited*. It would be easy to spot the error if the sentences simply said *The committee gave prizes to I* or *Mary invited I*, but when the sentence contains elements that separate the verb or the preposition from the pronoun object, it becomes harder to see the error at once. The question writers know this fact and exploit it in all exams. When you see a compound subject or object (that is, two or more subjects or objects joined by *and*), look carefully at the case of pronouns. Imagine how the sentence would read with just the pronoun (*Mary invited I?*).

PRONOUNS IN APPOSITION

An *appositive* is a word or phrase or clause in apposition—that is, placed next to another so that the second explains the first.

Margaret, my sister, and my oldest brother, Hugh, are in New York.

In this sentence, *sister* is in apposition to *Margaret* and *Hugh* is in apposition to *brother*. A pronoun in apposition is in the same case as the noun or pronoun to which it is in apposition. Thus in a sentence like *The outfielders, Jack, Joe, and I, are ready to play*, the *I*, which is in apposition to the subject, *outfielders*, is subjective. But in a sentence like *The class elected three representatives, Jack, Joe, and me*, the objective *me* is correct because it is in apposition to *representatives*, which is the object of the verb *elected*.

WHO AND WHOM

The demons of case are *who* and *whom*. Your test may not ask you to choose between them at all, but it may do so more than once. If you understand how to deal with *who* and *whom*, questions about the case of other pronouns should give you no trouble. The problem is always the same: Is the pronoun a subject or an object? Is it *I, he, she, who* or *me, him, her, whom*?

Use *who* for a subject, *whom* for an object:

Who is going to the store? (subject of sentence)
Whom are you going with? (object of preposition *with*)
Whom did they choose? (object of verb *choose*; *they* is the subject of the sentence)

If you have trouble with sentences that are questions, it may help to rephrase the sentence as a statement:

You are going with whom.
They did choose whom.

And it may also help if you substitute *I/me* or *he/him* for *who/whom*.

He is going to the store.
Are you going with *him?*
Did they choose *him?*

Before going on to nastier examples of *who* and *whom*, we need to define three more terms: *clause, independent clause*, and *dependent clause*. A *clause* is a group of related words containing a verb and its subject. An *independent clause* can stand by itself as a sentence. A *dependent clause*, though it has a subject and a verb, cannot stand by itself as a complete sentence.

I spoke. (one independent clause with a subject and a verb)

I spoke and she listened. (two independent clauses—*I spoke/she listened* would be complete sentences)

I spoke while she listened. (one independent clause—*I spoke*—and one dependent clause—*while she listened*—which, though it has a subject and a verb, is not a complete sentence)

The girl who is dressed in red is rich. (one independent clause—*The girl is rich*—and one dependent clause—*who is dressed in red*)

The easier questions with *who* and *whom* occur in sentences with only one clause. In sentences with more than one clause, the case of the pronoun (*who* or *whom*) is determined by its use in its own clause. Before you can decide between *who* and *whom*, you must be able to isolate the clause in which the pronoun appears.

1. He will give the book to whoever wants it.
2. He will give the book to whomever Jane chooses.
3. He will give the prize to whoever deserves it.
4. He will give the prize to whomever he likes.

In sentence 1, there are two clauses: *He will give the book to* and *whoever wants it*. The whole second clause (*whoever wants it*) not the pronoun *whoever* is the object of the preposition. In this second clause, *whoever* is the subject, *wants* is the verb, and *it* is the object. If you find this sort of sentence difficult, isolate the clause and substitute *he/him* for *who/whom* or *whoever/whomever*. Here *he wants it* should be easy to recognize as preferable to *him wants it*.

In sentence 2, there are again two clauses: *He will give the book to* and *whomever Jane chooses*. Again the whole clause is the object of the preposition, but the subject of the second clause is *Jane*, the verb, *chooses*, and *whomever*, the object of the verb *chooses*. (Jane chooses *him*, not Jane chooses *he*.) Sentences 3 and 4 follow the same principles. In sentence 3, *whoever* is the subject of the second clause; in sentence 4, *he* is the subject and *whomever* is the object of *likes*.

Remember that *whom* by itself will be the object of a preposition like *to*. (*To whom* did he give the book?), but in this sentence there is only *one* clause.

There is one more complication. You will sometimes find sentences in which a parenthetical expression occurs with the *who/whom* clause. Phrases like *I think, we know, they believe, he supposes, they say, one imagines* are, in fact, independent clauses and do not affect the case of *who/whom* in a separate clause.

1. He is a man who I think should be in prison.
2. He is a man, one assumes, who is sick.
3. Her husband is a man whom I think she has misunderstood.
4. He is a student whom we know the teachers dislike.
5. They will pay a large fee to whoever they decide is most qualified.

All of these sentences have three, not two, clauses. When deciding on the case of *who* or *whom*, we must pay no attention to the parenthetical phrases *I think, one assumes,* and *we know*. The *who/whom* clauses are *who should be in prison, who is sick, whom she has misunderstood,* and *whom the teachers dislike*. In the first two, *who* is the subject. In sentences 3 and 4, *whom* is the object of the verbs *has misunderstood* and *dislike*. There are two traps in sentence 5, the preposition *to* and the phrase *they decide*, but the clause is *whoever is most qualified*. The whole clause is the object of the preposition *to* and *they decide* is a separate clause. Therefore, it must be *whoever* (*he* is most qualified) because *whoever* is the subject of the clause.

POSSESSIVE ERRORS

The third case of English nouns and pronouns is the possessive, which is used, logically enough, to show possession: *my, your, his, her, its, our, their, whose.* Remember that the possessive form of the pronoun *it* is *its* without an apostrophe. With the apostrophe, *it's* is a contraction and means *it is.* Remember, too, that *their* is the possessive form of the pronoun *they,* while *there* is an adverb meaning *in that place.*

As a rule, use the possessive case before a gerund, that is, a verb used as a noun. Gerunds are formed by adding *-ing* to verb stems: *going, eating, writing, borrowing.* Like nouns, they are used as both subjects and objects.

1. I don't like my brother's borrowing so much money.
2. I don't mind his eating so much ice cream.
3. I don't approve of his driving with such worn-out tires.
4. I recommend his seeing a doctor.

In these sentences, *borrowing, eating, driving,* and *seeing* are gerunds, preceded by possessive forms. If the first sentence had said *brother* rather than *brother's,* it would seem to say *I don't like my brother* rather than *I don't like his borrowing so much.* Similarly, if sentence 2, 3, or 4 had used *him* instead of *his,* the meaning of the sentences would be changed. If an exam question offers you a choice between a possessive and an objective pronoun before a gerund, look carefully at what the sentence is saying. It is likely that the possessive is the better choice.

EXERCISE 2: CASE

Choose the correct form in each of the following sentences. The answers are on page 111.

Part A

1. The study suggests that (we, us) New Englanders are not practical.

2. Everybody at the table chose steak except Tom and (I, me).

3. I don't mind (him, his) using the car.

4. It was (I, me) who telephoned the fire department.

5. Why does he object to (us, our) standing here?

6. It is difficult to imagine how such an invention will affect you and (I, me).

7. Let's you and (I, me) invest together in this project.

8. I'm going to complain about (him, his) talking so loudly.

9. The Secret Service is worried about the (president, president's) riding in an open car.

10. They will award the trophy to one of the finalists, either Jack or (I, me).

Part B

1. The woman (who, whom) was recently elected to the board of directors has been with the company for some years.

2. The accountant (who, whom) we understand did not wish to be interviewed has been asked to appear at the trial.

3. (Who, Whom) do you suppose will buy this car?

4. (Who, Whom) do you suppose the company will choose?

5. Let me speak to (whoever, whomever) is waiting for the general.

6. Let me speak to (whoever, whomever) the general hopes to convince to join his campaign.

7. (Whoever, Whomever) I think deserves the prize always seems to lose.

8. They will give the job to (whoever, whomever) they decide is most likely to support their position.

9. They will give the job to (whoever, whomever) they decide they can agree with about prices.

10. Do you really care about (who, whom) you dance with?

3. AGREEMENT

An agreement error is the faulty combination of a singular and a plural. Agreement errors occur between subjects and verbs and between pronouns and their *antecedents* (the word, phrase, or clause to which a pronoun refers).

All the grammar exams test agreement frequently, and on some tests as many as one-fourth of the questions test for errors of agreement.

SUBJECT AND VERB AGREEMENT

Use a singular verb with a singular subject and a plural verb with a plural subject. The key to seeing errors of subject-verb agreement is identifying the subject correctly. Often, the sentences will try to mislead you by separating the subject and verb.

1. The *sound is* beautiful. (singular subject/singular verb)

2. The *number seems* to increase. (singular subject/singular verb)

3. The *sound* of birds singing and crickets chirping all about the sunlit lakes and woods *is* beautiful. (singular subject/singular verb)

4. The *number* of boats pulling waterskiers on the lakes *seems* to increase every summer. (singular subject/singular verb)

Sentences 1 and 2 here are easy, but in sentences 3 and 4, the plurals that come between the singular subjects and the verbs may make the reader forget that the verbs must be singular to agree with the singular subjects.

In sentences where there are two or more subjects joined by *and*, use a plural verb. Do not confuse compound subjects (two subjects joined by *and*) with prepositional or parenthetical phrases introduced by such words or phrases as *with, as well as, in addition to, along with, in the company of, not to mention,* and the like. A singular subject, followed by a phrase of this sort, still takes a singular verb.

1. The actress and the director *are* in the dressing room.

2. The chairman of Mobil, as well as the president of Texaco and the vice president of Gulf, *is* attending the meeting.
3. The fullback, accompanied by two ends, two guards, and the 340-pound tackle, *is* leaving the field.
4. The conductor, with his 125-piece orchestra, two small brass bands, and the Mormon Tabernacle Choir, *is* ready to begin the concert.

In the first example, there are two subjects (*actress* and *director*) joined by *and,* so the verb is plural. But in the second, third, and fourth sentences, the subject is singular (*chairman, fullback, conductor*), and all the plurals that intervene between the subject and the verb do not change the rule that the verb must be singular to agree with the singular subject.

Two singular subjects joined by *and* (a compound subject) must have a plural verb, but two singular subjects joined by *or, nor, either . . . or, neither . . . nor* take singular verbs.

1. Mary *and* Jill *are* in the play.
2. Mary *or* Jill *is* in the play.
3. *Neither* Mary *nor* Jill *is* in the play.

In sentences with *either . . . or, neither . . . nor,* if one subject is singular and one is plural, the verb agrees with the subject nearer the verb.

1. Neither the hunter nor the *rangers are* in sight.
2. Neither the rangers nor the *hunter is* in sight.
3. Either the dog or the *cats are* in the yard.
4. Either the cats or the *dog is* in the yard.

In sentences 1 and 3, the subjects nearer the verb are the plurals *rangers* and *cats,* so the verb is plural. In sentences 2 and 4, the singular subject is nearer the verb, and the verb is singular.

When the following words are used as subjects, use a singular verb: *anyone, anybody, anything, someone, something, everyone, everybody, everything, no one, nobody, nothing, either, neither, each, another, many a.*

1. *Everyone* in thc class of six hundred students *is* going on the field trip.
2. *Everybody* in the four western states *is* concerned about the election.
3. *Either* of the answers *is* correct.
4. *Neither* of the teams *has* won a game.
5. *Each* of the contestants *has* won a prize.
6. *Many a* man *has* gone astray.

Notice that many of these sentences begin with the singular subject which is followed by a prepositional phrase with plurals. The exam sentences will often use this structure, hoping that the plurals in the prepositional phrase will distract you from the real point—that the subject is singular. The sentences on the exam may be much longer than these examples so that the verb is even farther away from the singular subject.

> *Everybody* in the crowded shopping center, in the food stores, and in the specialty shops, as well as those who filled the department stores down the street, *was* looking for bargains.

When the subject is *none,* and the meaning is *not one* or *no one else,* use a singular verb. In some instances, the rest of the sentence will make it clear that the plural is more appropriate, but it is more likely that a sentence on the exam which uses *none* as the subject is testing your ability to see that *none* is usually singular.

1. None of the players *is* ready.
2. None of the twenty-two starting players on the two teams *is* ready.
3. None *is* so foolish as a man who will not listen to advice.
4. None *are* so foolish as men who will not listen to advice.

In the first three examples, *none* means *no one* and the verb is singular. In sentence 4, the plural *men* makes it clear that *none* must also be a plural.

Collective nouns like *jury, team, orchestra, crowd, family, Yale*— that is, nouns in which a singular form denotes a collection of individuals—usually take a singular verb. If the collection is thought of as a whole (The jury is deliberating), the verb is singular. If the sentence makes it clear that the members are thought of as acting separately, the verb is plural (My family have settled in five different states).

Watch carefully for agreement errors in sentences with the phrases *the number* or *a number* as subjects. *The number* is singular, but it is likely to be followed by a prepositional phrase with plurals. So long as *the number* is the subject, use a singular verb.

1. *The number* of bugs in my gardens and lawns *is* enormous.
2. *The number* of tests in my classes this semester *is* larger than last year's.
3. *The number* of people killed every year in highway accidents, drownings, and airplane crashes *has* increased every year since 1942.

A number can take either a singular or plural. Use a plural when *a number* means *many*.

1. *A number* of tests *are* given in this class.
2. *A number* of bugs *are* crawling on my roses.
3. *A number* of theories to account for the high incidence of lung disease *have* been discussed in the study.
4. *A number* that many people consider to be unlucky *is* thirteen.

In the first three examples, *a number* means *many* and the verbs are plural. In sentence 4, *a number* refers to one number (thirteen), and the verb is singular.

Be wary of nouns based on Latin and Greek that form their plurals with *a* at the end. *Criteria* is a plural (one criterion, two criteria) as are *data* (one datum), *phenomena* (one phenomenon), and *media* (one medium).

1. The media *are* guilty of sensationalism.
2. The criteria for admission *are* listed in the catalog.

The tests will frequently include agreement errors in sentences in which the verb precedes the subject, often by using an opening of *There is* or *There are*.

1. There *are* hidden away in a lonely house out on the heath a brother and sister living alone.
2. There *is* in London and New York newspapers a self-satisfaction that is not found in the papers of smaller cities.

Both of these sentences are correct, though it would be easy to miss the agreement error if the first had used *is* and the second, *are*. Do not let the singular nouns in the prepositional phrases in the first sentence or the plurals in the second distract you from finding the subjects of the verbs—the compound subject *brother and sister* in the first and the singular *self-satisfaction* in the second. The test writer's technique here is like that in those sentences that pile up plurals between a singular subject at the beginning of the sentence and the verb at the end. But in this case, the verb comes first.

PRONOUN AGREEMENT

Since personal pronouns have distinctive singular and plural forms (*he/they, his/their, him/them*), pronoun agreement errors are as common as noun-verb agreement errors. The number (that is, singular or plural) of a pronoun is determined by its *antecedent* (the word, phrase, or clause to which it refers), and pronouns must agree in number with their antecedents. Most of the rules that apply to the agreement of nouns and verbs also apply to the agreement of pronouns and their antecedents.

1. The *workers* finished *their* job on time.
2. The *group* of workers finished *its* job on time.
3. The *men* earn *their* money.
4. The *man* earns *his* money.
5. The *men* who earn *their* money are tired.

In sentence 1 here, the plural *their* agrees with the plural *workers*. In sentence 2, the singular *its* agrees with the singular subject, the collective noun *group*. In sentences 3 and 4, the antecedents are *men* and *man,* so the pronouns are *their* and *his*. In sentence 5, the antecedent to the pronoun *their* is *who*. To determine whether *who* is singular or plural, we must look at its antecedent. In this sentence, it is the plural *men*.

In the subject-verb agreement questions, so long as you know whether the subject is singular or plural, you should have no trouble. In pronoun agreement questions, you must know what word is the antecedent of the pronoun and whether that word is singular or plural. As the following sentences will demonstrate, these questions are more difficult.

1. Rosen is the only one of the five American musicians *who have entered* the competition *who is* likely to win a medal.
2. The leader of the senators *who are* gathered to discuss the tax on oil is the only one *who represents* an oil-producing state.

In the first sentence, the antecedent of the first *who* is the plural *musicians*. Therefore, *who* is plural and the correct verb is *have*. But the antecedent of the second *who* is *one* (and the antecedent of *one* is *Rosen*), and so the verb in this clause must be the singular *is*. In the second sentence, the antecedent of the first *who* is the plural *senators* (thus, *are*) while the antecedent of the second *who* is the singular *one* (thus, *represents* not *represent*).

Use a singular pronoun when the antecedent is *anyone, anybody, anything, someone, somebody, something, everyone, everybody, everything, no one, nobody, either, neither, each, another, one, person, man, woman, kind, sort.*

1. *None* of the girls in the class finished *her* assignment on time.
2. *Everybody* on the men's team has *his* weaknesses.
3. *Neither* of the women paid *her* bills.
4. *Each* of the boys ate *his* ice cream.
5. *One* of the twenty men in the upper balcony dropped *his* program into the orchestra.

When two or more antecedents are joined by *or* or *nor*, the pronoun should agree with the nearer antecedent.

1. Neither the mother nor the *daughters* brought *their* cars.
2. Neither the daughters nor the *mother* brought *her* car.

EXERCISE 3: AGREEMENT

Choose the correct form in each of the following sentences. Answers are on page 112.

1. None of the candidates who (is, are) campaigning in New Hampshire (is, are) willing to speak to that organization.

2. Either the general or the sergeant-at-arms (is, are) responsible for greeting the new Greek minister.

3. None of the applicants who (has, have) failed to submit photographs (is, are) likely to be called for an interview.

4. Mr. Lombardi, as well as his wife and three children, (was, were) found before midnight.

5. The newly discovered evidence, together with the confirming testimony of three eyewitnesses, (make, makes) his conviction certain.

6. The criteria for admission to Yale Law School in New Haven (includes, include) a score of above 600 on the test.

7. Precise and symmetrical, the basalt columns of the Devil's Postpile in the Sierras (looks, look) as if (it, they) had been sculpted in an artist's studio.

8. Neither the teacher nor the student (is, are) in the classroom.

9. Mr. and Mrs. Smith, in addition to their four children, (is, are) vacationing in Orlando.

10. Jack is one of eight quarter-milers who (has, have) reached the final heat.

11. The number of penguins that (is, are) killed by DDT (increases, increase) each year.

12. Either I or Mary Jane (is, are) going to Detroit.

13. Everyone in the theater, filled with more than six hundred people, (was, were) bored.

14. Neither Sally nor the twins (has, have) finished (her, their) practice teaching.

15. Neither the twins nor Sally (has, have) finished (her, their) practice teaching.

16. Neither she nor I (was, were) dancing, for we felt tired.

17. The president, no less than all the other members of the first family, (enjoy, enjoys) bowling.

18. The number of books about corruption in the government written by participants in the Watergate affair (seem, seems) to grow larger every month.

19. A number of the books about Watergate (has, have) been translated into Russian.

20. The data used in determining your federal tax (is, are) to be submitted with your letter of appeal.

REVIEW EXERCISE: SECTIONS 1, 2, and 3

Some of the following sentences may be correct. Others contain problems covered in Sections 1, 2, and 3 of the Grammar and Usage Review. There is not more than one error in any sentence.

If there is an error, it will be underlined and lettered. Find the one underlined part that must be changed to make the sentence correct. Choose (E) if the sentence contains no error. Answers are on page 113.

1. No one but the president, secretary, and me was at the
        A   B   C
   meeting, and we voted unanimously to spend all of the money
                                 D
   in the treasury. No error.
                E

2. Many a young man of twenty-five or thirty have dreamed of
                                     A
   retiring at fifty, but few, when they reach that age, find
                                   B
   that the sum they had thought could support them is adequate.
                  C   D
   No error.
    E

3. Having lived for two years near both the highway and the
   <u>A</u>   <u>B</u>
   airport, I am used to the noises of cars and planes, which no
                                                        <u>C</u>
   longer disturb my sleep. No error.
          <u>D</u>   <u>E</u>

4. The book's public-relations prose, its long-windedness, and
              <u>A</u>   <u>B</u>
   its tendency uncritically to list ideas ultimately makes it
                <u>C</u>   <u>D</u>
   a wholly useless study that should never have been published.
   No error.
   <u>E</u>

5. It is depressing to realize that in a country as rich as this,
                            <u>A</u>   <u>B</u>
   thousands of people live out their life without ever having
                                  <u>C</u>   <u>D</u>
   enough to eat. No error.
                 <u>E</u>

6. My family includes several serious and responsible members,
             <u>A</u>
   my sister and I, for example, but even we have had next to no
   <u>B</u>   <u>C</u>   <u>D</u>
   influence on public life. No error.
                             <u>E</u>

7. The result of all the tests, according to the surgeon, was not
                               <u>A</u>   <u>B</u>
   likely to alarm either her husband or her. No error.
   <u>C</u>   <u>D</u>   <u>E</u>

8. Some smaller players will tackle only whoever comes near them,
                                  <u>A</u> <u>B</u>
   while others will tackle whoever they can catch. No error.
               <u>C</u>   <u>D</u>   <u>E</u>

9. Though the first question on the test seemed simple, there were
                                         <u>A</u>   <u>B</u>
   simply too many questions for me to finish on time. No error.
   <u>C</u>   <u>D</u>   <u>E</u>

10. There are several runners on the team who are faster in the
                                          ‾‾‾   ‾‾‾‾‾‾
                                           A   B
shorter races than the runners of the opposing team, but in
‾‾‾‾‾‾
  C
the field events, they are best. No error.
                          ‾‾‾‾ ‾‾‾‾‾‾‾‾
                           D   E

4. VERBS

When you look up a verb in the dictionary, you will find an entry
like the following:

eat, v.t. (ate, eaten, eating)
chop, v.t. (chopped, chopping)
be, v.i. (was or were, been, being)
go, v.i. (went, gone, going)
run, v.i.,t. (ran, run, running)

The *v.* indicates that the word is a verb, and the *t.* or *i.* that it is
transitive (that is, takes an object) or intransitive (that is, does not
take an object). Some verbs, like *run,* can be either intransitive (I run
faster than David) or transitive (I run a factory in Kansas City).

The present infinitive of the verb is formed by adding the preposition *to* to the form given first (*to eat, to chop, to be, to go, to run*), and
most verbs (though *not* the verb *to be*) form their present tenses from
the infinitive (*I eat, I chop, I go, I run*). The second form of the verb,
given in the parentheses, is the past tense (*ate, chopped*), and the
third is past participle (*eaten, chopped*), the form which is combined
with an auxiliary to form the perfect tenses (*I have eaten, I have
chopped, I will have gone*). The *-ing* form is the present participle.

VERB TENSES

To deal more fully with verb errors, we will need to review and
define some additional terms. Each verb has *number, person, voice,*
and *tense. Number* is simply singular or plural. The three *persons* of a
verb are first (*I, we*), second (*you*), and third (*he, she, it, they*).
Active (I hit the ball) and passive (The ball was hit by me) are the
voices of verbs. If the subject of a verb performs the action of the
verb, the verb is *active,* while if the subject receives the action, the

verb is *passive*. The *tenses* of a verb are the forms that show *the time* of its action or state of being. Most of the verb errors that appear on the exams are errors of agreement or errors of tense.

The following chart gives the tenses of the verbs *to be* and *to chop*.

PRESENT TENSE: ACTION OR STATE OF BEING IN
THE PRESENT

	Singular	*Plural*
first person	I am/I chop	we are/we chop
second person	you are/you chop	you are/you chop
third person	he, she, it is/he, she, it chops	they are/they chop

PAST TENSE: ACTION OR STATE OF BEING
IN THE PAST

	Singular	*Plural*
first person	I was/I chopped	we were/we chopped
second person	you were/you chopped	you were/you chopped
third person	he, she, it was/he, she, it chopped	they were/they chopped

FUTURE TENSE: ACTION OR STATE OF BEING
IN THE FUTURE

	Singular	*Plural*
first person	I will be/I will chop	we will be/we will chop
second person	you will be/you will chop	you will be/you will chop
third person	he, she, it will be/he, she, it will chop	they will be/they will chop

PRESENT PERFECT TENSE: ACTION IN PAST TIME IN RELATION TO PRESENT TIME

	Singular	*Plural*
first person	I have been/I have chopped	we have been/we have chopped
second person	you have been/you have chopped	you have been/you have chopped
third person	he, she, it has been/ he, she, it has chopped	they have been/they have chopped

PAST PERFECT TENSE: ACTION IN PAST TIME IN RELATION TO ANOTHER PAST TIME

	Singular	*Plural*
first person	I had been/I had chopped	we had been/we had chopped
second person	you had been/you had chopped	you had been/you had chopped
third person	he, she, it had been/ he, she, it had chopped	they had been/they had chopped

FUTURE PERFECT TENSE: ACTION IN A FUTURE TIME IN RELATION TO ANOTHER TIME EVEN FURTHER IN THE FUTURE

	Singular	*Plural*
first person	I will have been/I will have chopped	we will have been/we will have chopped
second person	you will have been/ you will have chopped	you will have been/you will have chopped
third person	he, she, it will have been/he, she, it will have chopped	they will have been/they will have chopped

There should be no trouble with the present, past, and future tenses, but some examples of the perfect tenses may be helpful. Remember that the *present perfect* tense is used to describe action in *past* time in relation to the present. An example of a *past* tense is *I chopped wood last week.* An example of a *present perfect* tense is *I have chopped wood every Tuesday for three years.* That is, the wood chopping is an action begun in the past and continuing to the present. An example of a *past perfect* tense is *I had chopped wood every Tuesday until I bought a chain saw.* That is, the woodchopping was an action in the past that preceded another past action, buying a chain saw. In this sentence, *had chopped* is a *past perfect tense,* and *bought* is a *past* tense. An example of the future perfect tense is *By 1995, I will have chopped enough wood to heat six houses.* That is, the woodchopping will continue into the future but will be past in 1995.

Almost all verb tense errors on the exam occur in sentences with two verbs. Always look carefully at the tenses of the verbs in a sentence. Does the time scheme make sense? Is it consistent and logical? Since tense reflects the time of the actions, there can be no single rule about what tenses should be used. Meaning, in this case, the time scheme of the action, will determine tense. Sometimes the meaning will require a change of tense. For example,

Yesterday, I ate breakfast at seven o'clock, and tomorrow I will eat at nine.

We have both a past (*ate*) and a future (*will eat*) in this sentence, but other words which explain the time scheme (*yesterday, tomorrow*) make it clear that both a past and a future tense are necessary. On the other hand, consider this example.

In the seventeenth century, the performances at public theatres took place in the afternoon, and the actors dress in splendid costumes.

In this sentence, the change from the past (*took*) to the present (*dress*) makes no sense. Both verbs refer to past actions (*in the sixteenth century*); both should be in the past tense (*took, dressed*).

To spot errors in verb tense, you must look carefully at the verbs and the other words in the sentence that establish the time scheme. Adverbs like *then, subsequently, before, yesterday,* and *tomorrow,* and prepositional phrases like *in the dark ages* and *in the future,* work with the verbs to make the time of the actions clear.

The following are sentences very much like those used on examinations to test verb tenses. Which of the italicized verbs are incorrect?

1. The winds blew sand in the bathers' faces, so they gathered up their towels and *will leave* the beach quickly.
2. The new variety of plum was developed by Burbank who *begun* to work with fruits after the Civil War.
3. In the year 2010, I *am* fifty years old.
4. I *had spoke* with her briefly many times before, but today's conversation was the first in which she *spoke* frankly about her political ambitions.

All but one of the italicized verbs are incorrect. In the first sentence, the shift to the future tense (*will leave*) makes no sense after the two other verbs in the past tense. The verb should be *left.* In the second sentence, the past tense, *began,* or better, the past perfect, *had begun,* is necessary. The *am* of the third sentence should be *will be,* a future tense. In the fourth sentence, *had spoke* incorrectly tries to form the past perfect tense using the past tense (*spoke*) instead of the past participle *spoken.* The second *spoke* is a correct use of the past tense.

Participles, the form of the verb used as an adjective, have only two tenses, present (*going, chopping, eating*) and past (*having gone, having chopped, having eaten*), but tense errors are possible. Be sure that sentences with a participle have a coherent time sequence. A sentence like *Eating my lunch, I took the car to the gas station* makes sense if you eat and drive at the same time. If your meaning is *after lunch,* you must write *Having eaten my lunch, I took the car to the gas station.*

We expect a simple sentence that begins in the past tense to continue to refer to action in the past.

1. Greek sailors in the first century *thought* that their ships *traveled* faster with light ballast and small sails.
2. Egyptian astronomers *believed* that the sun *rose* when the jackal *howled*.

In both of these sentences, all the verbs are, rightly, in the past tense. But there is one kind of sentence which occasionally appears on advanced grammar exams which works differently.

1. Greek sailors in the first century *discovered* that the prevailing winds in the Ionian Sea *blow* from east to west.
2. A handful of ancient astronomers *realized* that the earth *revolves* about the sun and the moon *circles* the earth.

In these sentences, though the main verbs are in the past tense (*discovered, realized*), the verbs in the subordinate clauses are in the present tense (*blow, revolves, circles*). Because the action or state the clauses describe continues to be true (the earth still revolves around the sun) the present tense is correct. Logical meaning is the key to tense. Sentences like these will occur infrequently and are likely to appear in the sentence correction form of question.

SUBJUNCTIVES

In dependent clauses expressing a condition that is untrue or contrary to fact (*if I were sick, if he had arrived five minutes earlier*) the verb is said to be subjunctive, and its forms are different from those of the verbs in statements of fact. The following are examples of subjunctive forms of the verb.

If I *were* sick . . .
If I *arrive* on time . . .   (present tense)

If I *had been* sick . . .
If I *had arrived* on time . . .   (past tense)

If he *were* here . . .
If he *arrives* on time . . .   (present tense)

If he *had been* here . . .

If he *had arrived* on time . . .   (past tense)

For the exams, what you must remember about subjunctive verbs is that *would have* should never be used in the *if* clause. The question will probably be like one of the following:

1. If Holmes <u>would have arrived</u> a few minutes sooner, the murderer would not have escaped.
   - (A) would have arrived
   - (B) did arrive
   - (C) had arrived
   - (D) arrives
   - (E) would arrive

2. If the economic situation <u>would have improved</u> in the
                                          A
   first three months of this fiscal year, the banks <u>would</u>
                                                         B
   <u>not have had</u> to <u>foreclose on</u> so many mortgages. <u>No error.</u>
          C   D   E

In question 1, choice (C) is the correct answer. The contrary-to-fact clause (*if*) requires a past subjunctive form. In question 2, the error is choice (A). (Never use *would have* in the *if* clause.) The correct form of the verb in this clause is *had improved*.

LIE/LAY, RISE/RAISE, SIT/SET

Lie is an intransitive verb (that is, it takes no object) meaning *to rest* or *to recline*. *Lay* is a transitive verb (it must have an object) meaning *to put* or *to place*. The confusion between the two verbs probably arose because the past tense of the verb *to lie* (to recline) is the same as the present tense of the verb *to lay* (to place).

Yesterday I *lay* in bed till noon.
intransitive verb—past tense—no object

I *lay* the paper on the table.
transitive verb—present tense—object (paper)

	Present Tense	Past Tense	Past Participle	Present Participle
to rest, to recline *intransitive*	lie	lay	lain	lying
to place, to put *transitive*	lay	laid	laid	laying

1. I like *laying* my head in a pile of sand when I am *lying* on the beach.
2. I *laid* the book on the table and *lay* down on the couch.
3. I have *laid* the book on the table.
4. I have *lain* in bed all morning.

Like *lie, rise* and *sit* are intransitive verbs. Like *lay, raise* and *set* are transitive verbs.

	Present Tense	Past Tense	Past Participle	Present Participle
to go up, to ascend *intransitive*	rise	rose	risen	rising
to lift *transitive*	raise	raised	raised	raising
to be seated *intransitive*	sit	sat	sat	sitting
to put *transitive*	set	set	set	setting

1. I *raise* the window shade and watch the sun *rise*.
2. I *raised* the shade after the sun had *risen*.
3. The sun *rose* before I had *raised* the shade.
4. *Raising* the shade, I watched the sun *rising*.

EXERCISE 4: VERBS

Choose the correct verb form in the following sentences. Answers are on page 113.

1. If you (had, would have) eaten fewer potato chips, you would not be ill now.

2. In 1620, Philips discovered that a candle lighted at only one end (lasts, lasted) longer than one lighted at both ends.

3. I (waited, have waited) for her on the platform.

4. I (have waited, had waited) for her for two hours when she arrived at noon.

5. He (will go, will have gone) to the city tomorrow.

6. If I (were, was) thinner, I would buy a new wardrobe.

7. The thief climbed up the trellis, opened the window, and (steps, stepped) quietly into the room.

8. The letters (lying, laying) on the table have been (lying, laying) there for a week.

9. I (lay, laid) my briefcase on the table and (lay, laid) down on the couch.

10. In this car, the windows (rise, raise) at the press of a button.

11. (Sitting, Setting) the flowers on the table, she noticed the cat (setting, sitting) on the chair nearby.

12. At nine o'clock, a grill (rises, raises) to prevent any entry into the vault.

13. When I reach retirement age in 1995, I (will be, will have been) sixty years old.

14. When I reach retirement age in 1995, I (will work, will have worked) for the post office for thirty years.

15. If you (had been, were) more careful, you would not have dented the fender of the car.

16. If you (had been, were) more careful, you would make fewer mistakes.

5. MISPLACED PARTS, DANGLING MODIFIERS

MISPLACED PARTS

The grammatical errors discussed in parts 1, 2, and 3 are likely to be tested in a question which asks you to identify an error in a single sentence. The first part of this section discusses misplaced parts of the sentence. Since a misplaced part is often awkward but not, strictly speaking, a grammatical error, the questions testing for misplaced parts usually present five versions of the same sentence and ask you to select the sentence that is not only grammatically correct but also clear and exact, free from awkwardness and ambiguity. This form of question may also, of course, be used to test for the kinds of error already discussed.

A well written sentence will be clear and concise. Given a choice between two sentences which say all that must be said and are error free, choose the shorter version. This is *not* to say that any shorter sentence is the right answer. Sometimes a shorter sentence will have a grammatical error, omit part of the original thought, or change the meaning. Here is a sample question.

Fifteen women have formally protested their being overlooked for promotion.
(A) their being overlooked for promotion.
(B) themselves being overlooked for promotion.
(C) their overlooking for promotion.
(D) overlooking themselves for promotion.
(E) themselves as overlooked for promotion.

Answer (C) is the shortest of the five choices here, but it is the wrong answer. It changes the meaning by leaving out *being*. The right answer is choice (A), for a reason you already know—the possessive (*their*) before the gerund (*being overlooked*). The shorter version, then, is not always the best answer, but the right answer will be as short as it can be without sacrificing grammatical correctness and clarity of content.

The basic rule for dealing with misplaced parts of the sentence is *Keep related parts together.* Avoid any unnecessary separation of closely related parts of the sentence. Avoid odd or unnatural word

order. Keep modifiers as near as possible to the words they modify.
Be especially careful with the adverbs *only, just, almost, nearly, even, hardly,* and *merely.* Their placement can be crucial to the meaning of a sentence. Look closely at the following two sentences.

1. I almost walked to the park.
2. I walked almost to the park.

There may, at first, appear to be no difference between sentence 1 and sentence 2. But in sentence 1, *almost* clearly modifies *walked.* In sentence 2, it modifies the phrase *to the park.* The meaning of sentence 1 is either *I almost walked (rather than rode, or hopped, or ran)* or *I almost walked (but then decided not to).* The meaning of sentence 2 is *I did walk (but not quite as far as the park).*

Place modifying words, phrases, and clauses in positions that make clear what they modify.

1. I bought a jacket in a Westwood shop *made of leather.*
1. I bought a jacket *made of leather* in a Westwood shop.

2. The soprano had dreamed of singing at the Met *for many years.*
2. *For many years,* the soprano had dreamed of singing at the Met.

3. The committee decided *after the next meeting* to hold a dance.
3. The committee decided to hold a dance *after the next meeting.*

4. The ice cream cone I licked *rapidly* melted.
4. The ice cream cone I licked melted *rapidly.*
4. The ice cream cone I *rapidly* licked melted.

In the first version of sentences 1, 2, and 3, the placement of the italicized phrases makes the meaning of the sentence unclear, but the revisions place the phrases closer to the words they modify. In the first version of sentence 4, the adverb *rapidly* may modify either *licked* or *melted,* but it is not clear which meaning is intended. The two revised versions are clear, with two different meanings.

The normal word order in an English clause or sentence is subject-verb-object: *The dog bit the boy.* Although there are bound to be times when another word order is necessary, keep in mind that the clearest sentences will move from subject to verb to object and keep the three elements as close as possible. One type of question that appears on several exams presents the problem of lack of sentence clarity when there are several modifiers of the same word. Normally we want to keep the subject close to the verb, but if the subject has modifiers we also must keep these modifiers close to the subject. The following is a typical question of this sort. Which is the best version of the underlined portion of the sentence?

The tuba player, unlike the drummer, whose arms and hands must be strong, relying upon the power of his lungs, is likely to have an unusually well developed chest.

(A) The tuba player, unlike the drummer, whose arms and hands must be strong, relying upon the power of his lungs, is likely

(B) Unlike the drummer, whose arms and hands must be strong, and relying upon the power of his lungs, the tuba player is likely

(C) Relying upon the power of his lungs unlike the drummer, whose arms and hands must be strong, the tuba player is likely

(D) Because of relying upon the power of his lungs, unlike the drummer, whose arms and hands must be strong, the tuba player is likely

(E) Unlike the drummer, whose arms and hands must be strong, the tuba player, relying upon the power of his lungs, is likely

The subject here is *player* and the verb is *is*. There are two units modifying the subject (*player*): *unlike the drummer, whose arms and hands must be strong* and *relying on the power of his lungs*. How can we place both of these elements close to the subject and at the same time avoid separating the subject from the verb? The best we can do is to put the subject between the two modifiers. By putting the longer of the two modifiers at the beginning, we reduce the length of the separation of subject and verb. The best choice, then, is (E).

DANGLING MODIFIERS

Dangling modifiers are phrases that have nothing to modify. They most frequently occur at the beginning of a sentence and are usually verbals: participles (verbal adjectives), gerunds (verbal nouns), and infinitives.

Participles

A participle is a verb used as an adjective. The present participle ends in *-ing* (*eating, seeing, writing,* for example), while the past participle is that form of the verb used to form the perfect tense (*eaten, seen, written,* for example). Whenever you see a sentence that begins with a participle, check to be sure that the participle logically modifies the subject that immediately follows the comma that sets off the participial phrase. In the following sentences, the first version begins with a dangling participle. The revised versions correct the sentence to eliminate the error.

1. *Waiting* for the bus, the sun came out.
   While we were waiting for the bus, the sun came out.

2. *Fishing* for trout, our canoe overturned.
   While we were fishing for trout, we overturned our canoe.
   Fishing for trout, we overturned our canoe.

3. *Having finished* chapter one, chapter two seemed easy.
   After I had finished chapter one, chapter two seemed easy.
   Having finished chapter one, I found chapter two easy.

4. *Having had* no soup, the salad was welcome.
   Because I had no soup, the salad was welcome.
   Having had no soup, I found the salad welcome.

Sentences 1 and 2 use present participles; sentences 3 and 4 use past participles. The second of the two revisions of these sentences illustrates that a sentence can begin with a participle that does not dangle, and the exams will probably contain sentences that begin with a participle used correctly. But you may be sure that they will also contain sentences with dangling participles to test your ability to recognize this error.

Gerunds

Gerunds, verbal nouns, look like participles, but they are used as nouns rather than adjectives. In the sentence *Waiting for the bus is very boring, waiting* is a *gerund,* used as a *noun* and the subject of the sentence. But in the sentence *Waiting for the bus, I became bored,* *waiting* is a *participle,* used as an *adjective* and modifying the subject, *I.* The following sentences contain dangling gerunds, corrected in the revision that follows.

1. By changing the oil regularly, your car will run better.
   By changing the oil regularly, you can make your car run better.
2. By working very hard, better grades will result.
   By working very hard, you will get better grades.
3. After sneezing, my handkerchief was useful.
   After sneezing, I found my handkerchief useful.
   After I sneezed, my handkerchief was useful.

Infinitives

An *infinitive* is the simple, uninflected form of a verb, usually written with the preposition *to; to go* is an infinitive, while *goes* or *going* are inflected forms, that is, with additional sounds (*es, ing*) added to the infinitive. Dangling infinitives show up much less frequently on the exams than dangling participles or gerunds, but the principle of the error is the same. As with dangling participles and gerunds, you can correct a sentence with a dangling infinitive by making sure that the subject of the sentence that follows the comma is what the infinitive really modifies. The first version of the following sentences contains a dangling infinitive, corrected in the revisions.

1. To play the violin well, constant practicing is necessary.
   To play the violin well, you must practice constantly.
2. To make cookies, sugar and flour are needed.
   To make cookies, you need sugar and flour.

Prepositional Phrases and Elliptical Clauses

An *ellipsis* is the omission of a word or words. An *elliptical clause* or *phrase* is one in which the subject and verb are implied, but omitted. For example, in the sentence *When in New York, I stay at the Plaza,* the implied subject and verb of *When in New York* are *I am,* but they have been omitted. It is acceptable to use an ellipsis like this, but if the implied subject does not follow, the phrase will dangle.

1. Though rich and beautiful, her marriage was a failure.
2. While on guard duty, her rifle was lost.
3. When a very young child growing up in Brooklyn, his father sent him to summer camp in New Hampshire.
4. On the ship's observation deck, three gray whales were sighted.

The first three of these sentences begin with dangling elliptical clauses. Adding *she was* in the first and second clause and *he was* in the third, that is, filling in the ellipsis, will correct the sentences. The fourth sentence illustrates that even a prepositional phrase may dangle. An observer, not the three whales, is much more likely to be on this ship's observation deck. Dangling modifiers are, like this one, often not only incorrect but ridiculous too. Whenever you see a sentence that begins with a participle, gerund, elliptical phrase, or infinitive, look very carefully to see whether or not the phrase dangles. And remember that some will be correct.

EXERCISE 5: MISPLACED PARTS, DANGLING MODIFIERS

All of the following sentences contain misplaced parts or dangling modifiers. Rewrite each sentence to eliminate the errors. Answers are on page 115.

1. After making a par despite a very bad drive, the crowd cheered loudly for Nancy Lopez.

2. Having failed to read the book carefully, his remarks in class were either imperceptive or irrelevant.

3. By keeping your eye on the ball and not on your partner, the overhead may become your most consistent shot.

4. Hoping to win a place on the team, her free-skating performance must be first-rate.

5. To do well in this exam, both stamina and concentration are absolutely essential.

6. For months we had anticipated seeing Elton John's performance, and to get the best possible view of the stage, our seats were on the center aisle in the front row.

7. When only eight years old, he sent his son to boarding school in Arizona.

8. Though only five feet four, his quickness of reflex and the uncanny accuracy of his volley have made him the best doubles player on the team.

9. At temperatures below 250 degrees, you should stir the boiling syrup very briskly.

10. I have never, if I remember correctly, been in Venice in October.

11. By applying the insecticide carefully, damage to the environment can be avoided.

12. I just have enough money to pay my telephone bill.

6. PARALLELISM

Errors of parallelism will occur when two or more linked ideas are expressed in different grammatical structures. In a sentence like *I am interested in nuclear physics, to play tennis, and going to the theatre,* each of the three elements of the series is in a different grammatical form: a noun, an infinitive, and a gerund phrase. To make the series parallel, one would use any *one* of the forms three times.

I am interested in nuclear physics, tennis, and theatre.
(three nouns)

I am interested in studying nuclear physics, playing tennis, and going to the theatre.
(three gerunds)

I like to study nuclear physics, to play tennis, and to go to the theatre.
(three infinitives)

To find errors of parallelism, look first to be sure there are two or more ideas, words, or phrases that are similar; then check to see that the coordinate ideas are expressed by the same part of speech, verb form, or clause or phrase structure. The first version of the following sentences is *not* parallel. The revisions that follow each sentence correct the parallelism errors.

1. I admire *his cheerfulness* and *that he perseveres.*
    I admire *his cheerfulness* and *his perseverance.*

2. *To dance* and *singing* were his favorite pastimes.
    Dancing and *singing* were his favorite pastimes.
    To dance and *to sing* were his favorite pastimes.

3. *Her cleverness* and *that she looks innocent* helped her escape.
    Her cleverness and *innocent appearance* helped her to escape.

4. *To ship* a package by air freight is more expensive than *if you send* it by parcel post.
    To ship a package by air freight is more expensive than *to send* it by parcel post.

The following are common parallelism errors in the examinations. In the examples, the first version is in error; the revision or revisions correct the sentence.

Unnecessary Shifts in Verb Tenses

1. She *bought* her ticket at the box office and *sits* in the first row.
    She *bought* her ticket at the box office and *sat* in the first row.

2. Every day he *runs* five kilometers and *swam* half a mile.
    Every day he *runs* five kilometers and *swims* half a mile.
    Every day he *ran* five kilometers and *swam* half a mile.

Unnecessary Shifts from an Active to a Passive Verb

1. John *plays* tennis well, but ping-pong *is played* even better by him.
    John *plays* tennis well, but he *plays* ping-pong even better.

2. The editor *wrote* his article in thirty minutes, and it *was typed* by him in five.

The editor *wrote* his article in thirty minutes and *typed* it in five.

Unnecessary Shifts in Person

We divide personal pronouns into three classes: the first person (singular, *I;* plural, *we*), the second person (*you*), and the third person (singular, *he, she, it, one;* plural, *they*). Though it is possible that a sentence will refer to more than one person (*I* went to Florida, and *she* went to Georgia), in sentences where the change of person is not part of the meaning, the pronouns should be consistent. The first version of each of the following sentences is incorrect.

1. *One* should drive slowly and *you* should keep your eyes on the road.

   One should drive slowly and keep *one's* eyes on the road.

   You should drive slowly and keep *your* eyes on the road.

2. To win at poker, *a player* must know the odds and *you* must observe your opponents carefully.

   To win at poker, *you* must know the odds and observe your opponents carefully.

   To win at poker, *a player* must know the odds and observe *his or her* opponents carefully.

Parallelism errors are likely to occur in a list or series. In the following examples, the second version of the sentences corrects the parallelism errors.

1. The game has three steps: *getting* your pieces to the center, *capturing* your opponent's pieces, and you must *end* with a throw of double six.

   The game has three steps: *getting* your pieces to the center, *capturing* your opponent's pieces, and *ending* with a throw of double six.

2. I talked on, trying to be *charming, gracious,* and *to keep* the conversation going.

   I talked on, trying *to be* gracious and charming and *to keep* the conversation going.

The second example begins with a series of two adjectives (*charming, gracious*), but the expected third adjective is an infinitive. The revised version eliminates the series and makes the two infinitives (*to be, to keep*) parallel.

Sentences incorporating a series set up expectations of parallel structures. In a series of three or more, the first two elements will establish a pattern. Assume a series is to include three parts: *mow the grass, weed the garden,* and *empty the trash.* One can say: (1) *I want you to mow the lawn, weed the garden, and empty the trash* or (2) *I want you to mow the lawn, to weed the garden, and to empty the trash.* In (1), the series begins with the infinitive using *to,* and the *to* is understood in the next two parts. The series is *mow, weed, empty.* In (2), the *to* is used with all three verbs. But if the sentence read *I want you to mow the lawn, weed the garden, and to empty the trash,* the parallelism would be lost.

Do not expect every element in parallel structures to be identical all the time. It is proper, for example, to say *I want you to wash the kitchen and the bathroom, go to the store, and cash a check at the bank.* The parallel elements here are *to wash, (to) go,* and *(to) cash,* but other elements within the series are different.

One sure sign of a sentence that must have parallel grammatical constructions is the use of *correlatives.* Correlatives are coordinating conjunctions used in pairs to express similarity or equality in thought. Whenever any of the following correlatives are used, they should be followed by similar grammatical constructions. Memorize this list, and whenever you see these words in a sentence on the exam, you can be very sure that parallelism is one of the problems in the question.

both . . . and	first second
not only . . . but also	not merely . . . but
not only . . . but	not so much . . . as
not . . . but	as much . . . as
either . . . or	more . . . than
neither . . . nor	less . . . than

In a sentence with *both . . . and,* look first to see exactly what the grammar is immediately after the *both;* then make sure the same structure follows the *and.*

In the following examples, the first version illustrates an error, corrected in the revision or revisions.

1. The opera is *both* a complex work *and* original.

   The opera is *both* complex *and* original.
   both, adjective, *and,* adjective

   The opera is *both* a complex *and* an original work
   both, article, adjective, *and,* article adjective

2. He *not only* is selfish *but also* deceitful.

   He is *not only* selfish *but also* deceitful
   not only, adjective, *but also,* adjective

   He *not only* is selfish *but also* is deceitful.
   not only, verb, adjective, *but also,* verb, adjective

3. The book is *not only* about pigs *but also* flowers.

   The book is *not only* about pigs *but also* about flowers.
   not only, preposition, noun, *but also,* preposition, noun

4. The letter is *either* for you *or* your husband.

   The letter is for *either* you *or* your husband.
   either, pronoun, *or,* pronoun, noun

   The letter is *either* for you *or* for your husband.
   either, preposition, pronoun, *or,* preposition, pronoun, noun

Note that in the fourth sentence the corrected versions are not identical (for *you*/for *your husband*). The parallel must be in structure, but one part may contain additional words. It is correct to write *The letter is either for you or for your handsome first husband,* since both *either* and *or* are followed by prepositional phrases beginning with *for.*

EXERCISE 6: PARALLELISM

If there is an error in the following sentences, choose the underlined lettered part in which the error occurs. Some of the sentences will contain no errors. Answers are on page 116.

1. Because I grew up in Switzerland, I read and speak both French
   A   B   C   D
and German. No error.
           E

2. It is not his reckless spending of my money but that he spends
   A   B
it on other women that has led me to file for divorce. No error.
C   D   E

3. Educational reform is now being brought about by students who
                                  A
are more concerned with the value of their education than
                                  B
getting a piece of paper with B.A. written on it. No error.
     C   D   E

4. A person's aptitude for foreign languages is important to
      A   B
State Department examiners, but, on this exam, it is your
                                           C
ability to read French that will make the difference. No error.
                        D   E

5. Law school not only enables one to practice law, but also
                 A   B
teaches you to think more clearly. No error.
   B   C   D   E

6. I want you not only to paint and sand the screens but also
           A   B   C
to put them in the cellar. No error.
D   E

7. What one expects to get out of a long term investment should be
     A   B   C
considered carefully before you see your broker. No error.
                 D   E

8. Come to the next class meeting prepared to take notes, to
   A   B
speak briefly, and with some questions to ask. No error.
     C   D   E

9. Her grace and charm, her ability to see both sides of a
                         ——————
                             A
   question, and her willingness to accept criticism are
                  ——————————   ——
                       B   C
   qualities that I especially admire. No error.
            ————   ————————
             D   E

10. We must look closely both at the data in this year's report
       ———————— ——————— ——————————
          A   B   C
    and the results of last year's analysis. No error.
                         ——————   ————————
                           D   E

11. The process of natural selection requires that animals be able
                                    ———————————
                                         A
    to adapt to changing climates, to discover new foods,
             —————————————————
                    B
    and defend themselves against their enemies. No error.
    —————————————————   ————   ————————
              C   D   E

12. The new employee soon proved himself to be not only capable
                     ———— ——————————— ——————
                       A   B   C
    but also a man who could be trusted. No error.
             ————————————————————————   ————————
                        D   E

13. As soon as school ended, he jumped into his car, drove to the
    ——————   ————
       A   B
    pool, changes his clothes, and swam twenty laps. No error.
          ———————   ————   ————————
             C   D   E

14. To complete your application, you must fill out three forms,
                                 ———
                                  A
    pay the enrollment fee, submit a recent photograph, and
    ———   ——————
     B   C
    enclose a copy of your high-school transcript. No error.
    ———————   ————————
       D   E

15. I must remember to buy soap and a toothbrush,
                    ——————————————————————————
                              A
    to have the car washed, to order my Christmas cards and gift
    —————————————————————— ———————————————————————————————————
              B   C
    subscriptions, and cash a check before the bank closes.
    ——————————   ————————————————
         C   D
    No error.
    ————————
       E

REVIEW EXERCISE: SECTIONS 4, 5, and 6

Some of the following sentences may be correct. Others contain problems covered in Sections 4, 5, and 6 of the Grammar and Usage Review. There is not more than one error in any sentence.

If there is an error, it will be underlined and lettered. Find the one underlined part that must be changed to make the sentence correct. Choose (E) if the sentence contains no error. Answers are on page 117.

1. <u>Laying aside</u> his guns, the western hero seems <u>to lose</u> his
   A   B
   distinguishing feature, and <u>he became</u> <u>like</u> anyone else.
                               C   D
   <u>No error.</u>
   E

2. Timur's campaigns <u>were initiated</u> less from geopolitical
                      A
   considerations <u>than the need</u> to provide plunder for his army,
                  B
   <u>which resembled</u> a vast mobile city existing <u>only for conquest</u>
   C   D
   and pillage. <u>No error.</u>
                E

3. In calling <u>Vanity Fair a "novel without a hero,"</u> Thackeray
             A
   <u>suggests</u> that none of his characters, <u>not even Amelia or</u>
   B   C
   <u>Dobbin, is</u> completely admirable. <u>No error.</u>
   C   D   E

4. The psychosomatic origin of migraine headaches <u>has been</u>
                                                   A
   <u>suspected</u> for years, but <u>it was not</u> until 1970 that doctors
   A   B
   <u>realized</u> that a patient's thinking about pain <u>is</u> likely to prolong
   C   D
   an attack. <u>No error.</u>
              E

5. The fog of myth and superstition <u>was dispelled</u> not by professors
                                        A
   <u>but men like</u> Prince Henry the Navigator and his captains
       B
   <u>who went out</u> to explore the globe <u>and to chart</u> the known world.
       C   D
   <u>No error.</u>
       E

6. <u>Raising the window shade slowly</u>, the bright sunshine <u>poured</u>
              A   B
   into the room and <u>illuminated</u> the broken crystal <u>lying</u> on the
                          C   D
   floor. <u>No error.</u>
              E

7. <u>Having narrowly missed colliding with another car</u> while trying
                          A
   to change lanes on the freeway, all three of my passengers
   told <u>me</u> that <u>I was</u> a <u>terrible driver.</u> <u>No error.</u>
        B   C   D   E

8. The Prince was <u>embarrassed but not injured</u>
                              A
   when a demonstrator broke through the <u>cordon</u> of security
                                            B
   <u>guards</u> and splashes red paint on <u>his</u> white suit. <u>No error.</u>
        C   D   E

9. After beginning at the bottom <u>as a stockboy</u>, <u>he</u> <u>rose</u> to the
                                       A   B   C
   presidency of the store <u>in only eight years.</u> <u>No error.</u>
                                   D   E

10. You must be very careful <u>to read the instructions</u> on the test
                                    A
    booklet, <u>to mark the correct space</u> on your answer sheet, and
                    B
    <u>stop writing</u> as soon as the proctor <u>announces</u> the end of the
        C   D
    exam. <u>No error.</u>
              E

7. AMBIGUOUS PRONOUNS

In conversation and in informal writing, we often use pronouns that have no single word as their antecedent. *This* happens all the time, for example, the *this* that begins this sentence. It refers to the general idea of the preceding sentence but not to a specific noun. In the exams, you should regard a pronoun that does not have a specific noun or word used as a noun as its antecedent as an error. This sort of error is more likely to occur in the kind of question which gives you choice of revisions. The correct answer will either get rid of the ambiguous pronoun or supply a specific antecedent. Which is the best version of the following sentence?

1. The sun was shining brightly, *which* pleased me.
2. The sun was shining brightly, and *this* pleased me.
3. The sun was shining brightly, and *that* pleased me.
4. Because the sun was shining brightly, *this* pleased me.
5. There was bright sunshine, and *this* pleased me.

The fifth is the best version, for the pronoun *this* has a specific antecedent (*sunshine*). In the first four sentences, none of the pronouns has a specific antecedent. A revision like *That the sun was shining brightly pleased me* would also be correct, since this version simply removes the ambiguous pronoun. The four wrong answers demonstrate that you cannot correct an ambiguous pronoun by substituting another pronoun. The ambiguity will remain until you revise to supply a specific antecedent or to get rid of the pronoun altogether.

You must also be careful with sentences with a pronoun and a choice of antecedents. In a sentence like *Mark told Luke that he owed him five dollars,* we cannot know for certain who owes money to whom. A sentence with an ambiguity of this sort may appear in a question asking you to select an underlined error.

For many years, the American consumer preferred a cola to a
                                                    A   B

lemon, orange, or grapefruit flavored drink; recent surveys show a surprising rise in the consumption of it. No error.
C   D   E

The error here is choice (D), the ambiguous pronoun *it* which may refer to any one of four flavors.

EXERCISE 7: AMBIGUOUS PRONOUNS

All of the following sentences contain ambiguous pronouns. Identify the ambiguous pronoun and revise the sentence to eliminate the error. Answers are on page 118.

1. I came in fifteen minutes late, which made the whole chemistry class incomprehensible to me.

2. I want to go to law school because this is the best way to prepare myself for a career in politics.

3. I wrote checks for my phone bill, the gas bill, and my union dues, and this made my account overdrawn.

4. He ate a salad, a pizza, an order of chili, and a large wedge of apple pie in only seven minutes, and, needless to say, this gave him indigestion.

5. I bought a radio and a record player at the second-hand store, but when I plugged it in, it would not work.

6. Both Dave and Vince were scheduled to work Saturday morning, but because his car wouldn't start, he didn't appear until noon.

7. I am told that I think clearly and write well, and these are important in historical studies.

8. Marine iguanas have armored skin, strong claws, and sharp teeth, and this makes them seem ferocious, though they are harmless vegetarians.

8. OTHER ERRORS OF GRAMMAR

Chances are that seventy-five percent of the grammar errors on the exam you take will be errors of case, agreement, verb tense, parallelism, or misplaced parts, and most of these errors will appear more than once. The errors discussed in this section occur regularly, though usually only once or twice in each exam.

SENTENCE FRAGMENTS

A complete sentence must be an independent clause. Do not assume that a subject and a verb automatically make a complete sentence. *I go,* though it is only two words long, is a complete sentence, while *When he had finished eating his dinner, had pushed back his chair, placed his napkin by his empty wine glass, and risen from the table* is not. It is a dependent clause, a sentence fragment. All of the following are sentence fragments.

1. Hoping to be elected on either the first or second ballot.
2. Because the jurors had very carefully examined the evidence presented in the twenty-two days of testimony.
3. The runners from six South American countries, together with the volleyball teams from Canada, Cuba, and the United States.

To complete sentence one, we must add a subject and verb either in an independent clause following this dependent clause or by changing *Hoping* to *He hoped, She hoped, Carol hoped,* or something of the kind. The *Because* at the beginning of the second sentence marks it as a dependent clause. The third sentence has no main verb.

DOUBLE NEGATIVES

It's hard to miss the double negative in a sentence like *I don't want no peas.* The errors are much less obvious with other negative adverbs such as *hardly, but, scarcely, seldom, rarely,* and the like. When you see these words in a sentence, be on the lookout for a double negative like the following.

1. I spent ten dollars on gasoline, and now I don't have hardly any money.
   (Correct to: *I have hardly any money*)

2. In the twilight, a batter can't hardly see a fastball.
   (Correct to: *can hardly see*)

3. I don't have but a dollar, and that will not scarcely pay my check.
   (Correct to: *I have but . . . will scarcely pay*)

OMISSION OF NECESSARY WORDS

Good writing is concise. Given a choice on the exam between two grammatically correct sentences whose meaning is the same, you should choose the shorter version. But be sure there are no necessary words missing. When we read carelessly, sentences like these (which are *not* correct) appear to be complete.

1. People who read rapidly can easily and often have overlooked important details.
2. He always has and, I'm afraid, always will eat like a pig.

Both of these sentences need two main verbs and try to do the work with one. The verbs *have overlooked* and *will eat* are complete, but we cannot say *can overlooked* or *has eat*. We must write *can easily overlook and often have overlooked* and *always has eaten and . . . always will eat.* In a sentence like *He always does and always will eat like a pig,* we need not repeat the verb *eat,* but when the auxiliary verbs require different forms of the verb, the sentence must include both forms.

Watch very carefully for a missing preposition in sentences with two adjectives joined by a conjunction and followed by prepositions, phrases like *bored by and hostile to, fearful of and concerned about.* There are prepositions missing in the following sentences.

1. He doesn't like watching football games, but he is impressed and enthusiastic about some of the cheerleaders.
2. I am uninterested and bored by shopping for clothes.

We cannot say *impressed about* or *uninterested by.* So we must say *impressed by and enthusiastic about* and *uninterested in and bored by.*

Be especially wary with comparisons. Be certain that the two elements that are compared are equivalent. You cannot say *The man's time in the hundred meters was much faster than the woman* because the two elements being compared are different—*time* versus *woman.* The sentence must read *The man's time in the hundred meters was much faster than that of the woman* or *The man's time in the hundred meters was much faster than the woman's.*

What words must be added to correct the following sentences?

1. He is, sensibly, more interested in getting a good job than a rich wife.
2. The amount of vitamin C in eight ounces of tomato juice is much greater than eight ounces of milk.
3. There are far fewer single parents in Maine, Vermont, and New Hampshire than Massachusetts or Connecticut.

Sentence 1 needs a phrase like *than in getting a rich wife.*
Sentence 2 should end with *than that in eight ounces of milk.*
Sentence 3 should read *than in Massachusetts or Connecticut.*

You must often include *any* or *any other* after comparisons using *than* or the phrase *different from.* Your exam is likely to ask you to choose among the five versions of a sentence like this.

The poetry of Keats is different from any English poet.
(A) different from any English poet.
(B) different than any English poet.
(C) different from that of any English poet.
(D) different from that of any other English poet.
(E) different from any English poet's.

There are several problems here. To begin with, the preferred English idiom is *different from* rather than *different than.* And both choices (A) and (B) have missing words, since, as they stand, they make a comparison between *poetry* and a *poet.* The right answer must add *that of* or make *poet* possessive. The difference between choices (C) and (D) is the addition of *other* in choice (D). The *other* is necessary, since Keats was also a poet. For this reason, choice (D) is the correct answer. Choice (E) would also need to add *other* to be correct.

The difference between *any* and *any other* is a difference in meaning. Had the sentence been about a Latin poet, say Virgil, it might read *The poetry of Virgil is different from that of any English poet* without the *other.* If I say *Evans is faster than any other runner at Yale, and Jones is faster than any runner at Yale,* I am also telling you that Evans is a runner at Yale and Jones is not. Any sentence appearing on the exam will make its meaning clear; chances are the right answer will include the phrase *that of any other.*

Another favorite form of question testing the same error is a sentence with a *like* . . . or *unlike* . . . at the beginning or end.

1. Like Shelley, Byron's poetry is sensuous.
2. Like New York, Chicago's traffic is snarled on Friday afternoons.
3. The market in Boston never closes, like New York.
4. Her bank account is never overdrawn, unlike her husband.

In all of these sentences, the two compared elements are not parallel. The first sentence compares *Byron's poetry* with *Shelley,* not with *Shelley's poetry,* and the second compares *New York* and the *traffic* in Chicago. Any of the following revisions will correct the first sentence.

Like Shelley, Byron wrote sensuous poetry.
(*Shelley* = *Byron*)

Like Shelley's, Byron's poetry is sensuous.
(*Shelley's poetry* = *Byron's poetry*)

Like that of Shelley, Byron's poetry is sensuous.
(*Shelley's poetry* = *Byron's poetry*)

Similarly, the fourth sentence, which compares a *bank account* to a *husband,* must be revised. Either of the following is correct.

Her bank account is never overdrawn, unlike her husband's.
Her bank account is never overdrawn, unlike that of her husband.

DIRECT AND INDIRECT QUESTIONS

Direct questions are followed by question marks. Indirect questions are questions within a sentence that is not a question.

Direct: Did you hear my new record?
Indirect: I asked if you heard my new record.

Direct: The premier asked, "How can we save Venice?"
Indirect: The question is how we can save Venice.

In direct questions, the verb usually precedes the subject. In indirect questions, the subject should precede the verb. Thus, in a sentence like *I wonder how I can afford to buy a new car*, where the question is indirect, the subject (*I*) comes before the verb (*can afford*). In a direct question, *How can I afford a new car?*, the verb (*can*) precedes the subject.

LIKE AND AS

Like is a preposition, that is, a word used to connect a noun or pronoun to another element of the sentence. We speak of the noun or pronoun as the object of the preposition and phrases such as *like me* or *like New York* as prepositional phrases. *Like* should be followed by a noun (*like the wind*) or a pronoun (*like her*). It should not be used in place of the conjunction *as* to introduce a clause with a subject and verb or an implied verb. All of the following are correct.

1. As you said, he is overweight, like me.
2. Like zinnias, marigolds are easy to grow.
3. Marigolds are easy to grow, as zinnias are.
4. He is as fast as I. (The verb *am* is understood.)
5. He is fast, like me.
6. As I said, peaches taste good, as summer fruits should.

WHO, WHICH, AND THAT—RESTRICTIVE AND NONRESTRICTIVE CLAUSES

Given a choice among *who, which,* or *that*, use *who* when the antecedent is a single human being (*the man who, John Smith, who*) or a group thought of as individuals (*the lawmakers who, the players who, the jurors who*). Use *that* or *which* for a group thought of as a group (*the senate that; the team, which; the jury that*).

Conservative grammarians distinguish between *which* and *that*, using *that* in defining or restrictive clauses and *which* in nondefining or nonrestrictive clauses. A restrictive clause identifies or defines the noun it modifies, while a nonrestrictive clause merely describes or adds information.

1. The novel *that he wrote in 1860* was not published until 1900.
   (restrictive clause)

2. The novel *The Guardian, which he wrote in 1860,* was not published until 1900.
   (nonrestrictive clause)

3. The musicians *who missed two rehearsals* played badly.
   (restrictive clause)

4. The musicians, *who rehearse every day,* are on stage.
   (nonrestrictive clause)

The pronoun *who* can introduce either a restrictive or a nonrestrictive clause. If the clause is nonrestrictive, it should be set off by commas. Though it is extremely unlikely that a test will ask you to discriminate between the use of *that* and *which,* the point may appear in a sentence with a second and more obvious sort of error. But you should be alert to the possibility of a question that asks you to decide about the use of commas with a *who* clause, especially on the ACT exams, which test punctuation more frequently. Sentences with a human antecedent wrongly using *which* or *that* instead of *who* are common.

EXERCISE 8: OTHER ERRORS OF GRAMMAR

Answers are on page 118.

Part A

Identify the sentence fragments in the following.

1. Representing the farm belt attitude toward price subsidies, the delegations from Kansas, Nebraska, and Iowa, as well as food processors from Texas, Louisiana, and Georgia.

2. So David wept.

3. The Colt Company, a leader in the industry, and celebrated for introducing the first energy-efficient nine-room house at a cost under sixty thousand dollars.

4. Is he?

5. When glaciers ground extensive tracts of the granite to a highly polished finish.

Part B

All of the following sentences contain errors described in Section 8. Identify the error and correct the sentence.

1. The price of meat has gone up steeply in the past six months, according to an unofficial government survey, but there is some consolation for yogurt eaters; yogurt prices haven't risen hardly at all.

2. While calculating their income tax returns, people can and often have made mistakes.

3. During the Renaissance, Venice was wealthier and more important than any city in the world.

4. I wonder how can we finish both the painting and the window-washing in a single day.

5. People have and probably will say for many years to come that Mead's *Coming of Age in Samoa* should be required reading for anyone interested in anthropology.

6. I invested my money in the bank, which pays a higher rate of interest than any other in the city.

7. What Congress decides today will determine the kind of world people must live in the future.

8. The Orsinis hoped to establish their influence throughout Tuscany like the Borgias did in Rome.

9. The embassy claimed that the rights of Soviet Jewish citizens are no different from any Russians.

10. If you use two tablespoons of soy sauce, you will not need scarcely any salt.

11. Scientists argue that water plants can be as effective, if not more effective than chemicals in water purification.

12. The question is when can we afford to take the time to finish the report.

13. He never has and never will be able to play left field as well as Williams.

14. He bought the turkey at Jack's Ranch Market that offered a special price on poultry.

15. Despite their inventive plots and catchy melodies, the musical plays of Sondheim are less popular and less frequently recorded than Cole Porter.

16. As Spain, France was eager to send its navigators to Africa and America.

17. Her trills are as good or better than those of any other soprano.

18. The predators follow the herds of zebra who migrate more than fifteen hundred miles each year.

19. Like the senator explained, what transpired in Chicago in the 1930s now happens all over the country.

20. I am puzzled about how can he afford to make the payments on his cars and a boat while his income is so small.

9. ERRORS OF DICTION, IDIOM, AND STYLE

DICTION

The cause of a diction error, the choice of the wrong word, is not knowing exactly what each word means. Obviously, the more words you know, the fewer diction errors you will make. But the usage sections of the exams are not intended to test the range of your vocabulary, and the words that are misused are rarely obscure or difficult. They are much more likely to be words we all know—or think we know—but confuse with words that look or sound similar. A list of words that are easily mixed up can go on for pages. You should be aware of the following examples, but don't try to memorize the list. Just be sure when you are taking a test to read *each word* carefully.

allude (refer to)—elude (escape from)
allusion (reference)—illusion (false or misleading appearance)
invoke (ask solemnly for)—evoke (summon)
afflict (cause suffering to)—inflict (impose)
aggravate (intensify)—irritate (annoy)

anxious (apprehensive)—eager (ardent)
fortuitous (accidental)—fortunate (lucky)
detain (confine, delay)—retain (keep, hire)
precede (go before)—proceed (advance, continue)
there (in that place)—their (belonging to them)—they're (they are)
its (of it)—it's (it is)

Fewer/Less, Many/Much, Number/Amount

Use *fewer* (not *less*), *many* (not *much*), and *number* (not *amount*) with items that can be counted or numbered.

fewer gallons, many gallons, the number of gallons

Use *less, much,* and *amount* with items that cannot be counted or numbered.

less gasoline, much gasoline, the amount of gasoline

Between/Among

Use *among* with three or more persons or things. When there are only two, use *between*.

The estate was divided between his wife and his daughter.
The vote was split among the three candidates.

Affect/Effect

Affect is a verb meaning *to influence.* As a verb, *effect* means *to bring about,* but as a noun *effect* means a *result* or an *influence.*

1. The *effect* (result) of his decision was to *effect* (bring about) a change in the voting laws that has *affected* (influenced) every candidate for office.

2. Her decision will not *affect* single taxpayers, but it will have some *effect* on married couples.

In the second sentence, both *affect* and *effect* mean *influence,* but *affect* is a verb and *effect* a noun.

IDIOM

This Grammar and Usage Review began by saying that you must not choose your answers by the *it-sounds-right/it-sounds-wrong* principles, but unless you have memorized every idiom in the English language—and no one has—there is nothing to rely on in choosing between idioms except the it-sounds-right principle. Should I say *agree with, agree to,* or *agree upon?* Depending upon the sentence, any one of the three may be right.

I *agree with* your opinion
The plaintiff *agreed to* pay damage of one hundred dollars.
The committees have *agreed upon* a compromise.

Idioms are the usual way in which educated people put words together to express thought. Careful speakers or writers say *different from,* not *different than,* and *other than,* not *other from.* Most of the idiom problems arise from the use of propositions. Since prepositions are so often insignificant words (*to, from, of, by*), it is easy to miss an obvious idiom error if you read carelessly.

There are no rules for idiom, and as the example of *agree* illustrates, idiom will often depend upon meaning. The more advanced tests will occasionally use an idiom uncertainty to distract you from a real error. Which is the better of these two sentences?

1. The issue is *how can we make our streets free of crime.*
2. The issue is *how we can make our streets free from crime.*

Is it *free from* or *free of?* Neither sounds wrong, and, in fact, either is acceptable. The sentence is really testing word order with an indirect question, and sentence 2 (*we can*) is the better sentence.

One choice the exams often ask you to make is between a three-word phrase made up of a noun or adjective followed by a preposition and a gerund (a word ending in *-ing*) or a similar phrase with the same noun or adjective followed by an infinitive (the preposition *to* and the verb): *hope of going* or *hope to go; ability in running* or *ability to run; afraid of jumping* or *afraid to jump.* You must, finally, depend upon your ear and the context, but if neither version sounds clearly right or wrong, choose the infinitive. It is the better percentage play.

Apes have demonstrated some *ability for reasoning deductively.*
Apes have demonstrated some *ability to reason deductively.*

There are some established English idioms which appear regularly on standardized examinations. The *correct* idioms are given *first.*

different from not *different than*
die of not *die from*
try to not *try and*
except for not *excepting for*
in regard to not *in regards to*
plan to not *plan on*
prior to not *prior than*
type of not *type of a*

STYLE

To this point, we have been concerned with errors of grammar, usage, diction, and idiom. With errors of this sort, you can point to a problematical single word or phrase and identify an error. In some questions, you will be asked to choose between several versions of a sentence, none of which contains a specific error of grammar or usage. One of the answers will be better than the others for reasons of style, that is, because it conveys meaning with superior precision, conciseness, clarity, or grace.

Between an awkward sentence that is grammatically correct and a smoother sentence with a grammatical error, you must always prefer the correct version. But when neither of the two sentences has an error, you must base your decision on style. *Verbosity,* or unnecessary wordiness, is the most tested stylistic weakness, especially on ACT exams. In sentence correction questions, you will often be able to eliminate three of the five sentences for grammar or usage errors and have to decide between two grammatically correct sentences, one of which is less verbose.

After the shipment of bananas had been unloaded, a tarantula's nest was discovered by the foreman in the hold of the ship.

- (A) After the shipment of bananas had been unloaded, a tarantula's nest was discovered by the foreman
- (B) After unloading the shipment of bananas, a tarantula's nest was discovered by the foreman
- (C) Having unloaded the shipment of bananas, a tarantula's nest was discovered by the foreman
- (D) After the shipment of bananas had been unloaded, the foreman discovered a tarantula's nest
- (E) After the shipment of bananas had been unloaded, the foreman discovers a tarantula's nest

Choices (B), (C), and (E) cannot be right—choices (B) and (C) because of the dangling gerund and dangling participle, choice (E) because of the improper verb tenses (a past perfect and a present). Both choices (A) and (D) are grammatical, but because it uses the passive voice, choice (A) is wordier than choice (D). Given a choice like this, prefer the sentence in the active voice. It is impossible to write the same sentence using a passive verb without using at least two more words than the active voice requires.

   I hit the ball. (four words, active)
   The ball was hit by me. (six words, passive)

You should note also the ambiguity in choice (A) in that you are not sure if the *foreman,* the *nest,* or both are in the *hold* of the ship.

   In our eagerness to be expressive, we sometimes waste words by saying the same thing twice.

1. His prose is *clear* and *lucid.*
2. The *annual* celebration *takes place every year.*
3. Her argument was *trivial,* and *it had no importance.*

There are many phrases which take two or more words to say what one word can say equally well. *Due to the fact that* takes five words to say what *because* says in one. A verbose sentence will use a phrase like *his being of a generous nature* using six words where a phrase like *his generous nature* would say the same thing in three and *his generosity* in two. The following are examples of verbose phrases and formulas with a concise alternative.

VERBOSE	CONCISE
due to the fact that	because
owing to the fact that	because
inasmuch as	because
which was when	when
for the purpose of + gerund for the purpose of eating	to + verb to eat
in order to + verb in order to fly	to + verb to fly
so they can + verb so they can appreciate	to + verb to appreciate
not + negative adjective not useless	positive adjective useful
each and every	every
he is a man who	he is
... is a ... that soccer is a game that	is soccer is
the truth is that the truth is that I am tired	often omit altogether I am tired
the fact is that the fact is that you were late	often omit altogether you were late
it is it is money that talks	often omit altogether money talks
there are there are some flowers that are poisonous	often omit altogether some flowers are poisonous
in a situation where	where
in a condition where	where

EXERCISE 9: ERRORS OF DICTION, IDIOM, AND STYLE

Answers are on page 120.

Part A

All of the following sentences contain an error of diction or idiom. Identify the error and correct the sentence.

1. Led by the oldest graduate present, with classes more or less in chronological order, the alumni parade winds it's way from Weld Hall to the Ford Theatre, where the annual meeting is held.

2. Governor Smith's way of running the state is noticeably different than Governor Eliot's.

3. There are fewer cars on the road, less accidents, and a lower death rate since the gasoline shortage.

4. Since his speeches usually have considerable affect on the Senate, the president will speak tonight.

5. The squabbles between the four original New England states delayed the calling of a convention.

6. I will plan on attending the meeting if I am not delayed.

7. Inflicted with poor eyesight and hearing as a result of her indigent childhood, she nevertheless rose to be the top money winner in women's badminton.

8. By calling her client's widowed mother, the lawyer hoped to effect the jury, but the strategem had no effect.

Part B

All of the following sentences are verbose. Cross out all the unnecessary words without changing the meaning of the sentences.

1. Though trailing thirty-one to ten, the team showed great resiliency and an ability to bounce back; when the fourth quarter ended, the score was thirty-one to thirty.

2. She is so compulsive about avoiding noise that she refuses to begin to do her homework until there is total and complete silence in the dorm.

3. When I look back in retrospect on all that has happened, it is clear that I made the right decision.

4. At the present moment in history, there are now over two thousand unregistered handguns in Alpine County alone.

5. Raised in a well-to-do and affluent suburb of New York, she was unable to adjust to the lack of physical comforts in rural Saskatchewan.

6. Unless the president presents a workable and practicable program to conserve and keep energy from being wasted, none of the New England states is likely to support him.

7. The true facts of the case made it clear that he was obviously a victim of a hideous injustice.

8. The subtle distinctions and nice discriminations of her philosophical essays are too fine for any but the most learned and erudite to understand, even with several rereadings.

9. Many dramatists and playwrights, Congreve among them, wrote about the elegance and corruption of the Restoration society.

10. The photography of the mountainous hill regions where the peasants live is beautiful; unfortunately, the film opened when the potential audience to whom it might have appealed had sated its appetite for travelogues.

REVIEW EXERCISE: SECTIONS 7, 8, and 9

If there is an error of grammar, diction, or verbosity in the following sentences, choose the underlined and lettered part in which the error occurs. Some of the sentences will contain no errors. Answers are on page 121.

1. Gordon's novel, written with an eye to conservative readers,
                              A
has less scenes of action and more with moral lessons than
    B   C
any other work published this year. No error.
    D   E

2. An independent clause <u>can stand alone</u> as a <u>sentence;</u>
         A B
a dependent clause <u>occupies</u> a subordinate position and
         C
cannot <u>by itself</u> be a complete sentence. <u>No error.</u>
         D E

3. Though his lawyer <u>argued his case</u> cogently, concisely, and
         A
<u>forcefully,</u> Jones was <u>still</u> found guilty <u>and sentenced</u> to
 B C D
three years in jail. <u>No error.</u>
         E

4. Since the mountains in California are higher <u>than New York,</u>
         A
I and my cousins <u>who like to ski</u> <u>will prefer</u> <u>to spend</u> the
         B C D
winter on the west coast. <u>No error.</u>
         E

5. The courtly lover of Provence worshipped both <u>the Virgin</u> and
         A
an earthly lady and <u>paid his</u> tribute <u>to her</u> in <u>ornate</u> lyric
         B C D
poems. <u>No error.</u>
     E

6. Although he <u>took</u> careful notes, <u>studied</u> in the library every
         A B
night, and <u>wrote</u> two extra papers, this industry <u>did not effect</u>
         C D
his grade in the class. <u>No error.</u>
         E

7. <u>Like</u> a large room, the American continent once offered
 A
an exhilarating spatial freedom, impressing western settlers
         B
<u>first with</u> its sublime beauty and afterwards with
 C
<u>its opportunities for exploitation.</u> <u>No error.</u>
         D E

8. When the Queen entered, the <u>musicians which were</u>
                                 A

    on the stage withdrew quietly, but the actors were <u>too surprised</u>
                                                         B

    <u>to be able</u> <u>to know what to do.</u> <u>No error.</u>
       C   D   E

9. I have <u>no interest</u> and <u>no intention</u> to become involved with
              A   B

    this <u>foolish debate</u> about priorities <u>in</u> Central America.
           C   D

    <u>No error.</u>
      E

10. We will <u>have to start for home</u> much earlier this week, <u>for there</u>
                   A   B

    are <u>not but two or three hours</u> of good driving conditions
                    C

    <u>if we leave</u> after two o'clock. <u>No error.</u>
       D   E

10. PUNCTUATION

This section will certainly not tell you all you ought to know about punctuation to write well. It will describe the kind of punctuation errors that appear most often on the examinations. You are not likely to find sentences that test the use of the dash or the colon or that ask you whether to put the comma inside or outside a parenthesis. But you must know the difference between a comma and a semicolon. The ETS (Educational Testing Service) exams (SAT, GMAT, GRE, NTE, CBEST, and many others) rarely test for punctuation errors, and when they do, the question is likely to be on the use of the semicolon. The ACT English usage exam, however, does include questions on a variety of comma errors, on the use of the apostrophe, and on the semicolon and colon.

The comma is used to indicate a slight separation of sentence elements. The semicolon indicates a greater degree of separation, and the period marks the end of a sentence. The punctuation errors that will appear most frequently on the exams are the use of a comma where a semicolon is needed and the use of a semicolon where a comma is needed. In compound sentences, that is, sentences with two independent clauses, a semicolon and a comma are *not* interchangeable.

Punctuate the following sentences with either a comma or a semicolon.

1. I had come to China to buy silk and I was not planning to buy anything else.
   I had come to China to buy silk I was not planning to buy anything else.

2. I got my needles from Frankfurt while my threads came from London.
   I got my needles from Frankfurt my threads came from London.

In both examples, the first version needs a comma before the conjunction (*and, while*). In the second version, a semicolon should follow *silk* and *Frankfurt*. The principle is the same in both. With two independent clauses joined by a conjunction, use a comma. With two independent clauses that are not joined by a conjunction, use a semicolon.

Now punctuate the following sentences with either a comma or a semicolon.

1. I looked for a house for sale on the lake hoping to be able to finish my book there.
2. They bundled themselves into the car waved once and drove away.
3. He was not at all interesting a man who talked endlessly about himself and how much money he had.

All three sentences need commas and only commas: after *lake* in sentence 1, after *car* and *once* in sentence 2, and after *interesting* in sentence 3. All of the clauses after the commas are dependent, that is, they cannot stand by themselves as complete sentences. If they were set off by semicolons, they would be sentence fragments.

The ACT tests include punctuation questions more often than other exams. The following is an example of the ACT question form.

The editorials in *Ghost Magazine* are
infuriating to some <u>readers; delightful</u>
1

1. A. NO CHANGE
   B. readers. And
   C. readers,
   D. readers; or

to others. <u>Nevertheless, its</u> circulation
2
has grown more rapidly than that of any
other fantasy magazine.

2. F. NO CHANGE
   G. Nevertheless its
   H. Nevertheless, it's
   J. Nevertheless it's

The correct answers here are 1. (C) and 2. (F). You must use a comma after *readers*. If you use a period or a semicolon, the phrase *delightful to others* is a sentence fragment. In 2, the punctuation is correct. The possessive of the pronoun *it* is *its; it's* is a contraction of *it is*. The comma marks the slight pause after the introductory word *Nevertheless*.

The following is a brief summary of the rules governing commas, semicolons, and colons.

COMMA

Use a comma:

1. in a series of three or more with a single conjunction.

   He bought red, green, and blue neckties.
   I must stop at the bank, have the car washed, and leave my shirts at the laundry.

2. to set off parenthetic expressions.

   The result, I imagine, will be in the paper.
   The check, you will be glad to know, is in the mail.

3. to set off nonrestrictive relative clauses.

   In 1600, when *Hamlet* was first acted, the Globe was London's largest public theatre.
   Montpelier, Concord, and Augusta, which are all small cities, are the capitals of the northern New England states.

4. to separate the two parts of a sentence with two independent clauses joined by a conjunction.

The film is over, and the audience has left the theatre.
The mayor is present, but the governor is not here.

5. to set off introductory words, phrases, or clauses.

Unfortunately, he left his wallet in the car.
Having looked in the glove compartment, he discovered his wallet was missing.

6. to set off appositives.

Mr. Smith, the mayor, called the meeting to order.
The leading batter in the league is John Jones, the first baseman.

Do *not* use a comma to join two independent clauses not joined by a conjunction. Use a period or a semicolon.

Her novels are always best sellers; they are translated into three languages.
The boat crossed the lake in fifteen minutes; the canoe took two hours.

Each of these sentences could be written as two sentences with periods at the end. If a conjunction were added, a comma would replace the semicolons.

Her novels are always best sellers, *and* they are translated into three languages.
The boat crossed the lake in fifteen minutes, *but* the canoe took two hours.

SEMICOLON

Use a semicolon:

1. to separate two independent clauses in a compound sentence when there is no conjunction between them.

The hurricane came ashore near Lake Charles; its winds were measured at more than one hundred miles per hour.

The warnings were broadcast early in the day; thus, there was no loss of life.

2. to separate a series when one or more of the elements of the series contains commas.

He bought a red, a green, and a blue tie; three button-down shirts; and a pair of penny loafers.
We will stop in Maumee, Ohio; Erie, Pennsylvania; Albany, New York; and Amherst, Massachusetts.

COLON

Use a colon after an independent clause:

1. to introduce a series.

The following vegetables should be planted in March: radishes, carrots, leeks, turnips, and cabbage.

In this sentence, the clause before the colon is independent. In a sentence like *In March, you should plant radishes, carrots, leeks, turnips, and cabbage* where there is no independent clause before the series, you must *not* use a colon.

2. to join two independent clauses when the second amplifies or interprets the first.

A preliminary step is essential to successful whipped cream: you must chill the bowl and the beaters.

3. to introduce a quotation.

Every English schoolchild knows the opening line of *Twelfth Night:* "If music be the food of love, play on."

OTHER MARKS OF PUNCTUATION

Dash

Use a *dash* to indicate an abrupt break and to set off parenthetical elements already broken up by commas.

I believe—no, I know—he is guilty.

I—er—you—er—forget it!

The general—overdecorated, overconfident, overweight—spoke to the troops on the benefits of self-sacrifice.

The speech—the harangue, I should say—lasted for three hours.

Apostrophe

Use an *apostrophe* to indicate the omission of a letter or letters in a contraction (*I'm, I've, you'd, don't, who's, we're*).

Form the possessive of singular nouns by adding *'s* (*tiger's, cat's, man's*). Form the possessive of plural nouns by adding just the apostrophe (') if the plural ends in *s* (*tigers', cats', dogs'*). Form the possessive of plural nouns that do not end in *s* by adding *'s* (*mice's, men's, children's*).

EXERCISE 10: PUNCTUATION

In the left-hand column, you will find a passage in a "spread-out" format with various words and phrases underlined. In the right-hand column, you will find a set of responses corresponding to each underlined portion. If the underlined portion is correct as it stands, mark the letter indicating "NO CHANGE." If the underlined portion is incorrect, decide which of the choices best corrects it. Consider only underlined portions; assume that the rest of the passage is correct. Answers are on page 121.

Anything it seems is worth
                1
fighting about when there's
money to be made. How else can
we explain the public-relations
war being waged between the
plastics and paper industries
over the best kind of grocery
bag to use. If you've been to the
        2
supermarket lately, you know
what we're talking about.

1. A. NO CHANGE
   B. Anything, it seems is worth
   C. Anything it seems, is worth
   D. Anything, it seems, is worth

2. F. NO CHANGE
   G. bag to use? If
   H. bag to use; if
   J. bag to use! If

Alongside those <u>tried trusty</u>
3
<u>and true brown</u> paper bags that
3
Americans have relied on and
treasured since 1883, you'll see a
lump of limp, shapeless, non-
biodegradable plastic containers
that the plastic lobby would try
to convince you is the way to go.

Their argument is that plastic
bags are more easily <u>portable—</u>
4
<u>at least, for those who go to the</u>
4
<u>store on foot</u>—because they have
4

<u>handles; that</u> they don't leak all
5
over the place when something
wet gets loose; and that they can
just as easily be used as garbage
containers as the paper variety.
They are also cheaper for the
supermarket, at about 2.6 cents
apiece, compared with 4.4 cents
for paper bags, and they require
less storage space.

The obvious response to this
propaganda barrage is that paper
bags stand on their <u>own, so to</u>
6
<u>speak, in your trunk, are bio-</u>
6
<u>degradable, make a better waste</u>
6
<u>container can</u> be cut up and used
6

3. A. NO CHANGE
   B. tried, trusty, and
      true, brown
   C. tried trusty, and
      true brown
   D. tried, trusty and
      true brown

4. F. NO CHANGE
   G. portable, at least, for
      those who go to the
      store on foot—
   H. portable—at least for
      those who go to the
      store on foot—
   J. portable, at least, for
      those, who go to the
      store on foot,

5. A. NO CHANGE
   B. handles that
   C. handles, that
   D. handles—that

6. F. NO CHANGE
   G. own so to speak in
      your trunk, are bio-
      degradable, make a
      better waste container,
      can
   H. own, so to speak, in
      your trunk; are bio-
      degradable; make a
      better waste container;
      can
   J. own, so to speak, in
      your trunk, are bio-
      degradable, make a
      better waste container,
      can

to wrap books, packages, or
parcels, or to make Halloween
masks; and—here's the telling
          ———————
             7
punch—are actually cheaper
—————
   7
overall because supermarket
checkers can pack them
18 percent faster than
the plastic.

Surveys have been conducted,
                    —————————
                        8
of course, and it turns out, not
————————————————————————————
             8
too surprisingly, that those who
————————————————
       8
live alone in city apartments—
typically singles, old people, and
just about anyone who lives in the
middle of Manhattan or
San Francisco—prefer plastic.

The rest of us—suburbanites the
             ———————————————————
                    9
pro-plastic folks disparagingly
———————————————————————————————
              9
call us—are quite happy with
———————
  9
our brown paper bags, thank you,
and we're still a majority.

7. A. NO CHANGE
   B. masks; and here's the
      telling punch; are
   C. masks, and, heres the
      telling punch, are
   D. masks, and—here's
      the telling punch—
      are

8. F. NO CHANGE
   G. conducted, of course,
      and it turns out not
      too surprisingly
   H. conducted of course,
      and it turns out not
      too surprisingly
   J. conducted of course,
      and it turns out,
      not too surprisingly

9. A. NO CHANGE
   B. us—"suburbanites" the
      pro-plastic folks
      disparagingly call us—
   C. us—"suburbanites,"
      the pro-plastic folks
      disparagingly call us—
   D. us—suburbanites, the
      pro-plastic folks
      disparagingly call us—

REVIEW EXERCISE: SECTIONS 1–10

When you take a grammar exam, you must be able to recognize the kind of error that is being tested for. Certain words or sentence structures should warn you at once of the kind of error likely to occur in the sentence. All of the following words or structures should alert you at once to one or two likely errors. What are these errors? Answers are on page 122.

1. a sentence beginning with a participle

2. a sentence beginning with *Both*

3. a sentence containing a series

4. a sentence beginning with *Either*

5. a sentence containing the word *not*

6. a sentence beginning with a prepositional phrase with *Like*

7. a sentence containing the phrase *a number*

8. a sentence beginning with *Everybody*

9. a sentence containing the word *who*

10. a sentence containing the verb *look*

11. a sentence beginning with the word *One*

12. a sentence beginning with the word *None*

13. a sentence beginning with an elliptical phrase

14. a sentence containing the word *criteria*

15. a sentence containing the word *almost*

16. a sentence containing the word *hardly*

17. a sentence containing a comparison

18. a sentence containing the verb *lie*

19. a sentence beginning with the word *If*

20. a sentence containing the phrase *as well as*

ANSWERS TO THE GRAMMAR AND USAGE REVIEW EXERCISES

EXERCISE 1: PARTS OF SPEECH, ADJECTIVES AND ADVERBS, LINKING VERBS, COMPARATIVES AND SUPERLATIVES

1. *Almost*—an adverb, modifying the adjective *every*.

2. *different*—an adjective, with the linking verb *appeared*.

3. *suddenly*—an adverb, modifying *appeared*. In this sentence *appeared* means *made an appearance* rather than *looked* and is not a linking verb.

4. *best*—the superlative. There are more than two players.

5. *better*—the comparative, with only two compared.

6. *bad*—an adjective, modifying *pie*. *Taste* here is a linking verb.

7. *noticeably*—an adverb, modifying the adverb *more*.

8. *sad*—an adjective, with the linking verb *feel*.

9. *seriously*—an adverb, modifying the verb *take*.

10. *aromatic*—an adjective, with the linking verb *smells*.

11. *almost*—an adverb, modifying the adjective *any*.

12. *carefully*—an adverb. In this sentence *look* means *examine* not *appear* and is not a linking verb.
    clearly—an adverb, modifying the adjective *visible*.

13. *largest*—the superlative. There are many antelopes.
    slowest—the superlative. Again, there are more than two.

14. *surely*—an adverb, modifying the verb *seemed*.
    inexhaustible—an adjective, modifying the noun *supply*. *Seemed* is a linking verb.

15. *steeply*—an adverb, modifying the verb *rise*.
    steep—an adjective, modifying the pronoun *it*, with the linking verb *look*.

EXERCISE 2: CASE

Part A

1. *we*—subject of the clause *we are not.*

2. *me*—object of the preposition *except.*

3. *his*—possessive, before the gerund *using.*

4. *I*—subjective case, agreeing with the subject *it.*

5. *our*—possessive, before the gerund *standing.*

6. *me*—object of the verb *affect.*

7. *me*—objective case, in apposition to the objective *us* (*Let's* = *Let us*).

8. *his*—possessive, before the gerund *talking.*

9. *president's*—possessive, before the gerund *riding.*

10. *me*—objective case, in apposition to *finalists,* the object of the preposition.

Part B

1. *who*—subject of the clause *who was elected.*

2. *who*—subject of the clause *who did not wish to be interviewed.* The *we understand* is parenthetical.

3. *Who*—subject of the clause *Who will buy this car.*

4. *Whom*—object of the verb *will choose.* The subject of the clause is *company.*

5. *whoever*—subject of the clause *whoever is waiting for the general.*

6. *whomever*—object of the verb *convince.*

7. *Whoever*—subject of the clause *Whoever deserves the prize.*

8. *whoever*—subject of the clause *whoever is most likely to support their position.*

9. *whomever*—object of the preposition *with.*

10. *whom*—object of the preposition *with.*

EXERCISE 3: AGREEMENT

1. *are, is*—The antecedent of *who* is the plural *candidates;* the subject of *is* is the singular *None.*

2. *is*—the singular *sergeant-at-arms* is the subject of the verb.

3. *have, is*—The antecedent of *who* is the plural *applicants;* the subject of *is* is the singular *None.*

4. *was*—The subject is the singular *Mr. Lombardi.*

5. *makes*—The subject is the singular *evidence.*

6. *include*—The subject is the plural *criteria.*

7. *look, they*—The subject is the plural *columns,* which is also the antecedent of *they.*

8. *is*—The subject is the singular *student.*

9. *are*—The subject is compound, *Mr. and Mrs. Smith.*

10. *have*—The antecedent of *who* is *quarter-milers.*

11. *are, increases*—The antecedent of *that* is the plural *penguins;* the subject of *increases* is the singular *number.*

12. *is*—The subject is the singular *Mary Jane.*

13. *was*—The subject is the singular *Everyone.*

14. *have, their*—The plural *twins* is the subject of *have* and the antecedent of *their.*

15. *has, her*—The singular *Sally* is the subject of *has* and the antecedent of *her.*

16. *was*—The subject is the singular *I.*

17. *enjoys*—The subject is the singular *president.*

18. *seems*—The singular *The number* is the subject.

19. *have*—*A number* here means *many,* so the verb is plural.

20. *are*—The subject *data* is plural.

REVIEW EXERCISE: SECTIONS 1, 2, AND 3

1. (E) The *me* is the object of the preposition *but;* the subject is the singular *No one,* so *was* is also correct.

2. (A) The phrase *many a young man* is singular. The plural would be *many men.*

3. (E) The agreement in this sentence is correct.

4. (D) The subject is plural, a compound subject with *and.*

5. (C) Since *thousands* is plural, *life* should be *lives.*

6. (B) The phrase *my sister and I* is in apposition to *members,* the object of *includes. I* should be *me.*

7. (E) The singular *was* is correct with the singular subject *result. Her* is the object of *alarm.*

8. (D) The subject of the last clause is *they,* the verb is *can catch,* and the object should be *whomever.*

9. (E) The adjective *simple* is correct with the linking verb *seemed.* The adverb *simply* modifies the adverb *too.*

10. (D) With a comparison of two teams, *better* not *best* should be used.

EXERCISE 4: VERBS

1. *had*—Never use *would have* in the *if* clause.

2. *lasts*—Since the discovery is a fact that continues to be true, use the present tense.

3. *waited*—There is nothing in the sentence to suggest a present time to which a present perfect tense is related, so only the past tense makes sense.

4. *had waited*—Here the other verb in the sentence is the past tense *arrived.* Action in past time in relation to another past time is expressed by the past perfect tense.

5. *will go*—The sentence expresses a simple future (*tomorrow*). The future perfect would be used only if the action were related to another time even further in the future.

6. *were*—Since the condition expressed in the *if* clause is untrue (I am not thinner), the present subjunctive should be used. *Was* is the past tense and not a subjunctive.

7. *stepped*—The first two verbs (*climbed, opened*) are in the past tense. There is no reason to change tenses, so the third verb should also be in the past tense.

8. *lying, lying*—The verb here is the intransitive *lie* (to rest). The participal form of *lie* is *lying*.

9. *laid, lay*—The first verb is the transitive verb *lay* (to place) in the past tense. The second verb is the intransitive verb *lie* (to recline) in the past tense. The first verb has an object (*briefcase*); the second has none.

10. *rise*—The intransitive verb *rise* in the present tense is correct here.

11. *Setting, Sitting*—The first verb is the transitive *set* with *flowers* as the object; the second verb, the intransitive *sit,* has no object.

12. *rises*—The intransitive verb *rise* in the present tense is correct here

13. *will be*—The future tense, not the future perfect, is correct here. There is no time even further in the future to which this verb is related.

14. *will have worked*—Here the future perfect is correct because the opening clause defines a time which is even further in the future. In sentence 13, 1995 is in the future but not further in the future than the time at which I will be sixty. But in the second sentence, 1995 will come at the end of the period of thirty years' work.

15. *had been*—The verb in the first clause is subjunctive because it describes a contrary-to-fact situation. The past tense of the verb in the second clause requires a subjunctive in the past tense in the first. In the present tense, this sentence would read: *If you were more careful, you would not dent the fender of the car.*

16. *were*—The correct verb here is the present subjunctive.

EXERCISE 5: MISPLACED PARTS, DANGLING MODIFIERS

There are several ways to rewrite these sentences and eliminate the errors. The following are a few of the possible revisions.

1. As it stands now, the participial phrase at the beginning of the sentence dangles and appears to modify the *crowd* rather than *Nancy Lopez*. One can correct the sentence by beginning *After she made a par* . . . or by leaving the participial phrase unchanged and writing *Nancy Lopez was cheered* after the comma.

2. The sentence also beings with a dangling participle. It can be corrected by beginning with *Because he failed* . . . or by writing *he made remarks in class that were* . . . after the comma.

3. Again, the error is a dangling participle. Revise the sentence to begin with *If you keep* . . . or write something like *you may make the overhead* . . . after the comma.

4. A dangling particple once more. The corrected sentence could begin *If she hopes to win* . . . or could say *she must give a first-rate free-skating performance* after the comma.

5. The error here is a dangling infinitive, which makes it appear that *stamina* and *concentration* are taking the exam. Either add a human agent in the first phrase (*For you to do well*) or begin the second with *you must have.* . . .

6. This is a very difficult sentence because the dangling infinitive is not at the beginning of the sentence but in the middle (*to get the best possible view*). As it stands, the *seats* not the ticket holders are getting the best view. By revising the last clause of the sentence to read *we bought seats on the center aisle* . . . , we eliminate the error.

7. The elliptical phrase here dangles, so the sentence suggests that the father is eight years old. To remove the error, we can remove the ellipsis and write *When his son was only eight years old.* . . . If we wish to keep the opening unchanged, we must write *his son was sent* . . . after the comma.

8. Like sentence 7, this sentence opens with a dangling elliptical phrase. The simplest way to correct the error is to write *Though he is only. . . .*

9. Here the prepositional phrase which begins the sentence seems to modify *you.* Beginning the sentence with the *you* clause and putting the prepositional phrase at the end will correct the error.

10. To avoid the unnecessary separation of the parts of the verb, begin the sentence with *If I remember correctly. . . .*

11. The opening elliptical phrase dangles. Write *By applying the insecticide carefully, you can avoid damage to the environment.*

12. The *just* is misplaced. Write *I have just enough . . .* so that *just* is next to the word it modfies.

EXERCISE 6: PARALLELISM

1. (E) The parallelism here is correct.

2. (B) With the correlatives *not . . . but,* the words after *but* should be parallel to those after *not: not his reckless spending . . . but his spending.*

3. (C) The phrase *more concerned with* should have a parallel after *than: than with getting.*

4. (A) Since the pronoun *your* is used later in the sentence (and cannot be changed, since it is not underlined) the first phrase in the sentence should read *Your aptitude.*

5. (C) Since the pronoun *one* is used earlier in the sentence, *you* should be *one.*

6. (E) The parallelism here is correct.

7. (A) Since the pronoun *you* is used at the end of the sentence, *one* should be *you.*

8. (D) The series of infinitives (*to take, to speak*) should be completed with another infinitive (*to ask some questions*).

9. (E) The series in this sentence maintains parallelism.

10. (C) With the correlatives *both . . . and,* the structure following should be parallel. The correct version is *at both the data.*

11. (C) To maintain the series of infinitives, the sentence should read *and to defend.*

12. (D) With the correlatives *not only . . . but also,* the sentence should read *not only capable but also trustworthy.*

13. (C) The past tense should be used in all the verbs—*ended, jumped, drove, changed, and swam.*

14. (E) The parallelism here is correct.

15. (D) The final verb in this series should be an infinitive (*to cash*) to be parallel with the others.

REVIEW EXERCISE: SECTIONS 4, 5, AND 6

1. (C) Since the main verb in the first part of the sentence is in the present tense (*seems*), there is no reason to shift to a past tense.

2. (B) With *less from* followed by *than,* the *from* should be repeated.

3. (E) The sentence is correct as given.

4. (E) The present tense of *is* is correct, since the subject is a medical fact that continues to be true.

5. (B) With the correlatives *not . . . but,* the *but* should be followed by the preposition *by* to be parallel.

6. (A) *Raising* is the right verb (not *rising*), but the phrase is a dangling participle. It looks as if the *sunshine* raised the shade.

7. (A) Another dangling particple. The *I* of the sentence, not the passengers, narrowly missed the collision.

8. (C) The other verbs of the sentence (*was, broke*) are in the past tense, so *splashed* is correct here.

9. (E) The beginning phrase modifies *he* and does not dangle.

10. (C) The series should have three infinitives: *to read, to mark,* and *to stop.*

EXERCISE 7: AMBIGUOUS PRONOUNS

All of the following are *possible* answers, but certainly not the only right response.

1. The *which* has no specific antecedent. To avoid the ambiguous pronoun, one might write *My coming in fifteen minutes late made . . .* or *I came in fifteen minutes late and found. . . .* One cannot correct the error by substituting another pronoun for the ambiguous *which.*

2. The ambiguous pronoun is *this.* The sentence can be corrected by simply omitting the phrase *because this is* and adding a comma after *school.*

3. The ambiguous pronoun is *this.* Effectively revised, the sentence would read *By writing checks for . . . I overdrew my account.*

4. The ambiguous pronoun is *this.* It can be eliminated by concluding the sentence with *and, needless to say, had indigestion.*

5. The antecedent of *it* could be either the radio or the record player. The simple solution is to say *when I plugged the radio* (or *the record player) in, it would not work.*

6. The antecedent of *his* and *he* is unclear. As in sentence 5, the solution is to use the noun (*Dave* or *Vince*) in place of *he.*

7. The *these* is ambiguous. One solution is to write *these abilities.*

8. The *this* is ambiguous. One could write *this appearance makes them seem ferocious* or *and they appear ferocious, though. . . .*

EXERCISE 8: OTHER ERRORS OF GRAMMAR

Part A

1. A fragment. There is no main verb, only a participle.

2. A complete sentence. *David* (subject) *wept* (verb).

3. A fragment. There is no verb.

4. A complete sentence. *Is* (verb) *he* (subject).

5. A fragment. The clause is dependent.

Part B

1. Double negative—*haven't risen hardly*.

2. Omission of necessary word—*can make*.

3. Omission of necessary word—Since Venice is a city, *any other city*.

4. Word order in indirect question—*how we can*.

5. Omission of necessary word—*have said*.

6. *Which* for *that*—The clause is restrictive, *bank that* (with no comma).

7. Omission of necessary word—*must live in in the future*.

8. *Like* for *as*—The clause has a subject and verb—*as the Borgias*.

9. Omission of necessary words—*different from those of any other*.

10. Double negative—*not need scarcely*.

11. Omission of necessary word—*as effective as*.

12. Word order in indirect question—*when we can*.

13. Omission of necessary word—*never has been*.

14. *That* for *which*—The clause is nonrestrictive—*Jack's Ranch Market, which*.

15. Omission of necessary words—*than those of Cole Porter*.

16. *As* for *like*—The sentence should begin with a prepositional phrase—*Like Spain*.

17. Omission of necessary word—*as good as*.

18. *Who* for *which* Zebras are not humans—*Zebra, which migrate*.

19. *Like* for *as*—The clause has a subject and a verb—*As the senator explained*.

20. Word order in indirect question—*how he can afford*.

EXERCISE 9: ERRORS OF DICTION, IDIOM, AND STYLE

Part A

1. *it's*—should be *its*. *It's* means *it is*.

2. *than*—The correct idiom is *different from*.

3. *less*—Since accidents can be numbered, it should be *fewer accidents*.

4. *affect*—*Affect* is a verb; the noun *effect* should be used here.

5. *between*—Since there are four states, use *among*.

6. *plan on attending*—The correct idiom is *plan to attend*.

7. *Inflicted*—The required word here is *Afflicted*.

8. *effect*—The first *effect* should be the verb *affect*. The second *effect* is correct.

Part B

1. *Resiliency* and *ability to bounce back* mean the same thing.

2. One could omit *to do*. *Total* and *complete* mean the same thing.

3. Since *retrospect* means *a looking back*, the prepositional phrase is unnecessary.

4. The phrase *At the present moment in history* is unnecessary with the use of *now*.

5. *Well-to-do* and *affluent* mean the same thing.

6. *Workable* and *practicable* mean the same thing. You also do not need both *conserve* and *keep from being wasted*.

7. Both *true* and *obviously* are unnecessary words here.

8. Either *subtle distinctions* or *nice discriminations* and either *learned* or *erudite* can be eliminated.

9. A *dramatist* is a *playwright*. One or the other is sufficient.

10. With *mountainous, hill* is unnecessary, and *potential* is equivalent to *to whom it might have appealed*.

REVIEW EXERCISE: SECTIONS 7, 8, AND 9

1. (B) *Less* should be *fewer*.

2. (E) The sentence is correct as given.

3. (B) *Forcefully* repeats *cogently*.

4. (A) The sentence should read *than those in New York*.

5. (C) The antecedent of *her* is ambiguous. It could be either *the Virgin* or *an earthly lady*.

6. (D) *Effect* should be *affect*.

7. (E) There is no error in this sentence.

8. (A) Since the musicians are human, the pronoun should be *who*.

9. (A) The sentence should read *no interest in becoming*.

10. (C) The *not* and *but* are both negatives. Eliminate *not*.

EXERCISE 10: PUNCTUATION

1. (D) The phrase *it seems* is parenthetical and should be set off by two commas.

2. (G) The sentence is a question.

3. (B) A series.

4. (H) The dashes set off an interrupting phrase. One could use commas instead of the dashes, but not one comma and one dash as in choice (G). No commas are needed after *least* and *those*.

5. (A) The semicolon here divides the parts of a series

6. (H) The parenthetical *so to speak* should be set off by commas. The series requires semicolons after *trunk, biodegradable,* and *container* because it contains commas within elements of the series.

7. (A) The dashes set off the interruption. Choice (C) omits the apostrophe in *here's*. The series has been written using semicolons, so the commas are inconsistent in choices (C) and (D).

8. (F) The phrases *of course* and *not too surprisingly* are parenthetical and each requires two commas

9. (C) The word *suburbanites* should be in quotation marks (quoting the pro-plastic folks) and set off from the subject of the clause by a comma.

REVIEW EXERCISE: SECTIONS 1–10

1. dangling participle.

2. either agreement (the subject will be plural) or parallelism with *both . . . and.*

3. parallelism.

4. either agreement (the verb will agree with the word nearer the verb) or parallelism with *either . . . or.*

5. double negative or parallelism with *not . . . but.*

6. confusion of *like* and *as* or parallelism with the prepositional phrase.

7. agreement—*a number* is singular.

8. agreement—*Everbody* is singular.

9. case of *who/whom*—confusion of *who/that/which.*

10. adverb for adjective—*look* is a linking verb.

11. agreement—*One* is singular—or change of person, the incorrect use of *your* later in the sentence.

12. agreement—*None* is singular.

13. dangling elliptical phrase.

14. agreement—*criteria* is plural.

15. placement of related words.

16. double negative.

17. parallelism—be sure like elements are compared—or omission of necessary words such as *other.*

18. *lie* versus *lay.*

19. tense of subjunctive verbs.

20. agreement—*as well as* is parenthetical and will not make a singular subject plural.

ANSWER SHEET FOR ENGLISH USAGE AND SENTENCE CORRECTION PRACTICE
(Remove This Sheet and Use It to Mark Your Answers)

PART I: ENGLISH USAGE

Set 1	Set 2	Set 3	Set 4
1 Ⓐ Ⓑ Ⓒ Ⓓ Ⓔ	1 Ⓐ Ⓑ Ⓒ Ⓓ Ⓔ	1 Ⓐ Ⓑ Ⓒ Ⓓ Ⓔ	1 Ⓐ Ⓑ Ⓒ Ⓓ Ⓔ
2 Ⓐ Ⓑ Ⓒ Ⓓ Ⓔ	2 Ⓐ Ⓑ Ⓒ Ⓓ Ⓔ	2 Ⓐ Ⓑ Ⓒ Ⓓ Ⓔ	2 Ⓐ Ⓑ Ⓒ Ⓓ Ⓔ
3 Ⓐ Ⓑ Ⓒ Ⓓ Ⓔ	3 Ⓐ Ⓑ Ⓒ Ⓓ Ⓔ	3 Ⓐ Ⓑ Ⓒ Ⓓ Ⓔ	3 Ⓐ Ⓑ Ⓒ Ⓓ Ⓔ
4 Ⓐ Ⓑ Ⓒ Ⓓ Ⓔ	4 Ⓐ Ⓑ Ⓒ Ⓓ Ⓔ	4 Ⓐ Ⓑ Ⓒ Ⓓ Ⓔ	4 Ⓐ Ⓑ Ⓒ Ⓓ Ⓔ
5 Ⓐ Ⓑ Ⓒ Ⓓ Ⓔ	5 Ⓐ Ⓑ Ⓒ Ⓓ Ⓔ	5 Ⓐ Ⓑ Ⓒ Ⓓ Ⓔ	5 Ⓐ Ⓑ Ⓒ Ⓓ Ⓔ
6 Ⓐ Ⓑ Ⓒ Ⓓ Ⓔ	6 Ⓐ Ⓑ Ⓒ Ⓓ Ⓔ	6 Ⓐ Ⓑ Ⓒ Ⓓ Ⓔ	6 Ⓐ Ⓑ Ⓒ Ⓓ Ⓔ
7 Ⓐ Ⓑ Ⓒ Ⓓ Ⓔ	7 Ⓐ Ⓑ Ⓒ Ⓓ Ⓔ	7 Ⓐ Ⓑ Ⓒ Ⓓ Ⓔ	7 Ⓐ Ⓑ Ⓒ Ⓓ Ⓔ
8 Ⓐ Ⓑ Ⓒ Ⓓ Ⓔ	8 Ⓐ Ⓑ Ⓒ Ⓓ Ⓔ	8 Ⓐ Ⓑ Ⓒ Ⓓ Ⓔ	8 Ⓐ Ⓑ Ⓒ Ⓓ Ⓔ
9 Ⓐ Ⓑ Ⓒ Ⓓ Ⓔ	9 Ⓐ Ⓑ Ⓒ Ⓓ Ⓔ	9 Ⓐ Ⓑ Ⓒ Ⓓ Ⓔ	9 Ⓐ Ⓑ Ⓒ Ⓓ Ⓔ
10 Ⓐ Ⓑ Ⓒ Ⓓ Ⓔ	10 Ⓐ Ⓑ Ⓒ Ⓓ Ⓔ	10 Ⓐ Ⓑ Ⓒ Ⓓ Ⓔ	10 Ⓐ Ⓑ Ⓒ Ⓓ Ⓔ
11 Ⓐ Ⓑ Ⓒ Ⓓ Ⓔ	11 Ⓐ Ⓑ Ⓒ Ⓓ Ⓔ	11 Ⓐ Ⓑ Ⓒ Ⓓ Ⓔ	11 Ⓐ Ⓑ Ⓒ Ⓓ Ⓔ
12 Ⓐ Ⓑ Ⓒ Ⓓ Ⓔ	12 Ⓐ Ⓑ Ⓒ Ⓓ Ⓔ	12 Ⓐ Ⓑ Ⓒ Ⓓ Ⓔ	12 Ⓐ Ⓑ Ⓒ Ⓓ Ⓔ
13 Ⓐ Ⓑ Ⓒ Ⓓ Ⓔ	13 Ⓐ Ⓑ Ⓒ Ⓓ Ⓔ	13 Ⓐ Ⓑ Ⓒ Ⓓ Ⓔ	13 Ⓐ Ⓑ Ⓒ Ⓓ Ⓔ
14 Ⓐ Ⓑ Ⓒ Ⓓ Ⓔ	14 Ⓐ Ⓑ Ⓒ Ⓓ Ⓔ	14 Ⓐ Ⓑ Ⓒ Ⓓ Ⓔ	14 Ⓐ Ⓑ Ⓒ Ⓓ Ⓔ
15 Ⓐ Ⓑ Ⓒ Ⓓ Ⓔ	15 Ⓐ Ⓑ Ⓒ Ⓓ Ⓔ	15 Ⓐ Ⓑ Ⓒ Ⓓ Ⓔ	15 Ⓐ Ⓑ Ⓒ Ⓓ Ⓔ

PART II: SENTENCE CORRECTION

Set 1	Set 2	Set 3
1 Ⓐ Ⓑ Ⓒ Ⓓ Ⓔ	1 Ⓐ Ⓑ Ⓒ Ⓓ Ⓔ	1 Ⓐ Ⓑ Ⓒ Ⓓ Ⓔ
2 Ⓐ Ⓑ Ⓒ Ⓓ Ⓔ	2 Ⓐ Ⓑ Ⓒ Ⓓ Ⓔ	2 Ⓐ Ⓑ Ⓒ Ⓓ Ⓔ
3 Ⓐ Ⓑ Ⓒ Ⓓ Ⓔ	3 Ⓐ Ⓑ Ⓒ Ⓓ Ⓔ	3 Ⓐ Ⓑ Ⓒ Ⓓ Ⓔ
4 Ⓐ Ⓑ Ⓒ Ⓓ Ⓔ	4 Ⓐ Ⓑ Ⓒ Ⓓ Ⓔ	4 Ⓐ Ⓑ Ⓒ Ⓓ Ⓔ
5 Ⓐ Ⓑ Ⓒ Ⓓ Ⓔ	5 Ⓐ Ⓑ Ⓒ Ⓓ Ⓔ	5 Ⓐ Ⓑ Ⓒ Ⓓ Ⓔ
6 Ⓐ Ⓑ Ⓒ Ⓓ Ⓔ	6 Ⓐ Ⓑ Ⓒ Ⓓ Ⓔ	6 Ⓐ Ⓑ Ⓒ Ⓓ Ⓔ
7 Ⓐ Ⓑ Ⓒ Ⓓ Ⓔ	7 Ⓐ Ⓑ Ⓒ Ⓓ Ⓔ	7 Ⓐ Ⓑ Ⓒ Ⓓ Ⓔ
8 Ⓐ Ⓑ Ⓒ Ⓓ Ⓔ	8 Ⓐ Ⓑ Ⓒ Ⓓ Ⓔ	8 Ⓐ Ⓑ Ⓒ Ⓓ Ⓔ
9 Ⓐ Ⓑ Ⓒ Ⓓ Ⓔ	9 Ⓐ Ⓑ Ⓒ Ⓓ Ⓔ	9 Ⓐ Ⓑ Ⓒ Ⓓ Ⓔ
10 Ⓐ Ⓑ Ⓒ Ⓓ Ⓔ	10 Ⓐ Ⓑ Ⓒ Ⓓ Ⓔ	10 Ⓐ Ⓑ Ⓒ Ⓓ Ⓔ
11 Ⓐ Ⓑ Ⓒ Ⓓ Ⓔ	11 Ⓐ Ⓑ Ⓒ Ⓓ Ⓔ	11 Ⓐ Ⓑ Ⓒ Ⓓ Ⓔ
12 Ⓐ Ⓑ Ⓒ Ⓓ Ⓔ	12 Ⓐ Ⓑ Ⓒ Ⓓ Ⓔ	12 Ⓐ Ⓑ Ⓒ Ⓓ Ⓔ
13 Ⓐ Ⓑ Ⓒ Ⓓ Ⓔ	13 Ⓐ Ⓑ Ⓒ Ⓓ Ⓔ	13 Ⓐ Ⓑ Ⓒ Ⓓ Ⓔ
14 Ⓐ Ⓑ Ⓒ Ⓓ Ⓔ	14 Ⓐ Ⓑ Ⓒ Ⓓ Ⓔ	14 Ⓐ Ⓑ Ⓒ Ⓓ Ⓔ
15 Ⓐ Ⓑ Ⓒ Ⓓ Ⓔ	15 Ⓐ Ⓑ Ⓒ Ⓓ Ⓔ	15 Ⓐ Ⓑ Ⓒ Ⓓ Ⓔ

CUT HERE

ANSWER SHEET FOR ENGLISH USAGE AND SENTENCE CORRECTION PRACTICE
(Remove This Sheet and Use It to Mark Your Answers)

PART III: ENGLISH USAGE

Set 1	Set 2	Set 3	Set 4

Set 1

1 Ⓐ Ⓑ Ⓒ Ⓓ
2 Ⓕ Ⓖ Ⓗ Ⓙ
3 Ⓐ Ⓑ Ⓒ Ⓓ
4 Ⓕ Ⓖ Ⓗ Ⓙ
5 Ⓐ Ⓑ Ⓒ Ⓓ
6 Ⓕ Ⓖ Ⓗ Ⓙ
7 Ⓐ Ⓑ Ⓒ Ⓓ
8 Ⓕ Ⓖ Ⓗ Ⓙ
9 Ⓐ Ⓑ Ⓒ Ⓓ
10 Ⓕ Ⓖ Ⓗ Ⓙ
11 Ⓐ Ⓑ Ⓒ Ⓓ
12 Ⓕ Ⓖ Ⓗ Ⓙ
13 Ⓐ Ⓑ Ⓒ Ⓓ
14 Ⓕ Ⓖ Ⓗ Ⓙ
15 Ⓐ Ⓑ Ⓒ Ⓓ
16 Ⓕ Ⓖ Ⓗ Ⓙ

Set 2

1 Ⓐ Ⓑ Ⓒ Ⓓ
2 Ⓕ Ⓖ Ⓗ Ⓙ
3 Ⓐ Ⓑ Ⓒ Ⓓ
4 Ⓕ Ⓖ Ⓗ Ⓙ
5 Ⓐ Ⓑ Ⓒ Ⓓ
6 Ⓕ Ⓖ Ⓗ Ⓙ
7 Ⓐ Ⓑ Ⓒ Ⓓ
8 Ⓕ Ⓖ Ⓗ Ⓙ
9 Ⓐ Ⓑ Ⓒ Ⓓ
10 Ⓕ Ⓖ Ⓗ Ⓙ
11 Ⓐ Ⓑ Ⓒ Ⓓ
12 Ⓕ Ⓖ Ⓗ Ⓙ
13 Ⓐ Ⓑ Ⓒ Ⓓ
14 Ⓕ Ⓖ Ⓗ Ⓙ
15 Ⓐ Ⓑ Ⓒ Ⓓ
16 Ⓕ Ⓖ Ⓗ Ⓙ
17 Ⓐ Ⓑ Ⓒ Ⓓ
18 Ⓕ Ⓖ Ⓗ Ⓙ

Set 3

1 Ⓐ Ⓑ Ⓒ Ⓓ
2 Ⓕ Ⓖ Ⓗ Ⓙ
3 Ⓐ Ⓑ Ⓒ Ⓓ
4 Ⓕ Ⓖ Ⓗ Ⓙ
5 Ⓐ Ⓑ Ⓒ Ⓓ
6 Ⓕ Ⓖ Ⓗ Ⓙ
7 Ⓐ Ⓑ Ⓒ Ⓓ
8 Ⓕ Ⓖ Ⓗ Ⓙ
9 Ⓐ Ⓑ Ⓒ Ⓓ
10 Ⓕ Ⓖ Ⓗ Ⓙ
11 Ⓐ Ⓑ Ⓒ Ⓓ
12 Ⓕ Ⓖ Ⓗ Ⓙ
13 Ⓐ Ⓑ Ⓒ Ⓓ
14 Ⓕ Ⓖ Ⓗ Ⓙ
15 Ⓐ Ⓑ Ⓒ Ⓓ

Set 4

1 Ⓐ Ⓑ Ⓒ Ⓓ
2 Ⓕ Ⓖ Ⓗ Ⓙ
3 Ⓐ Ⓑ Ⓒ Ⓓ
4 Ⓕ Ⓖ Ⓗ Ⓙ
5 Ⓐ Ⓑ Ⓒ Ⓓ
6 Ⓕ Ⓖ Ⓗ Ⓙ
7 Ⓐ Ⓑ Ⓒ Ⓓ
8 Ⓕ Ⓖ Ⓗ Ⓙ
9 Ⓐ Ⓑ Ⓒ Ⓓ
10 Ⓕ Ⓖ Ⓗ Ⓙ
11 Ⓐ Ⓑ Ⓒ Ⓓ
12 Ⓕ Ⓖ Ⓗ Ⓙ
13 Ⓐ Ⓑ Ⓒ Ⓓ
14 Ⓕ Ⓖ Ⓗ Ⓙ

CUT HERE

ENGLISH USAGE AND SENTENCE CORRECTION PRACTICE

PART 1: ENGLISH USAGE

DIRECTIONS

Some of the following sentences are correct. Others contain problems in grammar, usage, idiom, or diction (word choice). There is not more than one error in any sentence.

If there is an error, it will be underlined and lettered. Find the one underlined part that must be changed to make the sentence correct, and choose the corresponding letter on your answer sheet. Mark (E) if the sentence contains no error. The Answer Key for this English Usage section may be found on page 162, and the explanatory answers may be found beginning on page 163.

Set 1

1. Had you paid very close attention to the shape of the gem, or
   A
   had you looked carefully at the allegedly sterling silver
   B   C
   setting, you would of suspected that the ring was not an
   D
   antique. No error.
   E

2. If the election results are as Harris predicted, the new senator
   A
   will be the man whom the people believed made the better
   B   C   D
   showing in the televised debate. No error.
   E

3. None of sixty-five students majoring in economics
   A
   were prepared for the teacher's laying a trap for them
   B   C   D
   in the comprehensive exam. No error.
   E

4. If they <u>simply gave</u> the prize <u>to whoever</u> really deserves
          A   B

   it, the publishers who pay for publicity <u>would withdraw</u>
                                          C

   <u>their support</u>, and <u>there would be</u> no award at all. <u>No error.</u>
       C   D   E

5. It must be <u>she</u> <u>whom</u> he had in mind when he spoke of a
             A   B

   "well-trained, superbly conditioned athlete <u>who</u> <u>might have</u>
                                        C   D

   <u>captured</u> a spot on the Olympic team." <u>No error.</u>
     D   E

6. The reasons for his success are <u>that he works hard,</u>
                                          A

   <u>his good looks</u>, <u>that he exercises regularly,</u> and <u>that his</u>
       B   C   D

   <u>grandmother left</u> him four million dollars. <u>No error.</u>
     D   E

7. <u>You'd think</u> that people <u>smart and intelligent enough</u> to be in
     A   B

   business <u>by themselves</u> would have the sense to know the
               C

   value of monthly savings <u>at a guaranteed</u> high interest
                                    D

   rate. <u>No error.</u>
        E

8. The jury must first decide <u>whether or not the defendant was</u>
                              A   B

   in New York on August third, and then, how <u>can he</u> have had
                                        C

   the strength <u>to carry</u> a 200-pound body. <u>No error.</u>
            D   E

9. The art of American morticians <u>paints</u> death <u>to look like life,</u>
                                A   B

   sealing <u>it</u> up in watertight caskets and <u>spiriting</u> it away to
          C   D

   graveyards camouflaged as gardens. <u>No error.</u>
                                   E

10. Anyone of the compounds that can be produced from
    ‾‾‾‾‾   ‾‾‾‾‾‾‾‾‾‾‾‾‾
    A   B
    the leaves of this plant is dangerous, but the plant itself is not
                             ‾‾   ‾‾‾‾‾
                             C   D
    poisonous. No error.
              ‾‾‾‾‾‾‾‾
              E

11. None of the survivors who have now recovered consciousness
                          ‾‾‾‾‾‾‾‾
                             A
    remember hearing any unusual sound in the motor just before
    ‾‾‾‾‾‾‾‾ ‾‾‾‾‾‾‾   ‾‾‾‾‾‾‾‾‾
       B   C   D
    the plane crashed. No error.
                      ‾‾‾‾‾‾‾‾
                         E

12. *The Destructors* is an unusually powerful film about a group
                          ‾‾‾‾‾‾‾‾‾
                             A
    of cruel and idle young boys who destroy an old man's home
                                 ‾‾‾‾‾‾‾‾‾‾‾
                                     B
    for no other reason but because it is beautiful. No error.
                        ‾‾‾ ‾‾‾‾‾‾‾   ‾‾‾‾‾‾‾‾
                         C   D   E

13. Hoping to both cut taxes and reduce unemployment,
    ‾‾‾
                       A
    the Senate has recommended a bill that allows married couples
                                    ‾‾‾‾‾‾‾‾‾‾‾
                                         B
    not to declare the income of either the husband or the wife,
    ‾‾‾‾‾‾‾‾‾‾‾‾‾
         C
    depending upon which income is the lowest. No error.
                   ‾‾‾‾‾‾‾‾‾‾‾‾‾‾‾‾‾‾‾‾‾‾‾‾ ‾‾‾‾‾‾‾‾
                             D   E

14. It seems increasingly obvious that men's clothes are designed
    ‾‾‾‾‾‾‾‾‾‾‾‾‾‾‾‾‾‾‾‾‾‾‾‾
               A
    not to please the men who will wear them, but as status
                                       ‾‾‾‾‾ ‾‾‾‾‾‾‾‾‾
                                         B   C
    symbols that impress the people who will see them. No error.
    ‾‾‾‾‾‾‾‾‾‾‾‾‾‾‾‾‾‾‾‾‾   ‾‾‾‾‾‾‾‾‾‾‾‾‾ ‾‾‾‾‾‾‾‾
               C   D   E

15. Unlike Monet, Graham's oil paintings have few bright colors,
                   ‾‾‾‾‾‾‾‾‾‾‾‾‾‾‾‾‾‾‾‾   ‾‾‾
                            A   B
    are small, and depict only urban scenes. No error.
    ‾‾‾‾‾‾‾‾‾ ‾‾‾‾‾‾   ‾‾‾‾‾‾‾‾
        C   D   E

Set 2

1. While I was out of action with a broken arm, the nurses
   <u>   A   </u>
   tried to teach me to eat, write, and to shave with my left hand,
   <u> B </u>   <u> C </u>
   but I was never able to write or shave very well. No error.
                 <u> D </u>   <u> E </u>

2. If I had my way, that driver would be charged for criminal
   <u>   A   </u>   <u> B </u>   <u> C </u>
   negligence and drunken driving and spend at least six months
                        <u> D </u>
   in jail. No error.
      <u> E </u>

3. Most schools require students to take standardized tests that
                 <u>   A   </u>   <u>B</u>
   are used by admissions committees to evaluate one student
   against another with common criteria. No error.
   <u>   C   </u>   <u> D </u> <u> E </u>

4. If westerners acknowledge that the eastern United States
             <u>   A   </u>
   has wilderness areas, one probably thinks of the Blue Ridge
   <u>   B   </u> <u>   C   </u>
   Mountains or perhaps western Maine. No error.
           <u> D </u>   <u> E </u>

5. Paul Ramsey, a theologian at Princeton University, as well as
   Edward Leon, a philosopher and physician at the University of
   Chicago, have argued that test-tube fertilization is
        <u> A </u>
   a form of experimentation that is unethical, since the potential
   <u>   B   </u> <u> C </u>
   child cannot consent to the risks of the experiment. No error.
          <u> D </u>   <u> E </u>

6. Though in only her first year of research, Dr. Johnson has
   <u>   A   </u>   <u> B </u>
   discovered a formula that may effect the study of mathematics
   <u> B </u>   <u>   C   </u>
   all over the world. No error.
   <u> D </u>   <u> E </u>

7. By buying the economy-size packages of pasta, of muffin mix,
   —————
   A
   and detergent, shoppers can save as much as two dollars in
   —————   ————
   B   C
   less than one month. No error.
   —————   ————
   D   E

8. As they crossed the Atlantic, cheeses were probably made
   ———————————————   ———————————
   A   B
   by the colonists in the galley of the *Mayflower*. No error.
   ——————————   ——————————   ————
   C   D   E

9. Hospital patients prefer homemade recipes that are lower in
                      ——————————————————— ————   ————
                      A   B   C
   calories and cost, which is important to those with high
                      ————
                      D
   medical bills and weight problems. No error.
                                      ————
                                        E

10. The focus of the new newspaper and television advertisements
                       —————————————————————————————————
                       A
   will be the claim that prunes are not only low in fat but also
   ————   ——————   ————————
   B   C   D
   are the fruit highest in fiber. No error.
   ——————————————————————   ————
   D   E

11 When the Baseball Writers' Association announced that Willie
                    ————————
                    A
   McCovey, the top left-handed home run hitter in National
            ———
            B
   League history, had been elected to the Hall of Fame, nobody
                   ——————————————
                   C
   was at all surprised. No error.
   ———   ————
   D   E

12. A public-opinion survey commissioned as part of a federal
                           ————————————————————
                           A
   antinoise program at the airport indicates that none of
                                    —————
                                    B
   the residents of the surrounding area are seriously disturbed
                                        ——— ——————————————
                                        C   D
   by aircraft noise. No error.
                     ————
                     E

13. It was Cardinal Richelieu who decided to found the French
                     ———————————
                          A
    Academy when he learned that an eminent group of
            ——————————   ————————
                 B   C
    grammarians and intellectuals will meet in secret to exchange
                                   ——————————————————
                                           D
    views on literature. No error.
                         ————————
                             E

14. More than thirty countries from around the world have
    ——   ————
                          A   B
    submitted entries for the Best Foreign Language Film Award
    ————————
       B
    being presented at the ceremony six weeks from today.
    ————————————   ————————————————————
         C   D
    No error.
    ————————
       E

15. Like President Carter, President Reagan's cabinet was chosen
    ——————————————————   ——————————
             A   B
    from former allies in state politics, national party leaders,
    ————   ————————————————
     B   C
    personal friends, and seasoned political professionals. No error.
                          ——————————————————————————————   ————————
                                         D   E

Set 3

1. The decline in the industrial average was much smaller
       ——————————
           A
   in comparative terms to the 1929 decline because the Dow
   ——————————————————   ——
            B   C
   index stands at a much higher level today. No error.
         ——————   ————————
           D   E

2. To safeguard wildlife, the state of Florida will line its
   ———————————————   ———
          A   B
   highways with high fencing, forcing panthers to scoot
                               ——————   ————————
                                  C   D
   beneath the roads through specially designed animal
   underpasses. No error.
                ————————
                   E

3. The discovery of the existence of a fifth force could have
                                                   A
enormous impact on theoretical physicists who are trying to
                 B   C
develop a unified theory to explain the interactions of matter.
                                      D
No error.
 E

4. If the team is to qualify for the state championship, it
              A   B
cannot afford to make those kind of mental error. No error.
               C   D   E

5. Neither the violinists nor the harpist were accustomed to
                   A   B
playing modern music, and so the performance of the concerto
                       C
was a total failure. No error.
        D   E

6. Missing the forehand volley, a relative easy shot, Gonzalez
               A   B
fell behind early in the match, and he never recovered.
                              C   D
No error.
 E

7. The writer of allegory commonly invents a world in order to
                          A   B
talk about the world we live in; the symbolist uses the real
 B   C
world to reveal a world we cannot see. No error.
              D   E

8. When it is five o'clock in New York, it is only three in
                                              A   B
Texas, and it will be two o'clock in California, Washington,
            C
or Oregon. No error.
 D   E

9. <u>Some</u> begonias have huge flowers, <u>wonderfully colored;</u> <u>some</u>
     A   B   C
   have glorious foliage; and <u>some</u> provide a blaze of color, with
     C   D
   large clusters of small flowers. <u>No error.</u>
                                  E

10. The highest profits <u>are</u> likely <u>to be earned</u> by those investors
                            A   B
    <u>whom brokers claim</u> are willing to take risks <u>early in the</u>
             C   D
    <u>year.</u> <u>No error.</u>
      D   E

11. Northerners seem to believe that <u>we</u> Texans talk <u>oddly,</u> but
                                     A   B
    we think <u>it</u> is <u>them</u> who have the strange accents. <u>No error.</u>
            C   D   E

12. <u>To encourage better reading skills,</u> students in the public
                    A
    schools <u>are now required</u> by teachers to submit weekly
              B
    reports of <u>the books, magazines, and newspapers</u> <u>they have</u>
                                C   D
    <u>read.</u> <u>No error.</u>
      D   E

13. The legislators insist <u>that</u> charitable foundations have the
                               A
    <u>same, identical moral obligations</u> <u>as</u> private citizens
                   B   C
    or <u>publicly owned corporations.</u> <u>No error.</u>
                   D   E

14. University libraries across the nation use different methods
    to control crime, and the electronic system <u>that gives out</u>
                                                  A
    <u>a signal</u> <u>if a person leaves</u> the library with a book that has
      A   B
    not been checked out <u>was</u> one of <u>them.</u> <u>No error.</u>
                          C   D   E

15. The notion that Americans are conventional and Europeans are
    <u>free-spirited</u> <u>is</u> not only a dubious thesis <u>but also a trivial</u>
         A   B   C
    <u>one.</u> <u>No error.</u>
     D   E

Set 4

1. <u>Like Friedman warned</u> in the early seventies, taxes and the cost
            A
   of living <u>have risen</u> steadily <u>while</u> the value of the dollar abroad
            B   C
   <u>has steadily declined.</u> <u>No error.</u>
          D   E

2. Those musicians <u>having studied</u> under masters like Baker and
               A
   Hess are the ones who <u>ought</u> to become teachers when <u>their</u>
                    B   C
   performing careers <u>have ended.</u> <u>No error.</u>
                D   E

3. Either to bemoan the death of the counterculture or <u>to insist</u>
                                                    A
   that <u>it</u> still exists is <u>to commit</u> the same error, for a
        B   C
   counterculture never really <u>existed.</u> <u>No error.</u>
                    D   E

4. <u>Woven from fronds of cabbage palms and palmettos,</u>
                          A
   the natives of the islands <u>constructed</u> huts <u>that are</u>
                        B   C
   both rain proof in winter and cool in the <u>summertime.</u>
                                                D
   <u>No error.</u>
    E

5. <u>Though raised in conservative New Hampshire,</u> Miss Wegg
                        A
   <u>leads</u> a remarkably unconventional life in an environment
    B
   <u>totally</u> <u>unlike that</u> of her childhood. <u>No error.</u>
     C   D   E

6. Quicker at the net than any other player in the tournament,
   <u>A</u>
   his weak returns of service and <u>his tendency to double fault</u>
   <u>B</u>
   <u>under pressure</u> <u>have</u> prevented Simmons <u>from</u> reaching
      B   C   D
   the quarter finals. <u>No error.</u>
                   E

7. Neither the British archaeologists nor the American, Miss
   Hope, <u>have</u> discovered anything <u>with a</u> significance comparable
        A   B
   <u>to that of</u> the artifacts <u>unearthed</u> here twenty years ago.
      C   D
   <u>No error.</u>
     E

8. <u>Using the inland roads,</u> you will have to travel far <u>less</u>
          A   B
   miles, but the scenery, <u>such as it is,</u> is markedly inferior to
                          C
   <u>what you can see</u> on the coast. <u>No error.</u>
        D   E

9. <u>Unwilling to depend on you,</u> your brother, or even <u>I</u>, she
            A   B
   <u>has hired</u> a car at the airport and <u>has already driven</u>
      C   D
   to Cleveland. <u>No error.</u>
                 E

10. If you want to get ahead in this world, <u>one</u> must be ready
                                         A
    <u>to make</u> sacrifices, <u>to compromise,</u> and, when the situation is
       B   C
    unavoidable, <u>to tell</u> half-truths. <u>No error.</u>
              D   E

11. Between 1930 and 1945, most jazz improvisers played
    <u>not only the songs</u> of Gershwin, Rodgers, and Berlin,
           A

but also <u>those</u> <u>of</u> less well known writers <u>like</u> Wilder, Arlen, and
     B   C   D

Hunter. <u>No error.</u>
           E

12. Tommy Jones, together with Keeter Betts <u>on bass</u>
                                             A

and Jimmy Smith on drums, <u>are</u> performing at Newport <u>in</u> an
                               B   C

oblique, original, and <u>unwearyingly inventive</u> concert program.
                                            D

<u>No error.</u>
    E

13. The easiest way to get to Cnidus from Athens is not,
<u>as would seem likely</u>, to fly to Istanbul but <u>as a passenger</u> in
          A   B

the ships <u>that</u> <u>ply</u> between Rhodes and the Turkish coast.
             C   D

<u>No error.</u>
    E

14. Although the <u>councillor</u> had promised to support rent control,
                  A

it was <u>with no hesitation</u> and apparently with some pleasure
              B

<u>when</u> he cast his vote on the side of the landlords. <u>No error.</u>
  C   D   E

15. The quarterback, <u>with the trainer</u> and two doctors, <u>were</u>
                    A   B

<u>slowly walking</u> toward the bench <u>while</u> the crowd groaned
   B   C

<u>audibly.</u> <u>No error.</u>
  D   E

PART II: SENTENCE CORRECTION

DIRECTIONS

Some part of each sentence below is underlined; sometimes the whole sentence is underlined. Five choices for rephrasing the underlined part follow each sentence; the first choice (A) repeats the original, and the other four are different. If choice (A) seems better than the alternatives, choose answer (A); if not, choose one of the others.

For each sentence, consider the requirements of standard written English. Your choice should be a correct and effective expression, not awkward or ambiguous. Focus on grammar, word choice, sentence construction, and punctuation. If a choice changes the meaning of the original sentence, do not select it. The Answer Key for this Sentence Correction section may be found on page 162, and the explanatory answers may be found beginning on page 167.

Set 1

1. The series of articles is not only <u>about the sicknesses of a violent and materialistic society, but also how these ills can be remedied.</u>
   - (A) about the sicknesses of a violent and materialistic society, but also how these ills can be remedied.
   - (B) about the sicknesses of a violent and materialistic society, but also remedies for these ills.
   - (C) about the sicknesses of a violent and materialistic society, but also their remedy.
   - (D) about the sicknesses of a violent and materialistic society, but also about remedies for these ills.
   - (E) about the sicknesses of a violent and materialistic society, but also about remedying these ills.

2. Carrying the warm water across the yard to melt the ice on the <u>bird bath, the sparrows were gathered</u> only a few feet from me.
   - (A) bird bath, the sparrows were gathered
   - (B) bird bath, the sparrows gathered
   - (C) bird bath, the groups of sparrows were
   - (D) bird bath, the group of sparrows was gathered
   - (E) bird bath, I saw that the sparrows were gathered

3. This year's alumnae differ from last year's in the way they believe and give support to fund raising.
   (A) they believe and give support to fund raising.
   (B) it believes and gives support to fund raising.
   (C) it believes in and gives support to fund raising.
   (D) they believe in and support fund raising.
   (E) they believe in fund raising, and support it.

4. In addition to those of gasoline and sugar, the consumer must face higher wheat prices, which lead to more expensive meat and poultry.
   (A) the consumer must face higher wheat prices, which lead to more expensive meat and poultry.
   (B) the consumer must face the higher prices of meat and poultry caused by more expensive wheat.
   (C) higher wheat prices lead to more expensive meat and poultry, and the consumer must face these.
   (D) the higher wheat prices, which lead to more expensive meat and poultry, must be faced by the consumer.
   (E) the wheat consumer must face higher prices in meat and poultry.

5. When you see, instead of read, a play, it sometimes reveals new strengths and weaknesses.
   (A) it sometimes reveals new strengths and weaknesses.
   (B) new strengths and weaknesses are sometimes revealed to you.
   (C) you sometimes see new strengths and weaknesses.
   (D) sometimes new strengths and weaknesses are revealed.
   (E) new strengths and weaknesses are seen sometimes.

6. The doctor visits her patients once every three hours, which can be decreased as the danger lessens.
   (A) which can be decreased
   (B) a schedule that can be altered
   (C) which can be altered
   (D) to be decreased
   (E) and can be altered

7. She desperately <u>wanted, and in the second set nearly did, to win.</u>
   (A) wanted, and in the second set nearly did, to win.
   (B) wanted to win, and in the second set, she nearly did win.
   (C) wanted to, and in the second set nearly did, win.
   (D) wanted to win, and in the second set nearly did.
   (E) wanted to win, in the second set she nearly did.

8. <u>The appearance of a musical play—its sets, costumes, and lighting—is</u> as important as enjoying its songs.
   (A) The appearance of a musical play—its sets, costumes, and lighting—is
   (B) The appearance of a musical play—its sets, costumes, and lighting—are
   (C) Enjoying the appearance of a musical play—its sets, costumes, and lighting—is
   (D) In a musical play, the sets, costumes, and lighting are
   (E) The sets, costumes, and lighting of a musical play are

9. <u>Like many composers</u>, the operas of Mozart are more frequently performed in Italy than in France.
   (A) Like many composers
   (B) Like many other composers
   (C) Like the operas of many composers
   (D) Like those of many other composers
   (E) As many composers

10. Many people admire his lectures, but to me, <u>he is nothing else, in my opinion,</u> only a bore.
    (A) he is nothing else, in my opinion,
    (B) he is
    (C) he is nothing else except
    (D) he is nothing but,
    (E) he is nothing except

11. All of this trouble could have been avoided <u>if you would have planned who to ask</u> to speak before you rented the hall.
    (A) if you would have planned who to ask
    (B) if you planned who to ask
    (C) if you had planned whom to ask
    (D) if you had planned who to ask
    (E) if you planned whom to ask

12. Some young people work until they are exhausted; and this will surely prove injurious to their physical well-being later on in life.
    (A) exhausted; and this
    (B) exhausted; it
    (C) exhausted, which
    (D) exhausted, a practice that
    (E) exhausted, and it

13. I am both afraid and awed by her ability to reach important decisions and take action so quickly.
    (A) am both afraid and awed by her ability
    (B) both am afraid and awed by her ability
    (C) am both afraid of and awed by her ability
    (D) am both afraid and in awe of her ability
    (E) am afraid and also awed by her ability

14. The book contends that Othello is not a better play but more carefully constructed than King Lear.
    (A) that Othello is not a better play but more carefully constructed
    (B) Othello is not a better play but is more carefully constructed
    (C) not that Othello is better but a more carefully constructed play
    (D) that Othello is not a better play but a more carefully constructed one
    (E) not that Othello is better, but it is more carefully constructed

15. The house we rented had no garage, which meant we had to keep our boat on the front lawn.
    (A) which meant we had to keep
    (B) which meant keeping
    (C) and this meant we had to keep
    (D) so we had to keep
    (E) so we keep

Set 2

1. That your horse won at Bowie is not an indication of Kentucky Derby quality.
   (A) That your horse won at Bowie
   (B) Because your horse won at Bowie
   (C) Your horse winning at Bowie
   (D) If your horse won at Bowie
   (E) Winning results at Bowie

2. Every one of the tickets that was reserved for parents has been sold.
   (A) that was reserved for parents has
   (B) reserved for parents have
   (C) that were reserved for parents have
   (D) that were reserved for parents has
   (E) reserved for parents had

3. Neither salad oils nor butter has less calories than margarine.
   (A) has less calories than
   (B) has fewer calories than
   (C) have fewer calories than
   (D) are less in calories than
   (E) are fewer in calories than

4. Manning's article on *Nicholas Nickleby* is both the most dependable account and shortest guide to this difficult novel.
   (A) is both the most dependable account and shortest guide to
   (B) is both the shortest and most dependable account to
   (C) both is the most dependable account and shortest guide to
   (D) is both the most dependable account of and shortest guide to
   (E) is the most dependable account of and shortest guide to

5. Every one of the Socialist candidates have promised to support whoever wins the primary.
   (A) have promised to support whoever wins
   (B) has promised to support whomever wins
   (C) has promised to support whoever wins
   (D) have promised to support whomever wins
   (E) had promised to support whoever wins

6. The symbolical and experimental nature of modern fiction frequently relegates them to publication in magazines that have limited circulation.
   (A) relegates them to publication in magazines that have limited circulation.
   (B) relegate them to publication in magazines with limited circulation.
   (C) relegates them to publication in magazines of limited circulation.
   (D) relegates it to publication in magazines, which have limited circulation.
   (E) relegates it to publication in magazines with limited circulation.

7. Lured by the Florida sun, Canadians by the thousands descend annually into St. Petersburg each year.
   (A) Canadians by the thousands descend annually into St. Petersburg each year.
   (B) St. Petersburg receives thousands of Canadians each year.
   (C) St. Petersburg annually receives thousands of Canadians.
   (D) Canadians by the thousands descend on St. Petersburg each year.
   (E) thousands of Canadians descend into St. Petersburg each year.

8. Like Switzerland, the mountains of Colorado and Wyoming keep their snows for ten months.
   (A) Like Switzerland,
   (B) As Switzerland,
   (C) Like those in Switzerland,
   (D) Like the mountains which are in Switzerland,
   (E) Switzerland, like

9. At the door to the kitchen, he stopped to wipe the mud from his boots, ran a comb through his hair, and knocks loudly at the door.
   (A) and knocks loudly at the door.
   (B) and knocks loud at the door.
   (C) and knocked loudly at the door.
   (D) and then knocks loudly at the door.
   (E) knocking at the door loudly.

10. <u>Whoever makes the least mistakes or whoever</u> the wind reaches
    first is likely to win the sailing trophy.
    (A) Whoever makes the least mistakes or whoever
    (B) Whoever makes the least mistakes or whomever
    (C) Whoever makes the fewest mistakes or whomever
    (D) Whoever can make the least mistakes or whoever
    (E) Whoever makes the fewest mistakes or whoever

11. I especially admire <u>her eagerness to succeed, that she is willing to
    work hard, and her being optimistic.</u>
    (A) her eagerness to succeed, that she is willing to work hard,
        and her being optimistic.
    (B) that she is eager to succeed, willing to work hard, and that
        she is optimistic.
    (C) her eagerness to succeed, her willingness to work hard, and
        that she is optimistic.
    (D) her eagerness to succeed, her willingness to work hard, and
        her optimism.
    (E) her being eager to succeed, her being willing to work hard,
        and her being optimistic.

12. <u>Where the main purpose of the greenhouse is</u> to raise half-hardy
    plants for planting out in the garden or to grow flowering plants
    in pots for cut flowers and for bringing into the house.
    (A) Where the main purpose of the greenhouse is
    (B) When the main purpose of the greenhouse is
    (C) The main purpose of the greenhouse is
    (D) The main purpose of the greenhouse are
    (E) Where the main purpose of the greenhouse are

13. With his new knowledge of the processes of cell formation and
    reproduction, <u>nurserymen have now learned to induce sports</u> or
    mutations in plants.
    (A) nurserymen have now learned to induce sports
    (B) science has now learned to induce sports
    (C) the nurseryman has now learned to induce sports
    (D) science has now learned how to induce sports
    (E) scientists have now learned how to induce sports

14. The city plans to dismantle and move a fourteenth-century English church to Arizona which will give it the oldest church in the Western Hemisphere.
    (A) which will give it
    (B) and this will give it
    (C) which will give the city
    (D) and this will give the city
    (E) to give the city

15. Banking regulators have seized a savings bank in Georgia and charged that the institution both used deceptive lending and business practices and it misled its stockholders.
    (A) both used deceptive lending and business practices and it misled
    (B) both used both deceptive lending and business practices and that it misled
    (C) used both deceptive lending and business practices, misleading
    (D) used deceptive both lending and business practices, and misled
    (E) both used deceptive lending and business practices and misled

Set 3

1. More children are held in the Belmont City Jail than in any lockup in the state.
    (A) than in any lockup   (D) than any other
    (B) than in any other lockup (E) than any other lockup
    (C) than any

2. For three years, the rock group White Flag has virtually ignored Chicago, the city where they started in.
    (A) has virtually ignored Chicago, the city where they started in.
    (B) have virtually ignored Chicago, the city where they started in.
    (C) has virtually ignored Chicago, the city where it started.
    (D) has virtually ignored Chicago, the city where it started in.
    (E) have virtually ignored Chicago, the city where it started.

3. To whet the appetite for next week's Super Bowl, <u>NBC will show film clips of this year's best plays.</u>
   (A) NBC will show film clips of this year's best plays.
   (B) NBC will show film clips of this years' best plays.
   (C) this year's best plays will be shown in film clips by NBC.
   (D) film clips of this year's best plays will be shown by NBC.
   (E) this year's best plays in film clips will be shown by NBC.

4. Neither of the state's senators <u>is supportive or interested in</u> a constitutional amendment.
   (A) is supportive or interested in
   (B) is supportive of or interested in
   (C) are supportive of or interested in
   (D) support or are interested in
   (E) supports or are interested in

5. This semester I will <u>try and do my work as well or better</u> than anyone else in the class.
   (A) try and do my work as well or better
   (B) try and do my work better
   (C) try to do my work as well or better
   (D) try to do my work as well as or better
   (E) try and do my work as well as or better

6. While unlike savings bonds, <u>their principal value fluctuates, you will earn higher interest with government mortgage certificates.</u>
   (A) their principal value fluctuates, you will earn higher interest with government mortgage certificates.
   (B) their principle value fluctuates, you will earn higher interest with government mortgage certificates.
   (C) their principle value fluctuates, government mortgage certificates pay higher interest.
   (D) their principle value fluctuates, government mortgage certificates will pay you higher interest.
   (E) their principal value fluctuates, government mortgage certificates will pay you higher interest.

7. <u>Personally, I believe that we all will be happier</u> if there were no cars at all in the downtown area of the city.
   (A) Personally, I believe that we all will be happier
   (B) I believe we all would be happier
   (C) I personally believe that all of us will be happier
   (D) I believe that all of us would be more happy
   (E) I believe we will all be happier

8. To lose weight quickly on this diet, one must weigh every food portion carefully, exercise regularly, <u>and you should only drink</u> water, black coffee, or diet soda.
   (A) and you should only drink
   (B) drinking only
   (C) only drinking
   (D) and drink only
   (E) and one should drink only

9. <u>Different from any designs in the show,</u> Orlando Fashions Company exhibited a collection made entirely of nylon.
   (A) Different from any designs in the show,
   (B) Different from any other designs in the show,
   (C) With designs different from any in the show,
   (D) With designs different from any other in the show,
   (E) With designs different from any other designs in the show,

10. As Gordon's army advanced farther into the interior, <u>its supply line from the coast became more and more threatened.</u>
   (A) its supply line from the coast became more and more threatened.
   (B) it's supply line from the coast became more and more threatened.
   (C) it's supply line from the coast became more and more of a threat.
   (D) its supply line on the coast became more threatening.
   (E) its supply line from the coast became more of a threat.

11. The drug appears to have <u>no affect whatsoever in regards to</u> a patient's cold symptoms.
   (A) no affect whatsoever in regards to
   (B) no affect whatsoever in regard to
   (C) no affect whatsoever upon
   (D) no effect whatsoever on
   (E) no effect whatsoever regarding

12. He has been cheated several times <u>because of his being of a credulous nature.</u>
   (A) because of his being of a credulous nature.
   (B) because of his credibility.
   (C) because of his credulous nature.
   (D) because he is credulous.
   (E) because he is credible.

13. A very old plant in our gardens, <u>cornflowers appear in paintings made as early as in the fourth century.</u>
   (A) cornflowers appear in paintings made as early as in the fourth century.
   (B) paintings of cornflowers were made as early as the fourth century.
   (C) fourth century made paintings show cornflowers.
   (D) the cornflower appears in paintings made as early as the fourth century.
   (E) paintings of cornflowers have been made as early as in the fourth century.

14. None of the <u>terrorists who were seen in Libya in June have</u> been connected to the latest bomb threat.
   (A) terrorists who were seen in Libya in June have
   (B) terrorists, who were seen in Libya in June, have
   (C) terrorists who were seen in Libya in June has
   (D) terrorists, who was seen in Libya in June, have
   (E) terrorists, who were seen in Libya in June, will have

15. Paging through the cookware catalogue, <u>Jerry chose a matching skillet, teakettle, and saucepan as a prize for Janice and I or for whoever wins the contest.</u>

(A) Jerry chose a matching skillet, teakettle, and saucepan as a prize for Janice and I or for whoever wins the contest.

(B) Jerry chose a matching skillet, teakettle, and saucepan as a prize for Janice and me or for whoever wins the contest.

(C) Jerry chose a matching skillet, teakettle, and saucepan as a prize for Janice and me or for whomever wins the contest.

(D) a matching skillet, teakettle, and saucepan were chosen by Jerry as a prize for Janice and me or for whoever wins the contest.

(E) Jerry chose a matching skillet, teakettle, and saucepan for a prize for us or the contest winners.

PART III: ENGLISH USAGE

DIRECTIONS

In the left-hand column, you will find passages in a "spread-out" format with various words and phrases underlined. In the right-hand column, you will find a set of responses corresponding to each underlined portion. If the underlined portion is correct as it stands, mark the letter indicating "NO CHANGE." If the underlined portion is incorrect, decide which of the choices best corrects it. Consider only underlined portions; assume that the rest of the passage is correct as written. The Answer Key for this English Usage section may be found on page 162, and the explanatory answers may be found beginning on page 171.

Set 1: Passages I and II

Passage I

Before the summer games
of 1984, optimists believed the
Los Angeles Olympiad would
                          ——
                           1
produce a small profit. But no
———
 1
one guessed just how well the
plan for private-sector financing
would work. The latest audit
shows that the summer games
generated a whopping surplus of
two hundred and fifteen million
                   ——————————
                        2
dollars, this sum will likely grow
———————
   2
to two hundred and fifty million
dollars as Olympic coin sales
continue and two million dollars
in interest is added to the total
each month.

All of this money will be going
to good causes. The U.S. Olympic
         ——————————
              3

1. A. NO CHANGE
   B. will produce
   C. would deduce
   D. to produce

2. F. NO CHANGE
   G. fifteen million dollars
   H. fifteen million dollars;
   J. fifteen million dollars:

3. A. NO CHANGE
   B. causes; the
   C. causes, the
   D. causes including the
      following;

Committee, youth and athletic programs, and amateur American sports groups. In addition, the Los Angeles committee's board voted to donate seven million dollars to foreign Olympic committees, reimbursing them for their delegations' housing costs in
4
Los Angeles last summer.

4. F. NO CHANGE
   G. the costs for housing their delegations
   H. their delegations housing costs
   J. their delegation's housing costs

All of this stands in stark
5
contrast to the financing fiasco
5
in Montreal eight years before. Citizens there will be paying off their one billion dollar public debt for decades to come. And there was no surplus funds to
6
help sustain amateur athletics in Canada and Olympic committees elsewhere in the world. It is likely that in the future we will see fewer and fewer city govern-
7
ments taking on the financial risk of sponsoring the Olympic Games single-handed. The huge success of the 1984 summer games in Los

5. A. NO CHANGE
   B. in contrast starkly with
   C. contrasting to
   D. contrasting with

6. F. NO CHANGE
   G. there were no surplus
   H. they're were no surplus
   J. their were no surplus

7. A. NO CHANGE
   B. less and less
   C. a smaller and smaller number of
   D. a lesser and lesser number of

Angeles makes the privatization
8
option more attractive than ever.
8

8. F. NO CHANGE
   G. privatization options
   H. private financing
   J. the private financing

Passage II

Since the first of the year, the premiers of three of Canada's most important provinces, Rene Levesque of Quebec, William Davis of Ontario, and Peter Lougheed of Alberta, have announced their retirements. It may <u>be just a coincidence; a</u>
                                    9
series of independent decisions by long-time political leaders to yield the responsibilities of power. But it may also mark the end of a long period of estrangement between the national government in Ottawa and Canada's <u>relative</u>
                                    10
<u>autonomous</u> provinces.
      10

Levesque once led Quebec's separatist movement. But with as little as four percent of the province's voters now favoring separatism, Levesque has abandoned <u>it as</u> the key plank in
                    11
his platform. Meanwhile, Quebec voters appear to be leaning more toward the mainline national parties. Recent polls show the Liberals in the lead. And in last September's national elections half of the province's vote went to the Progressive-Conservative Party, <u>which had been led</u> by
            12

9. A. NO CHANGE
   B. just be a coincidence; a
   C. be just a coincidence, a
   D. just be a coincidence: a

10. F. NO CHANGE
    G. relatively autonomous
    H. relatedly autonomous
    J. relative

11. A. NO CHANGE
    B. them as
    C. it to be
    D. OMIT

12. F. NO CHANGE
    G. lead
    H. which had been lead
    J. led

French-speaking Quebequer
Brain Mulroney. In effect,
Mulroney's rise to power
in Ottawa left Levesque with
neither cause nor a future in
 ‾‾‾‾‾‾‾‾‾‾‾‾‾‾‾‾‾‾‾‾‾‾‾
          13
Quebec City.
   The one resignation that could
spell trouble for Mulroney

13. A. NO CHANGE
    B. neither cause or
       future
    C. neither a cause nor
       a future
    D. neither a cause nor
       future

is Davis. With his departure,
‾‾‾‾‾‾‾
  14
Ontario's normally Conservative

14. F. NO CHANGE
    G. is Davis's resignation
    H. is Davis's
    J. is that of Davis's

Legislature have come under the
          ‾‾‾‾‾‾‾‾‾‾‾‾‾‾
               15
control of a newly formed
coalition of Liberals and third-
party New Democrats. Provincial
politics in Canada don't necessarily reflect national trends, and
the Ontario alliance may not be
extendable nationwide. Having
fared very badly in September,
new strength in national opinion
‾‾‾‾‾‾‾‾‾‾‾‾‾‾‾‾‾‾‾‾‾‾‾‾‾‾‾‾
              16
polls has been shown by the
‾‾‾‾‾‾‾‾‾‾‾‾‾‾‾‾‾‾‾‾‾‾
        16
Liberals. It would be ironic if
‾‾‾‾‾‾‾‾
   16
Mulroney should have the middle
slip our from under him just as
his political flanks were being
secured by the retirements of two
of Canada's more contentious
provincial premiers.

15. A. NO CHANGE
    B. will have come under
    C. are now under
    D. has come under

16. F. NO CHANGE
    G. national opinion polls
       show new Liberal
       strength
    H. national opinion polls
       show new strength in
       the Liberal Party
    J. the Liberals have
       shown new strength
       in national opinion
       polls

Set 2: Passages III, IV, and V

Passage III

On your last camping vacation or fishing trip far from the bright lights <u>of the urban American city,</u>
₁
perhaps you gazed upward on a breathtakingly clear night and

1. A. NO CHANGE
   B. of the American city
   C. of urban American cities
   D. of the urban city

were struck <u>by awe</u> at the starry
₂

2. F. NO CHANGE
   G. with awe
   H. awesomely
   J. in awe

panorama. <u>If so,</u> you may be able
₃
to appreciate the elation of scientists at the California Institute of Technology, which has been given seventy million dollars to construct the world's largest telescope.

3. A. NO CHANGE
   B. If this is so,
   C. If so
   D. So

The generous donor is the W. M. Keck Foundation of Los Angeles, whose grant will pay for all but fifteen million dollars of the cost of building the telescope and an observatory to house it atop a dormant volcano in Hawaii. The telescope will have thirty-six mirrors with a total diameter of about thirty-three feet, which will permit study of a volume of space eight times greater <u>than the currently</u>
₄
<u>largest telescope,</u> on Palomar
₄

4. F. NO CHANGE
   G. than the currently largest telescope's
   H. than that visible with the currently largest telescope
   J. than the space that can now be seen by the currently largest telescope

Mountain in California.

A telescope is more than just an instrument <u>to look at stars.</u>
5

5. A. NO CHANGE
   B. to look for stars
   C. for looking at stars
   D. for the purpose of looking at stars

It's also a time <u>machine, the</u>
6
light it captures may have left a distant star billions of years earlier. The Keck scope is expected to pick up light from matter that is twelve billion years old, three quarters the estimated age of the universe. Small wonder, then, that the scientists <u>are</u>
7
<u>happy and gleeful.</u> The Keck
7
donation puts much more of the universe within their view. For now, the rest of the heavens can wait.

6. F. NO CHANGE
   G. machine—the
   H. machine: the
   J. machine; the

7. A. NO CHANGE
   B. are gleeful, and happy
   C. are gleeful
   D. are happily gleeful

Passage IV

I often wish that this phrase, "applied science," had never been invented. For it suggests that there is a sort of scientific knowledge of direct practical use, which can be studied <u>apart</u>
8
<u>from another sort</u> of scentific
8
knowledge, which has no practical use, and which is termed "pure

8. F. NO CHANGE
   G. as a part of
   H. apart and separate from
   J. as part

science." But there <u>is no more</u>
                              9
<u>total and complete</u> fallacy than
                  9
this. What people call applied
science is nothing but the
application of pure science to
particular classes of problems.
    <u>It consists</u> of deductions
         10
from those general principles,
established by reasoning and
observation, that constitute
pure science. No one can safely
make these deductions until he
has a firm grasp of the

<u>principles.</u>
    11

9. A. NO CHANGE
   B. are no more total
   C. is no more complete
   D. is no fallacy that is
       a more complete

10. F. NO CHANGE
    G. It consists
        (DO NOT begin
        new paragraph)
    H. They consist
        (DO NOT begin
        new paragraph)
    J. They consist

11. A. NO CHANGE
    B. principles, which are
        involved.
    C. principals that are
        involved.
    D. principals.

Passage V

These paragraphs may or may not be in the most logical order. The
last item of this passage will ask you to choose the most logical
order.

(1)

Many people mistakenly believe
they have insomnia. Because
they have not had eight full
hours of sleep, they think that
they are insomniacs. But there is
no evidence to support the
common belief that <u>everyone has</u>
                                    12
to get eight hours of sleep

12. F. NO CHANGE
    G. everyone have
    H. everybody have
    J. that everybody have

nightly. In fact, a few people
<u></u>
13
habitually sleep as little as two
hours a night and wake up
feeling fine. A much larger

13. A. NO CHANGE
    B. OMIT and begin
        sentence with
        A few
    C. Move to after
        habitually
    D. As a matter of fact,

number requires only five hours
<u></u>
14
of sleep each night, while
others must have ten hours to
feel refreshed.

14. F. NO CHANGE
    G. requires
    H. only requires
    J. require only

(2)

Another type of insomnia
occurs when something exciting
<u></u>
15
or something upsetting happens,
<u></u>
15
or is about to happen, in
someone's life. Fortunately, this
sort of insomnia is likely to
disappear naturally after the
crisis has passed. When insomnia
does not go away, it is possible
that sleeplessness is a sign of
physical or emotional illness.
Awakening early in the morning,
for example, is sometimes a sign
of depression, and this is a
<u></u>
16
potentially serious mental illness.

15. A. NO CHANGE
    B. something exciting or
        something upsetting
        happens
    C. something exciting or
        something upsetting
        happen,
    D. something exciting or
        upsetting happen

16. F. NO CHANGE
    G. OMIT
    H. which is
    J. that is

(3)

There is a type of insomnia in
which people believe that they
have had only a few minutes of
sleep, or no sleep at all. Though
these sufferers have not slept

well, they have probably had some sleep. Because periods of light sleep and wakefulness are often fused, the insomniac does not realize that they have been
₁₇
asleep. It is harder to judge
₁₇

time in a dark bedroom than in the daylight, so it is easy to overestimate the number of wakeful hours and to underestimate those spent sleeping.

17. A. NO CHANGE
    B. they were
    C. he or she has been
    D. he or she have been

18. Choose the sequence of paragraph numbers that will make the essay's structure most logical.
    F. NO CHANGE
    G. 1, 3, 2
    H. 2, 1, 3
    J. 3, 1, 2

Set 3: Passages VI and VII

Passage VI

Over the last few years, the home satellite dish industry has experienced such explosive growth that today it is being
₁
estimated that fifty thousand new
₁

1. A. NO CHANGE
   B. that it is being estimated today
   C. that today it is estimated
   D. that today it is currently estimated

receivers are being installed
₂
already this year. These bring an expansive range of programming to more than one million people

2. F. NO CHANGE
   G. have been installed
   H. will be installed
   J. will have been installed

every day of the week; many
                    ___
                     3
dish owners, however, are getting
mixed signals about the usefulness
of home dishes and the continued
availability of satellite-delivered
programming.

Now that several leading
pay-TV programmers are moving
ahead with plans to scramble
its service. The large investment
_____
    4
in a satellite dish is a
questionable one. Though some
dish owners mistakenly believe
that the scrambling of signals
is illegal, the Cable
Communications Act recognizes
that satellite programmers can
scramble to protect their services
                      _____
                           6
being used without authorization.
_____
    5

Criterion Cable Company has
long been concerned by protecting
                       _____
                            6
its services from unauthorized
use by commercial enterprises
as hotels, bars, and restaurants,
_____
              7
which in some cases have broken
the law by charging customers
for the privilege of viewing

3. A. NO CHANGE
   B. every day. Many
   C. every day of the week.
       (Begin new paragraph
       with *Many*)
   D. every day. (Begin new
       paragraph with
       Many)

4. F. NO CHANGE
   G. its services, the
   H. their services, the
   J. their services; the

5. A. NO CHANGE
   B. their service being
       used
   C. its services' being
       used
   D. their services from
       being used

6. F. NO CHANGE
   G. to protecting
   H. about protecting
   J. about how to protect

7. A. NO CHANGE
   B. such as hotels bars
       and restaurants
   C. like hotels, bars,
       and restaurants
   D. as hotels, bars
       and restaurants

programs which it has received
8

without charge. Scrambling is
the most efficient way to prevent
this unlawful activity.

8. F. NO CHANGE
   G. programs that it has
   H. programs that
       they have
   J. programs it has

Passage VII

   Larry Harmon has been Bozo
the Clown for thirty-five years.
He has played the character
himself on live television
and provides the voice for
9

twenty years of Bozo cartoons.
Now sixty, Harmon is still going
strong, and he thinks Bozo is
needed more than ever. That is
10

the reason why he is working
10

now to reintroduce Bozo to
youngsters in a TV show and
movie called *Bozo, Secret Agent.*
   Harmon not only urges people
11

to do something good for others,
but also to be good to themselves.

For example, he warns school
12

children about the danger of
drugs and at the same time

cheers them up. He's trying in
13

his own way to make the world a
13

safer, happier place to live.

9. A. NO CHANGE
   B. and he provides
   C. and is
   D. and has provided

10. F. NO CHANGE
    G. That is why
    H. This is why
    J. For this reason,

11. A. NO CHANGE
    B. urges people not only
    C. urges not only people
    D. both urges people

12. F. NO CHANGE
    G. He, for example,
    H. As an example, he
    J. He, as an example,

13. A. NO CHANGE
    B. He's trying to make
        in his own way
    C. Hes trying, in his
        own way, to make
    D. In his own way, he's
        trying to make

Interviewed at his home in Silver
$\overline{14}$
Lake, I asked him about retiring.
$\overline{14}$

14. F. NO CHANGE
    G. When interviewed
       at his home in
       Silver Lake
    H. Interviewing him
       at his home in
       Silver Lake
    J. Being interviewed
       at his home in
       Silver Lake

"Bozo will never retire," he said.
$\overline{15}$
He'll go smiling and in makeup to
that big circus in the sky.

15. A. NO CHANGE
    B. He said Bozo will
       never retire.
    C. Bozo will never
       retire he said.
    D. "Bozo will never
       retire"; he said.

Set 4: Passages VIII and IX

Passage VIII

The Voyager spacecraft, racing
toward an encounter with Uranus,
has already discovered a number
$\overline{1}$
of tiny moons orbiting the planet.
Ranging in size from twenty to
thirty miles in diameter,

1. A. NO CHANGE
   B. has already discovered
      the number
   C. have already
      discovered the number
   D. have already
      discovered a number

the spacecraft has discovered
$\overline{2}$
new moons that scientists had
$\overline{2}$
not been able to see with high-

2. F. NO CHANGE
   G. the spacecraft
      discovered new moons
   H. new moons have been
      discovered by
      the spacecraft
   J. new moons discovered
      by the spacecraft

powered telescopes. Because
                3
Uranus is so far from the sun and
so dimly lighted. And scientists

expect additional moons to be
                           4
discovered in the next few days.
    4
    Prior to this Voyager flight,

only five moons were detected,
        5

and these were much larger than
                             6
the new discovered satellites.
    6
None of the moons is in an area
that would endanger Voyager
being they are in orbits fifty
    7
thousand miles from the planet's
center. No photographs of the
new moons have yet been released
because the spacecraft is still so
far from Uranus that satellites
appear only as tiny specks
            8
of light.
    8

3. A. NO CHANGE
   B. telescopes, due to the
       fact that
   C. telescopes.
   D. telescopes because

4. F. NO CHANGE
   G. discovered
   H. to have been
       discovered
   J. will have been
       discovered

5. A. NO CHANGE
   B. five moons only
       were detected
   C. only five moons
       had been detected
   D. only five moons
       have been detected

6. F. NO CHANGE
   G. than new discovered
   H. than newly discovered
   J. than the newly
       discovered

7. A. NO CHANGE
   B. being it is
   C. because it is
   D. because they are

8. F. NO CHANGE
   G. are tiny specks
       of light only
   H. appears only as tiny
       specks of light
   J. will appear only as
       tiny specks of light

Passage IX

Born only a week ago, <u>according</u>
               ₉
<u>to a spokesman for Sea World,</u>
          ₉
a killer whale died last night.
When the whale was born, it
weighed three hundred pounds
and it appeared healthy.

9. A. NO CHANGE
   B. according to a Sea
      World spokesman,
   C. Move phrase to
      beginning of sentence
   D. Move phrase to end
      of sentence

<u>And three days later, however,</u>
          ₁₀
it displayed symptoms of a
respiratory ailment; it was moved
to an intensive-care pool but did
not respond to treatment.
    There is a high mortality rate
for whales born in captivity.
None of the four killer whales
<u>who were born</u> at Sea World
    ₁₁

10. F. NO CHANGE
    G. And three days later,
    H. Three days later,
       however,
    J. Three days after,

11. A. NO CHANGE
    B. that were born
    C. who had been born
    D. , which were born,

<u>have survived.</u> The only killer
    ₁₂
whale born in captivity to survive
was born in an aquarium in
Europe. Named Victor, the whale
<u>is now eight years old; and is</u>
               ₁₃

12. F. NO CHANGE
    G. has survived
    H. survive
    J. are surviving

13. A. NO CHANGE
    B. old and is featured
    C. old, and the whale is
       featured
    D. old; featured

<u>featured</u> daily with dolphins <u>in an</u>
  ₁₃   ₁₄
<u>aquatic show each day.</u>
        ₁₄

14. F. NO CHANGE
    G. each day in an
       aquatic show
    H. in an aquatic show
    J. every day in an
       aquatic show

ANSWER KEY FOR ENGLISH USAGE AND SENTENCE CORRECTION PRACTICE

PART I: ENGLISH USAGE

Set 1	Set 2	Set 3	Set 4
1. D	1. C	1. C	1. A
2. B	2. C	2. E	2. A
3. B	3. E	3. E	3. E
4. E	4. C	4. D	4. A
5. E	5. A	5. B	5. E
6. B	6. C	6. B	6. A
7. B	7. B	7. E	7. A
8. C	8. A	8. C	8. B
9. E	9. D	9. E	9. B
10. A	10. D	10. C	10. A
11. B	11. E	11. D	11. E
12. C	12. C	12. A	12. B
13. D	13. D	13. B	13. B
14. C	14. C	14. C	14. C
15. A	15. A	15. E	15. B

PART II: SENTENCE CORRECTION

Set 1	Set 2	Set 3
1. D	1. A	1. B
2. E	2. D	2. C
3. D	3. B	3. A
4. D	4. E	4. B
5. C	5. C	5. D
6. B	6. E	6. E
7. D	7. D	7. B
8. C	8. C	8. D
9. D	9. C	9. D
10. B	10. C	10. A
11. C	11. D	11. D
12. D	12. C	12. D
13. C	13. C	13. D
14. D	14. E	14. C
15. D	15. E	15. B

PART III: ENGLISH USAGE

Set 1		Set 2		Set 3		Set 4	
1. A	9. C	1. B	10. G	1. C	9. D	1. A	8. F
2. H	10. F	2. G	11. A	2. G	10. J	2. H	9. D
3. C	11. A	3. A	12. F	3. D	11. B	3. D	10. H
4. F	12. J	4. H	13. A	4. H	12. F	4. F	11. B
5. A	13. C	5. C	14. J	5. D	13. D	5. C	12. G
6. G	14. H	6. J	15. A	6. H	14. H	6. J	13. B
7. A	15. D	7. C	16. G	7. C	15. A	7. D	14. H
8. H	16. J	8. F	17. C	8. H			
		9. C	18. G				

ANSWERS TO ENGLISH USAGE AND SENTENCE CORRECTION PRACTICE

PART I: ENGLISH USAGE

Set 1

1. (D) The verb should be *would have suspected.*

2. (B) The correct form is *who,* subject of the clause *who made the better showing in the televised debate.*

3. (B) The verb should be the singular *was prepared* to agree with the singular subject *None.*

4. (E) There are no errors in this sentence.

5. (E) There are no errors in this sentence.

6. (B) The phrase should be made parallel with the others in the series: *that he is good looking.*

7. (B) *Smart* and *intelligent* mean the same thing. One of the terms should be deleted.

8. (C) In an indirect question, the pronoun should precede the verb: *he can.*

9. (E) The sentence is correct as given.

10. (A) *Anyone* should be two words: *Any one.*

11. (B) The verb should be the singular *remembers* to agree with the singular *None.* The plural is correctly used in *who have* to agree with the plural *survivors.*

12. (C) The idiom is *other than,* and the phrase should read *than that.*

13. (D) The comparative *lower* should be used with a comparison of only two incomes, those of husband and wife.

14. (C) With the correlatives *not . . . but,* the structure after *but* should be parallel to *to please,* an infinitive.

163

15. (A) The comparison in the prepositional phrase is to a painter, not his painting. The following phrase should begin with *Graham*.

Set 2

1. (C) The series of *to eat, write, and to shave* should be made up of parallel elements—either *to eat, to write, and to shave* or *to eat, write, and shave*.

2. (C) In this context, the idiom is *charged with*. To *charge for* is used to mean *to assess a cost*.

3. (E) The sentence is correct as given.

4. (C) The pronoun should be the plural *they* to agree with the plural *westerners*.

5. (A) The subject of the sentence is singular; the phrases following *as well as* are parenthetical and not part of a compound subject.

6. (C) The verb *affect* should be used. As a verb, *effect* means *to bring about; affect* means *to influence*.

7. (B) To keep parallelism in the series (*of pasta, of muffin mix*), you must also say *of detergent*.

8. (A) The *they* in the dependent clause at the beginning of the sentence refers to the *colonists,* but here it appears to refer to the *cheeses*.

9. (D) The *which* is an ambiguous pronoun.

10. (D) With *not only . . . but also,* the same structure must follow both correlatives: *not only low in fat . . . but also highest in fiber*.

11. (E) There are no errors in this sentence.

12. (C) An agreement error. *None* is singular.

13. (D) A tense error. The future tense makes no sense here where three other verbs are in the past tense.

14. (C) The present tense of the participle is inappropriate for an action to take place in the future; *to be presented* is better.

15. (A) The sentence compares a man (*President Carter*) and a group of people (*cabinet*). It should read *Like President Carter's*.

Set 3

1. (C) An error of idiom. With *smaller*, the *to* should be *than*.

2. (E) The sentence is correct as given.

3. (E) Remember that roughly one sentence in five on the tests will have no error.

4. (D) *Kind* is singular. Use *this kind* or *that kind*.

5. (B) An agreement error. Since the singular *harpist* is nearer the verb in a *neither . . . nor* construction, the verb is singular.

6. (B) The adverb *relatively* should be used to modify the adjective *easy*.

7. (E) This sentence contains no errors.

8. (C) With the present tense used twice already, there is no reason to change to the future tense. Use *it is* three times.

9. (E) The sentence is correct as given.

10. (C) The phrase *brokers claim* is parenthetical. The clause is *who are willing to take risks*, and *who* is the subject of the clause.

11. (D) The clause here is *it is they; they* is subjective with the verb *is*.

12. (A) The infinitive at the beginning of the sentence dangles.

13. (B) A verbosity error. Since *same* and *identical* mean the same thing, only one of the two should be used.

14 (C) A tense error. The present tense (*is*) should be used here.

15. (E) There are no errors in this sentence.

Set 4

1. (A) The clause should begin with the conjunction *As*, not the preposition *Like*.

2. (A) The phrase *who have studied* is necessary, parallel to *who ought* later in the sentence.

3. (E) The sentence is correct as given.

4. (A) The opening participial phrase dangles, evidently modifying *natives* rather than *huts*.

5. (E) The sentence contains no error.

6. (A) The opening phrase dangles, modifying *returns* rather than *he* or *Simmons*.

7. (A) The plural *have* should be singular to agree with the singular nearer the verb after *neither . . . nor*.

8. (B) With *miles, fewer* should replace *less*.

9. (B) The subjective *I* should be *me*, object of the preposition *on*.

10. (A) Since the sentence begins with *you,* there should be no change of person to *one*.

11. (E) The sentence is correct as given.

12. (B) The subject is singular; *are* should be *is*.

13. (B) With the correlatives *not . . . but* an infinitive should follow *but* to be parallel with *to fly*. The phrase *as would seem likely* is parenthetical.

14. (C) The *when* should be *that*.

15. (B) The singular subject *quarterback* requires the singular verb *was*.

PART II: SENTENCE CORRECTION

Set 1

1. (D) The *not only . . . but also* should both be followed by parallel constructions, *about* and a noun.

2. (E) Only choice (E) supplies an appropriate word (*I*) for the dangling participial phrase (*Carrying the warm water . . .*) to modify.

3. (D) Since *alumnae* is plural, the pronoun must be *they*. The preposition *in* must follow *believe*.

4. (D) The *those* of the opening phrase refers to *prices,* and unless *prices* follows, the phrase dangles. Though passive, choice (D) is better than choice (C), in which the antecedent of *these* is unclear.

5. (C) Since the sentence begins with *you,* the subject of the main clause should also be *you.*

6. (B) The pronoun *which* has no clear antecedent; *hours* cannot be *decreased,* choice (D), or *altered,* choice (E), but a *schedule* can be *altered.*

7. (D) In choice (D), the related words are kept together and the sentence is more concise than choice (B).

8. (C) The beginning of the sentence must parallel *enjoying.*

9. (D) The prepositional phrase at the beginning of the sentence must refer to *operas* not *composers,* either directly or by a pronoun (*those*). Since Mozart is a composer, *other* is also necessary.

10. (B) The shortest version here is correct.

11. (C) The verb in the *if* clause should be *had planned.* The pronoun *whom* is the object of *to ask.*

12. (D) Only choice (D) avoids the ambiguous pronoun error.

13. (C) The correlatives *both . . . and* should be followed by parallel words (the adjectives *afraid* and *awed*). The preposition *of* must follow *afraid.*

14. (D) The correlatives *not . . . but* should be followed by parallel structures (*a better . . . a more carefully*).

15. (D) In the first three answers, the pronouns have no specific antecedent. Choice (E), though shorter, changes the meaning.

Set 2

1. (A) *That your horse won* is a noun clause, a proper subject of the verb *is*. In choice (C), the gerund requires a possessive. There is an agreement error in choice (E).

2. (D) The antecedent of *that* is the plural *tickets*, but the subject of the sentence is the singular *one*. The verbs should be *were reserved* and *has*.

3. (B) With *neither . . . nor,* the subject of the verb is the singular *butter*. Since calories can be counted, *less* should be *fewer*.

4. (E) The first four answers have parallelism errors with the correlatives *both . . . and*. By eliminating the correlatives, choice (E) avoids the errors and is more concise.

5. (C) The singular subject (*one*) requires a singular verb (*has promised*). The pronoun should be *whoever,* subject of the clause *whoever wins the primary*.

6. (E) Though there are two adjectives, the subject of the sentence is the singular *nature,* so the main verb must be *relegates*. Since *fiction* is singular, the correct pronoun is the singular *it*. Both choice (D) and choice (E) avoid the agreement errors, but choice (D) is wordier and uses *which* and a nonrestrictive clause where a restrictive clause with *that* should be used (or the prepositional phrase).

7. (D) Choice (A) is wordy (*annually* means *each year*) and misuses the idiom *descend on*. But choices (B) and (C) make *lured* a dangling participle. The idiom (*descended into*) in choice (E) is wrong in this context.

8. (C) In choices (A) and (B), the two parts of the comparison (*Switzerland* and *mountains*) are not parallel. Choice (E) makes no grammatical sense. Choices (C) and (D) are grammatically correct but choice (D) is wordy.

9. (C) With the verb *knocked,* the adverb *loudly,* not the adjective *loud,* should be used. To maintain a logical sequence of verb tenses, the two past tenses (*stopped, ran*) should be followed by a third past tense (*knocked*).

10. (C) The subject of the first clause is *whoever,* but in the clause *whomever the wind reaches, wind* is the subject and *whomever* is the object. The adjective should be *fewest* not *least.*

11. (D) The problem here is parallelism. The most concise version of the sentence will use three nouns, *eagerness, willingness,* and *optimism.* Choice (E), though parallel, is wordier than choice (D).

12. (C) Choices (A), (B), and (E) are all sentence fragments and dependent clauses. In choice (D), the plural verb is an agreement error.

13. (C) Since the introductory phrase uses the singular *his knowledge,* the subject must be singular. Since *his* is the possessive case of *he,* the subject must also be a human, a *nurseryman,* not *science.*

14. (E) The error in choices (A), (B), (C), and (D) is the same, an ambiguous pronoun (*which* or *this*).

15. (E) There are parallelism errors with the correlatives *both . . . and* in choices (A) and (B). Choice (C), though grammatically correct, changes the meaning of the original sentence slightly. Choice (D) awkwardly separates the adjective *deceptive* from the words it modifies.

Set 3

1. (B) To maintain parallelism, *in* must follow *than.* Since the Belmont Jail is a lockup, the correct phrase is *any other.*

2. (C) Since *group,* a collective noun, is singular, the correct verb is *has,* and the correct pronoun is *it.* With *where,* the use of *in* is unnecessary.

3. (A) In choices (C), (D), and (E), the infinitive dangles. In choice (B), *years* is plural.

4. (B) With the singular subject *Neither,* the verb or verbs must be singular. Choice (A) omits the necessary word *of.*

5. (D) The correct idiom is *try to.* Choice (C) omits the necessary word *as.*

6. (E) The main clause must begin with *government mortgage certificates* to which *their* refers. The correct word here is *principal,* the noun meaning *face value,* not *principle.*

7. (B) With the *if* construction, the correct verb form is *would be.* The word *personally* is unnecessary.

8. (D) The series here is *one must* followed by a verb controlled by *must: weigh, exercise,* and *drink.*

9. (D) In choices (A) and (B), *different* modifies *Company.* The word *other* must be included. Choice (E) is wordy.

10. (A) The sentence is correct as given. *Its* (the possessive) is correct here. Choices (C), (D), and (E) all change the meaning of the original.

11. (D) The correct noun here is *effect.* The idiom is *effect on* or *upon.*

12. (D) The correct word here is *credulous* (trusting, believing) not *credible* (believable). Choice (D) is better than choice (A) or (C) because it is more concise.

13. (D) The main clause should begin with a singular plant to agree with the opening phrase *a very old plant.*

14. (C) The plural *were* is correct with the plural *terrorists.* The main verb is singular (*has*) to agree with the singular subject *None.* Since we cannot be certain from the context whether the clause is restrictive or nonrestrictive, the use or omission of commas is not an issue.

15. (B) *Me* is correct as the object of the preposition *for. Whoever* is the subject of the clause *whoever wins the contest.* The correct idiom is *as a prize,* not *for a prize.* While choice (D) correctly uses *me* and *whoever,* it creates a dangling participial phrase and suggests that the skillet, teakettle, and saucepan are paging through the catalogue.

PART III: ENGLISH USAGE

Set 1: Passages I and II

Passage I

1. (A) No change is needed.

2. (H) With two independent clauses, the semicolon is correct.

3. (C) The series in apposition should be introduced by a comma.

4. (F) Though choice (G) is not wrong, it uses one word more. The apostrophe here follows the *s,* as *delegations* is plural.

5. (A) In choices (C) and (D), some meaning is lost by the omission of *stark.* Choice (A) uses the correct idiom.

6. (G) With *funds,* the verb must be plural. *There* is correct; *they're* means *they are* and *their* is a possessive form of *they.*

7. (A) The phrase *fewer and fewer* is correct and concise.

8. (H) It is easy to coin a verb by adding *-ize* to an adjective or noun (*privatize*) and to coin a noun by adding *-ation* (*privatization*), but usually a clearer and often shorter way of saying the same thing already exists. The diction of *privatization option* is pretentious. The phrase *private financing* is clear and shorter.

Passage II

9. (C) The sentence requires a comma. With a semicolon, the second part of the sentence is a fragment without a main verb.

10. (G) The adverb *relatively* is needed to modify the adjective *autonomous.*

11. (A) The singular *separatism* is the antecedent of *it.* Omission of the phrase changes the meaning of the sentence.

12. (J) The past perfect tense is unnecessary here. The past tense of the verb *to lead* is *led. Lead* is the present tense or the noun for the metal, which is easily confused with *led.*

13. (C) The article *a* should follow both *neither* and *nor.*

14. (H) There is no need to repeat *resignation*. One can say either *that of Davis* (with no apostrophe) or, more concisely, *Davis's*.

15. (D) *Legislature* is a singular; the required tense is the perfect.

16. (J) The participial phrase at the beginning modifies *the Liberals*, not *strength* or *national opinion polls*. Without this change, the participle dangles.

Set 2: Passages III, IV, and V

Passage III

1. (B) Since *urban* means *of the city*, it is unnecessary here.

2. (G) The idiomatic preposition is *with*.

3. (A) The briefer *If so* should be followed by a comma.

4. (H) There must be a parallel to *volume of space* after the comparison. The most concise correct version uses the pronoun *that*. Choice (J) is grammatically correct but wordy.

5. (C) The idiom is *instrument for*.

6. (J) Use a semicolon between two independent clauses not joined by a conjunction.

7. (C) The adjective *gleeful* conveys the meaning by itself.

Passage IV

8. (F) *Apart from* is idiomatic. Choice (H) includes both *apart* and *separate*, which mean the same.

9. (C) Since *total* and *complete* mean the same thing, there is no reason to use both. The singular verb agrees with the singular subject, *fallacy*.

10. (G) The subject of the paragraph is still *applied science*. The antecedent of the pronoun *it* is the singular *science*.

11. (A) The correct word is *principle*. Chocies (B) and (C) are needlessly wordy.

12. (F) Either *everyone* or *everybody* can be used, but both are singular so the verb must be *has*.

13. (A) The phrase *In fact* should be retained at the beginning of the sentence, since the sentence is correcting the mistaken belief referred to in the first sentence. The phrase *As a matter of fact* is not wrong, but it takes five words to say what *In fact* says in two.

14. (J) *A number* is plural and calls for the plural *require*.

15. (A) The comma at the end of the clause is necessary in this case to set off the parenthetical phrase that follows. While this phrase need not be considered parenthetical, you can be sure that it is treated as such because of the comma after *happen* (which may not be changed because it is not underlined), which must be paired with a preceding comma to be correct.

16. (G) The phrase that ends the sentence can stand as an appositive. The other versions are needlessly wordy.

17. (C) The subject of the sentence is the singular *insomniac*. Only in choice (C) are the pronouns and the verb in agreement with their antecedent.

18. (G) Paragraph 2 begins with a reference to *another type* of insomnia, but paragraph 1 has not identified one. Paragraph 2 logically follows only paragraph 3, which does describe types of insomnia.

Set 3: Passages VI and VII

Passage VI

1. (C) The present tense here is correct and concise.

2. (G) The perfect tense in the first clause (*has experienced*) and the use of *already* indicate that the perfect tense should be used here.

3. (D) The content of the sentence after the semicolon and the use of *however* signal a change. The sentence is more logically a part of the second paragraph. Though grammatically correct, choice (C) is wordier than choice (D).

4. (H) The antecedent of the pronoun is plural (*programmers*). If the semicolon is used instead of the comma, the first clause is a fragment, a dependent clause.

5. (D) Since *programmers* is plural, the correct pronoun is *their*. The meaning of the sentence is not *to protect the services* but *to protect them from being used*.

6. (H) The correct idiom here is *concerned about*. Though choice (J) is not wrong, it is wordier than choice (H).

7. (C) With the series, there must be at least one comma (after *hotels*), and there can be a comma after *bars*. The preposition *like*, not the conjunction *as*, should be used here.

8. (H) The clause is a restrictive one. The verb and pronoun should be plural to agree with *commercial enterprises*.

Passage VII

9. (D) The consistent sequence of tenses here calls for the perfect tense.

10. (J) Only choice (J) avoids the use of an ambiguous pronoun.

11. (B) Since the *but also* is followed by an infinitive, the *not only* should also be followed by an infinitive. The correlatives are *not only . . . but also*, not *both . . . but also*.

12. (F) Beginning with *for example* keeps the subject and verb together.

13. (D) Beginning with *in his own way* keeps the subject and verb together.

14. (H) The subject of the sentence is *I*, so to avoid a dangling phrase, the opening must modify *I*, not *Bozo*.

15. (A) The sentence is correctly punctuated.

Set 4: Passages VIII and IX

Passage VIII

1. (A) In this context, *a number* (that is, *many*) is correct. The last

sentence of the paragraph makes it clear that the number has not yet been determined. The subject is the singular *spacecraft*.

2. (H) Since the participial phrase that begins the sentence refers to the *moons*, the *moons* must begin the main clause or the participle will dangle. Choice (J) has no main verb.

3. (D) If the first sentence ends at *telescopes*, the sentence beginning with *Because* is a fragment.

4. (F) With *expect*, the future infinitive is necessary.

5. (C) The past perfect tense is necessary to denote an action in a past time in relation to another past time (*Prior to this flight*).

6. (J) The article (*the*) is necessary. The adverb *newly* modifies the adjective *discovered*.

7. (D) The antecedent of *they* is the plural *moons*. The correct conjunction is *because*.

8. (F) The verb should be plural to agree with *satellites*.

Passage IX

9. (D) To keep the opening phrase close to the word it modifies, the parenthetical phrase should come at the end of the sentence.

10. (H) The *and* suggests continuation, but *however* suggests a change of direction in the discourse. The *however* should be used to indicate this change.

11. (B) The correct pronoun is *that*, modifying *whales*. The clause is restrictive.

12. (G) The subject of the verb is the singular *None*.

13. (B) The semicolon is not correct because there is no subject in the phrase *and is featured* . . . Choice (C) is wordy.

14. (H) With *daily*, *each day* or *every day* is unnecessary.

Part III: Writing Timed Essays Strategies and Practice

ESSAY WRITING STRATEGIES

A number of standardized tests include a writing sample. You are asked to respond to an essay question, under time constraints. In this section, we will present typical questions along with techniques for generating, organizing, and proofreading your writing.

To better appreciate the techniques presented, you should first understand the typical criteria and scoring procedures used to evaluate timed writing on standardized tests. The most popular method for evaluating national and state writing tests is "holistic" scoring. Faced with hundreds of essays and the problem of producing reliable scores, professional readers evaluate each essay with a "general impression" number that reflects the reader's overall conclusion. The scoring scale is usually 1 through 4 or 1 through 6 (with 1 being the lowest in both cases), and a passing essay is one receiving an "upper-half" score. On the 1–4 scale, an upper-half score is either a 3 or a 4. On the 1–6 scale, an upper-half score is a 4, 5, or 6.

Each essay is read and scored twice, by different people who are not aware of each other's scores. If the two scores are very different (a 3 and a 6, for example), the essay goes to a third reader. However, the incidence of divergent scores is generally quite low, mainly because the readers are employing similar criteria. In general, for reading timed essays—whether they are scored holistically or not—the criteria are as follows:

1. *Fullness of response:* Credit is given to an essay which responds fully to all parts of the question.

2. *Adequate details:* Credit is given to an essay in which generalizations are supported by specific details, reasons, and examples.

3. *Correct grammar, usage, and spelling:* Although occasional errors are allowed, credit is *not* given to essays that display frequent mistakes.

Understanding scoring procedures and criteria should help you to adjust your writing to the expectations of your readers. Remember that they will probably be reading carefully but quickly, perhaps spending no more than two or three minutes on your essay. Therefore, your most effective and successful writing will be clear and direct, allowing your readers to proceed efficiently. Also, remember that no reader will expect a perfect, polished essay. Under time constraints, even the best writer's effort is somewhat flawed.

THE NARRATIVE/DESCRIPTIVE ESSAY

One type of essay topic asks you to draw directly from personal experience, to show (describe) and tell about (narrate) a significant event in your life. Here is a sample topic:

We have all faced a number of important challenges. Write an essay about the most difficult challenge you faced recently. Discuss why the challenge was difficult; describe the way in which you prepared; and tell whether you were successful or unsuccessful in meeting the challenge.

In order to make sure that you will respond appropriately and fully to the question, *mark the key words*. Note that you must first select a *difficult challenge* from your recent experience. Do this quickly. Don't waste time worrying about whether the experience you select is "important" or "interesting" enough. Just get started. The question asks for a *three-part response* in which you *discuss* the *difficulty* of the challenge, *describe* your *preparation,* and *tell* the *results.* You must respond to all three parts. Responding insufficiently to any one of the parts will very likely result in a lower-half score.

For any timed writing task, you should work through three "stages" that lead to a competent finished product: (1) preparing to write, (2) writing, and (3) proofreading.

Preparing to Write

Inventing and organizing information at short notice, given only a few minutes, can be difficult and perhaps impossible unless you are ready with an effective technique. One technique that is well suited to the timed essay is the "cluster outline":

Step One: Jot down the experience *you* will discuss and the three aspects you must consider and draw a circle around each one.

Step Two: Consider each of the three subareas of "Running a 10K" and quickly jot down, in a cluster, whatever comes to mind (see following).

Step Three: Add more information to what you have so far. The additional information can (1) answer the question "Why?" or "How?" or "So What?" and (2) give a concrete example or "for instance."

Here is a completed cluster outline for "Running a 10K."

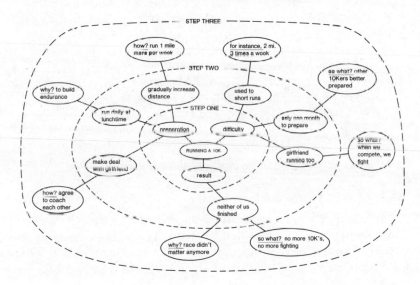

Mastering the cluster outline takes *repeated practice*. As you become more familiar with this technique, you should be able to jot down a wealth of information in a few minutes. (Note that you can use fragment sentences and abbreviations to save time.) Once your cluster outline is complete, you will have more than enough information, which will be clustered into categories for easy organization, and you will be ready to write your opening paragraph.

Writing

A strong opening paragraph is essential. One type of introduction, easy to master and very effective, is a GENERALIZE-FOCUS-SURVEY structure. This is a three- or four-sentence paragraph in which the first sentence generalizes about the given topic; the second sentence focuses on what you have chosen to discuss, and the last one or two sentences survey the particulars you intend to present.

Referring to the essay question and to your cluster outline, jot down (1) the central term from the given topic, (2) the term that names your subject, and (3) several aspects of your subject that you plan to discuss:

1. General term—   difficult challenge

2. Focused term—   running a 10K

3. Aspects to survey—   increasing distance
                        building endurance
                        maintaining relationship

Step One: In your first sentence, use the general term.

Difficult challenges can be physical and emotional.

Step Two: In your second sentence, focus on the subject you have chosen to discuss.

When I took on a tough physical challenge, *running a 10K,* I did not expect it to be emotional as well.

Step Three: Finally, survey the aspects you will discuss.

Increasing my running distance and *building endurance* taxed me physically. At the same time, I faced the emotional challenge of *maintaining a relationship* with my chief competitor, my girl friend.

An effective first paragraph tells your reader what to expect in the body of the essay. The GENERALIZE-FOCUS-SURVEY paragraph points toward the specifics you will discuss and suggests the order in which you will discuss them.

Writing the body of the essay involves presenting specific details and examples that are related to the aspects you have introduced. The body of the essay may consist of one longer paragraph or several shorter paragraphs. If you choose to break your discussion into several paragraphs, make sure that each paragraph consists of at least three sentences. Very short paragraphs may make your essay appear to be insubstantial and scattered.

Be realistic about *how much* you will be able to write. Your readers do not give more credit for longer essays. Although they want you to support your points adequately, they understand that you must write concisely in order to finish in time.

It will be sufficient to provide one substantial example or "for instance" for each aspect you discuss in the body of your essay. Here is an example of a two-paragraph body:

About a year ago, I was a "jogger" but not a "runner." I jogged three times a week, two miles each time, but wondered whether I had the ability to endure a run of over six miles—the demanding 10K. With the Independence Day 10K only a month away, I began a very difficult training program. I began running three miles daily for a week, then four miles, then five miles, and a week before the race I was running six miles a day. My friends warned me that I was driving myself too hard, and my constant exhaustion told me that as well. But pushing myself this hard seemed like the best way to build endurance and increase distance by the time of the race.

The physical challenge was at least matched by the emotional challenge in dealing with my girl friend. She had decided to train for the race as well, and I was afraid that because we were both so competitive we would be fighting constantly. So, early on, I made a deal with Jane. She would help me and I would help her. We'd support each other. There were moments every day when cooperating seemed almost impossible. Tired and sweating, we began to grumble at each other. But both of us quickly remembered the deal and stopped a potential argument. But restraining myself from arguing was hard work.

Notice that so far this essay deals with two of the three parts of the question. It discusses the difficulty of the challenge and describes the preparation. Notice also that not all of the details that are in the cluster outline are in the essay. You should not expect to or try to use every detail from your outline. Also, realize that as you write, new ideas and details will come up, and you should use them to your advantage.

As you prepare to write the conclusion, you should be paying special attention to time. You must allow enough time both to write the conclusion and to proofread. The conclusion may function to (1) *complete* your response to the essay question, (2) *add* information that was not introduced earlier, or (3) *point toward the future.* The following conclusion serves all three functions:

The day of the race arrived, and both of us were not really ready. We both felt that we had trained too hard and too often, and we were right. After running just three miles, we simply could not continue and dropped out. However, both of us agreed that learning to cooperate was more important than finishing the race. Once we dropped out of competition for the 10K, we stopped competing and fighting with each other as well.

Proofreading

Always allow a few minutes to proofread your essay for errors in grammar, usage, and spelling. Common problems in these areas are discussed in Part II of this book. To make sure that you do not proofread hastily, try this. With a sheet of paper, cover all but the first line of your essay. Read that line carefully. Then reveal and read the second line, and so forth. Using this method, you are more assured of focused and careful proofreading.

If you detect an error, line it out carefully and insert the correction neatly. Keep in mind, both while you are writing and while you are correcting, that your handwriting must be *legible.*

THE ANALYTICAL/EXPOSITORY ESSAY

Another type of essay topic asks you to explain and analyze an issue, problem, or quotation. This question may or may not ask you to draw from personal experience and background. Here is a sample topic:

Consider the following, written by Lewis Thomas:
We learn, as we say, by "trial and error." Why do we always say that? Why not "trial and rightness" or "trial and triumph?" The old phrase puts it that way because that is, in real life, the way it is done.

Thomas suggests that learning is a result of making mistakes rather than doing things correctly. Decide whether Thomas is right or not, and support your decision by discussing the role of trial and error with reference to a particular modern problem.

You may approach this question just as you would a narrative/descriptive question. First, *mark the key words* in the question. You must *decide* about Thomas and must *support* that decision by discussing a *particular modern problem.* To prepare to write, make a cluster outline:

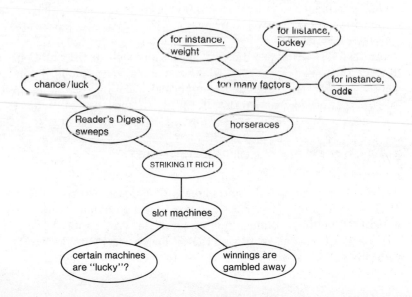

Notice several things about this cluster outline. First, it is much less extensive than the "Running a 10K" outline. This writer, spending a few minutes jotting down ideas and examples, could not think of more information than that which appears here. Knowing that he must not spend excessive time on the outline and trusting that he will discover more ideas while writing the essay, this writer goes ahead to compose the first paragraph. The GENERALIZE-FOCUS-SURVEY introduction proceeds as follows:

1. General term—   trial and error

2. Focused term—   striking it rich

3. Aspects to survey—   horseraces
                        Reader's Digest sweepstakes
                        slot machines

Following is a first paragraph based on this approach:

   Lewis Thomas claims that we learn through *trial and error.* However, he seems to be forgetting a modern problem that thousands of people are struggling with every day—the problem of beating the odds and *striking it rich.* They place their bets at the *racetrack,* mail their entries to the *Reader's Digest sweepstakes,* and fill casino *slot machines* with coins, learning nothing new from losing time and time again.

Note that this writer has taken a novel approach to the question. Rather than worrying about whether the "modern problem" he chooses is serious or dignified enough and choosing something he feels uncomfortable with, this writer picks an "unexpected" subject for which he has something to say and makes it fit the question.

Here is an example of a one-paragraph body:

   For every gambler's "trial," there is more often an "error" than a "triumph," so I would agree with Thomas that trial and error go together. Whether we "learn" from gambling losses is another matter. Conducting "research" at the Santa Anita racetrack this summer, I found that although every gambler was trying to pick a winner, and trying to keep relevant factors—

weight, jockey, odds—in mind, most groaned at the finish and then groaned again at the end of race after race. There were no more winning bets in the ninth race than there were in the first. Nobody learned a thing. As the racing season ends, these gamblers migrate to Las Vegas, where they pour money into slot machines, conducting trial after trial and suffering error after error and going home busted. Sitting at home, dejected, they fill out entries to the *Reader's Digest* sweepstakes and any other sweepstakes game that comes in the mail, only to receive nothing in response for the umpteenth time.

In the following conclusion, this writer adds new information, a new perspective, which follows from what he has written but which was not included in the earlier material.

Perhaps gamblers do learn, or should learn, something from their errors. They learn that gambling is fundamentally a matter of chance and luck, even for professionals. And after years of errors and wasted money, some of us learn that we shouldn't gamble at all.

REVIEW

Once again, the steps to writing a successful timed essay are as follows:

1. Read and mark the question/topic carefully.

2. Prepare to write by jotting down ideas and examples, perhaps in the form of a cluster outline.

3. Write an introductory paragraph using the GENERALIZE-FOCUS-SURVEY structure.

4. Write a body of one or more paragraphs, adding relevant examples and "for instances."

5. Write a concluding paragraph that adds new information, completes a full response, or points toward the future.

6. Proofread carefully, line by line, and make neat corrections if necessary.

SAMPLE ESSAYS

THE NARRATIVE/DESCRIPTIVE ESSAY

One common theme in science fiction and fantasy literature is "time travel," the power to travel in time and actually alter the past or the future. If you possessed the power to travel backward through the events of your own life, what single event from your own past would you change? Describe the event, explain why you would change it, and tell how the change would probably affect your present life and your future.

This question requires a three-part response. You must (1) describe the past event, (2) give reasons for your change, and (3) tell the effects of your change. You would begin by spending a few minutes sketching a cluster outline and constructing an opening paragraph in which you GENERALIZE-FOCUS-SURVEY.

1. General term—   time travel

2. Focused term—   finishing my master's thesis

3. Aspects to survey— the day I stopped writing
                       pressure from family to give it up
                       resulting career limitations

SAMPLE ESSAY

The first paragraph introduces the points the writer intends to discuss and addresses the question fully.

Some may wish to travel back in time to alter some great historical event, but I have a much more modest and personal wish. I would like to travel back fifteen years and pull out my unfinished master's thesis—"Educational Reform in the Eighteenth Century." If only I had written the final chapter of that piece and had earned my degree, my opportunities for career advancement would be much broader today. But my family convinced me to quit, back then, and now I regret the limitations of that decision.

Two weeks before my twenty-third birthday, I was still engrossed in research about eighteenth-century educators and was delighted to discover that even then people were concerned about the growth of young minds. In particular, I admired Descartes and was planning to write my final chapter about the applications of Cartesian philosophy to modern educational problems. However, as I was about to set pen to paper, a phone call from the school district and the offer of a full-time job teaching third grade left me confused about what to do.

Taking a full-time job would leave me no time to write. I was raising a family at the time, and housekeeping and teaching together would certainly occupy all my time. I discussed the choice with both my husband and my parents, and they advised me to set aside the thesis. "You can write some other time," they explained; "Jobs are scarce," they explained; "Nobody really cares about the eighteenth century anyway," they explained. Weak-willed and easily persuaded, I agreed.

Now I wish that I could change this decision, primarily because the lack of that master's degree has

Concrete details contribute to the clarity of the paragraph, along with transitions such as *in particular* and *however*.

A *concise* survey of the factors influencing the decision rather than an unnecessarily wordy, rambling one strengthens this paragraph.

Here the writer addresses the second part of the question, and she explains the reasons for the change directly and extensively.

limited the amount of my pay raises and has excluded me from a number of administrative and teaching opportunities available to those with a master of arts degree. Also, I realize now that my decision should have been my own, not based on the reasons of others. Because of my giving in to their reasons rather than following my own interests, I now feel like less of an individual than I might have been.

Here the writer addresses the third part of the question to assure a complete response and adds new information about her self-esteem that makes the conclusion stronger and fresher.

If I had finished that thesis, I would now be qualified to apply for the several professors' positions that just opened up at Wicker Community College. Securing one of these positions, I could look forward to a more intellectually stimulating career and to greater independence than I now enjoy. But most of all, finishing that thesis would have boosted the self-esteem that I still struggle with.

THE ANALYTICAL/EXPOSITORY ESSAY

"The typical human response to the unknown is fear and aggression."
Write an essay in which you agree or disagree with this statement, supporting your position with relevant examples.

This question requires two main elements: (1) a statement of your position and (2) supporting details. The cluster outline and the GENERALIZE-FOCUS-SURVEY first paragraph are appropriate for this writing task.

SAMPLE ESSAY

The writer adapts the GENER-ALIZE-FOCUS-SURVEY structure to the topic, announcing in the third sentence the details to be discussed.

The writer supplies supporting details in the form of a brief narrative. Note especially the vivid adjectives and active verbs.

The "fight or flight" response is supposed to be a quality of only lower animals. Humans are rational beings, supposedly, and do not mindlessly attack or run and hide when threatened. Or do they? Fourteen years ago, the families in my neighborhood behaved like animals when they brutalized an immigrant family trying to join the community. Faced with the "unknown" (in the form of a family with Eastern European customs and clothes), they responded with fear and aggression (taunts and broken windows in the dead of night).

I was raised in a small midwestern town full of middle American values. "Mom, the flag, and apple pie" were the ideals that my parents and their friends worshipped. When the Luzinskis moved to town, full of hope that they could share the "American dream" of opportunity and prosperity, they were met by smiling, courteous citizens until the sun set. I remember the nightly neighborhood meetings where angry neighbors claimed that the Luzinskis "didn't fit in" and organized groups to hide in the darkness, shouting insults at this new family and hurling rocks through their windows. After only two weeks of bruised hopes and shattered window panes, the Luzinskis quietly left.

The writer ties in the conclusion with the essay topic and strengthens the conclusion by adding new information about (1) Golding's novel and an analogous situation and (2) herself.

My community could not cope with the unknown; they were afraid of strangers disrupting their established values, and so they attacked. Like the little boys in Golding's *Lord of the Flies,* who are so frightened of the ominous jungle darkness that they blindly strike out at each other, these "lovers of liberty" savaged their fellow beings. I cannot help but conclude that such people, so typical of most ordinary citizens, represented a typical human response with their actions. I only hope that I am a less "typical" human than they were.

THE "CHOOSE BETWEEN OPTIONS" ESSAY

Read the following description of Considine and Burdett, possible hosts of a late night talk show on network television. Then write an argument for hiring either Considine or Burdett. Use the information in this description, along with these criteria:

1. The host must be popular with viewers thirty to fifty years old.
2. The host must have been a success on network television as a sketch comedian and a talk-show interviewer.

Considine started as a nightclub comedian twenty years ago when he was only nineteen years old. Although his humor at that time seemed shocking to all but the most radical members of his own generation, he is now regarded as not at all controversial. In 1969 he hosted a network comedy-variety program that featured sketches satirizing political issues, and although the show received top ratings, especially from young-adult viewers, it was cancelled because network executives objected to the comedy.

Since 1969 Considine has appeared in nightclubs around the world and has been a frequent guest and guest-host on late-night television. His recent TV special, "Remember the Sixties," was the most highly rated program of the year.

Burdett was an amateur comedienne and the homemaker for a family of four until at age forty she was encouraged by friends to turn to comedy full time. Since beginning to work in small, east-coast nightclubs five years ago, her popularity has risen rapidly. As the star of a situation comedy, "Anything Can Happen," she received rave reviews from critics, who referred to her as a comedic genius with a "hilarious perception of everyday life." Since the series ended last year, Burdett has been busy as the writer and director of her first feature film, occasionally dropping in on a late-night talk show and usually upstaging the host.

This question requires that you argue for *one* of the two possibilities. Note that you are *not* asked to "compare and contrast" Considine and Burdett. Rather, you should do the following: (1) Choose the person whose qualifications appeal most to you. (2) Emphasize the *strengths* of your choice. (3) Minimize the *weaknesses* of your choice.

SAMPLE ESSAY

The writer adapts the GENER-ALIZE-FOCUS-SURVEY struc-ture. However, he does *not* merely repeat the words in the question and description.

Clearly we must hire a personality who appeals to a broad and mature adult population and whose past success speaks for itself. Therefore, Considine is the best choice. He remains popular with the viewers who loved him in the sixties, and he brings experienced talent to late-night television.

Those teenagers and young adults who accounted for Considine's high ratings years ago are precisely the viewers who comprise our

The writer deduces general conclusions from the facts of the description that fit the persuasive purpose. The writer makes common-sense assumptions.

target audience of today. The twenty-year-old radical of 1969 is now the middle-aged, middle-class viewer who loves late-night television. Although these viewers no longer fight for controversial issues, they recall with happy nostalgia those days of political rebellion and "dangerous" comedy and identify with the heroes of their youth. Considine is one of those heroes, as the popularity of his "Remember the Sixties" special demonstrates.

Surely, Considine has lost none of the comedic talent that brought him tremendous early popularity. He continues to be in demand internationally, and he is invited back again and again for late-night appearances. His talent as a sketch comedian was remarkable in his first series and has matured since then.

The writer deflects the potential criticism that Considine's talent is not what it used to be.

Although the network rejected Considine before, times have changed. His comedy has mellowed and network tolerance has broadened. By hiring Considine, we bring to our viewers a legend of the past whose talent is still a hit.

The writer turns a possible weakness into a strength.

ESSAY WRITING PRACTICE

Following are examples of topics commonly used on several types of essay exam sections. Some topics are listed under specific exams; however, even if your exam is not specifically mentioned, you can be sure that the essay questions will be similar to the representative topics which follow. Note, for example, that many teacher competency and credentialing exams are very similar to CBEST and English Placement essay types. To practice essay writing realistically, you should use the following steps:

1. Determine the type of essay you will be required to write. This information will be listed in the official bulletin for your exam.

2. From the following sample topics, choose one closest in type to the essay you will be required to write.

3. Write an essay *using the time limit as given in your exam directions. Do not exceed this time limit in your practice.* (You may find it helpful to actually reduce the time by a few minutes during your practice.) Remember to make use of all of the strategies you've learned in the beginning of this section.

4. Give your completed essay to a qualified friend or teacher to evaluate. Have the evaluator complete one of the removable Essay Checklists (at the end of this section).

5. Review your essay with the evaluator, concentrating on any difficulties you have had.

6. Repeat this process until you feel comfortable producing essays of consistently high quality in the time allowed.

CBEST

On the written essay portion of the California Basic Educational Skills Test, you will have 60 minutes to write on two assigned topics. (Note that the exact allocation of time may change on future tests—at present *you* must divide the 60 minutes between the two essays. Check to ensure your understanding of the time allotment before you begin to organize your thoughts.)

You will have space for prewriting. It is recommended that you use this space to organize your thoughts, possibly using a cluster outline. Double check to determine how much space you have in which to write your essay. At present, the test provides two blank sides of 8½" by 11" paper per essay.

DIRECTIONS

In this section, you will have 60 minutes to plan and write two essays, one for each topic given. You may use the bottom of this page to organize and plan your essay before you begin writing. You should plan your time wisely. Read each topic carefully to make sure that you are properly addressing the issue or situation. YOU MUST WRITE ON THE SPECIFIED TOPIC. AN ESSAY ON ANOTHER TOPIC WILL NOT BE ACCEPTABLE.

The two essay questions included in this section are designed to give you an opportunity to write clearly and effectively. Use specific examples whenever appropriate to aid in supporting your ideas. Keep in mind that the quality of your writing is much more important than the quantity.

Your essays are to be written on the special answer sheets provided. No other paper may be used. Your writing should be neat and legible. Because you have only a limited amount of space in which to write, please do NOT skip lines, do NOT write excessively large, and do NOT leave wide margins.

Remember, use the bottom of this page for any organizational notes you may wish to make.

SAMPLE TOPICS

1. Few individuals are completely satisfied with themselves. If you could change one thing about yourself, what would it be and how would that change make you better?

2. Consider a very large purchase you have made sometime during your life. What was your reason for making that purchase, and what were either the positive or negative feelings you had afterward?

3. Recollect a family problem you once had to resolve. Describe how it affected you or your family, how you or your family intended to solve it, and how you were or were not able to solve it.

4. Throughout our formal education, each of us has taken "physical education" courses. Think back on these classes and choose one particular sport or activity that you learned in "physical education" that was particularly valuable to you. Describe why this sport or activity was so valuable.

5. Two opposite philosophies of living can be expressed in adages. One is, "You are your brother's keeper." The other is, "Live and let live." Choose the philosophy that you feel is prevalent in America today and give the reasons that you feel the philosophy is prevalent.

6. "Equal justice under the law may be a goal of the American judicial system, but it does not exist today in this country's courts. The legal system actually exists for the benefit of the rich."

   Explain why you agree or disagree with the sentiment expressed above, using examples from your reading, observations, or experiences.

7. Think of one machine in your life that you could never do without. Using specific examples, explain why that particular machine is so necessary for daily living.

8. Some have said that the quality of a society is best judged by whom it chooses for its heroes. Think of one "hero" held in high regard in our society today, and explain why you think that that particular hero reflects well, or poorly, on our society.

9. Some years ago, a businessman marketed the "Pet Rock," a simple rock sold in a gift box. Some called it a silly gift item, but it nevertheless sold in the millions.

   Briefly describe another silly but popular gift item sold today. Explain why you think it's silly, and then explain what you think makes it so popular.

10. Television is no doubt a powerful medium in American society. Some believe that television is a positive force, enlightening the populace with news while entertaining the nation with diverting programming. Critics of television claim it plays a more negative role, that its news is, in fact, shallow and its entertainment is of low quality.

Do you feel that, on the whole, television is a positive or negative force in our society? State your position—either positive or negative—and support it with appropriate examples from your experience or observations.

ENGLISH PLACEMENT AND PROFICIENCY TESTS

English Placement and Proficiency Tests vary in time allotment. Some are 20 minutes in length; others are 40 or 45 minutes. The topics may be of either a personal or a general nature but will always draw upon the writer's observations and experiences. One essay topic is given for the allotted time. Several representative English Placement and Proficiency Test essay questions follow.

DIRECTIONS

You will have 20 minutes to plan and write on the topic assigned below. Express your thoughts carefully, naturally, and effectively. Be specific. Remember that how well you write is as important as how much you write. DO NOT WRITE ON A TOPIC OTHER THAN THE ONE ASSIGNED BELOW.

SAMPLE TOPICS

1. Your senator has continually voted against a bill which you strongly support. Write a letter to your senator indicating your disappointment about her vote and why you feel she should change her position.

2. A recent independent study proposed that the most effective way to improve the quality of public education is to raise teachers' salaries—in some cases to as much as $57,000 per year. State your position on the issue and give your reasons for believing as you do.

3. Different individuals are fulfilled in different ways. Some achieve fulfillment through their work, some through their hobbies, others through their faith or religion, and still others through activities with family or friends. Indeed, the means for fulfillment are many and varied. What is your way of achieving fulfillment? Why is it particularly effective for you?

4. At the conclusion of H. G. Wells's *The Time Machine,* the protagonist travels into the far, far distant future to help the people of another society in their struggle to rebuild civilization. Though he takes with him three books, we do not know their titles. If you were helping another society build its civilization, what three books from our age would you take along? Why would those particular books be more important than any others?

5. Some critics of contemporary music have claimed that popular culture today is "junk"; they maintain that quality lasts and that most of what is produced today musically disappears very quickly. They cite the enduring works of Mozart, Beethoven, and Verdi, as well as those of Ellington, Gershwin, and the jazz greats whose compositions are still played today to support their contention that current pop music is, in most respects, garbage. State your position on this argument. Do you agree or disagree with the sentiments of these music critics? In either case, use specific examples from your observations or experiences to support your position.

6. Albert Einstein once said, "Genius is one percent inspiration and ninety-nine percent perspiration." Explain what you think is the meaning of this quotation. Do you agree or disagree with Einstein's message? In either case, use specific examples from your observations or experiences to support your position.

7. Presently, the federal government imposes a sixteen-cent tax on every pack of cigarettes. Some people maintain that this is an unfair levy on those who are addicted to smoking cigarettes. Supporters of the tax argue that the cigarette tax monies collected by government help to defray the cost of government research in cancer and heart disease, two of the killers caused by

cigarette smoking. State your position on this issue and give your reasons for believing as you do.

8. Sometimes a person, despite pressures or other influences, just has to say, "No!" Describe one particular time when you "had to say, 'No!' " Explain on what basis you made your decision. Describe the outcome of your decision.

9. Imagine that you are president of your local homeowners' association. You, together with your membership, are very distressed by the annual Medieval Faire, which is held on the outskirts of your community. The crowds attending the Faire constantly cause terrible traffic jams on the one road leading to your neighborhood as well as extensive litter on this road and others nearby. Since you, as well as most of your neighbors, moved to this community for its peacefulness and beauty, the crowds and litter are a problem you wish to resolve. To resolve this situation, write a letter to either (1) the directors of the Medieval Faire or (2) the supervisor of the Planning Commission that allows the event to take place.

10. Human beings are sometimes said to have personalities or traits very much like other animals. If you had to envision yourself as an animal (other than the human animal), which animal would it be? Why did you choose that particular animal? What qualities does it have that make it comparable to you? If you had to choose to actually *be* an animal (other than the human animal), which animal would you choose to be? Why would you choose that particular creature rather than any other? What qualities does it have that make it attractive to you?

LSAT

The unscored writing sample on the Law School Admission Test is a 30-minute writing exercise on one given topic. Typically, the writer must make a choice between two candidates for a particular position or two objects for a particular purpose, etc. It is not important to the reader which choice is made. What is important is how the writer supports that choice given the criteria and qualifications listed in the essay topic. Several representative LSAT topics follow.

SAMPLE DIRECTIONS AND TOPICS

1. Read the following descriptions of Arbour and Wolfe, two candidates for the position of Park Ranger for a national park. Then write an argument for hiring either Arbour or Wolfe. Use the information in the descriptions, along with these criteria:

   (1) A National Park Ranger must have a deep interest in preserving and protecting the wildlife of our parks.
   (2) A National Park Ranger must not only work well with the public but must be able to impart his or her extensive knowledge about plant and animal life in the national parks.

Arbour was born in the High Sierras thirty-five years ago and has lived there ever since. As an expert in the flora of the region, she often leads expeditions of naturalists into the wilderness, where they live in a survival situation for several weeks, consuming only what the forest provides. Indeed, her commitment to the plantlife of the area has earned her the honor of having a previously unknown type of fern named after her, a fern which she discovered some twelve years ago. Though she is somewhat shy and reclusive, her love for the park's flora often causes her to become animated in relating the interesting and notable facts about plantlife to those who accompany her in her travels through the park.

Wolfe received his Ph.D. in animal wildlife and has been a noted author on topics of wildlife for the past twenty years. A one time high school science teacher, he initiated and developed the Wildlife Retreats that now send over 100,000 high school students into the national parks for a week each year to study and appreciate the natural beauty of our land. Born and raised in New York City, he is an advisor at the Bronx Zoo and a trustee of the Museum of Natural History—Animal Division. He often laments, however, that his writing and advising chores keep him too far from his first love—the forest—which, because of his present commitments, he is able to visit only two weeks each year.

2. Read the following descriptions of the Comet and the Antelope, two automobiles being considered for purchase by the Acme Taxicab Company, which must buy 30 of one type of automobile. Then write an argument for purchasing either a fleet of Comets or a fleet of Antelopes. Use the information in the descriptions, along with these criteria:

(1) The automobile chosen must be not only comfortable but also extremely reliable because time spent in the maintenance bay lowers profits.

(2) The automobile chosen must get excellent gas mileage because most of the driving is done within the city.

The Antelope is a relatively new automobile, having been on the market for only one year. However, in that time it has impressed auto experts both with its handling and with its gas mileage. In an independent study, the Antelope was found to get 55 miles per gallon in highway driving and 48 miles per gallon in stop-and-go driving in the city. No other automobile comes close to achieving that many miles per gallon. The Antelope also has large trunk space as well as ample foot room in the front and back seats. The ride is smooth and easy, even over potholes and rough city streets. In a survey of 50 taxicab drivers in a neighboring city, 48 ranked the Antelope as "excellent."

The Comet is the classic taxicab. First manufactured in 1943, it has been the choice of cab companies for over 40 years for its excellent ride and long-term dependability. Designed and co-built by the owner of a New England cab company, the Comet typifies what a cab is often envisioned to be. Leather seats and extensive legroom for passengers (enough, in fact, for extra baggage) are two of the hallmarks of the Comet. Its heavy frame yields a smooth, comfortable ride, though its weight significantly decreases its miles per gallon (35 country/28 city). But of all its features, perhaps the most impressive is its longevity. Comets built in the 1950s are still driving city streets today. In fact, a recent study revealed that of all the automobiles on the road, Comets are the most problem free. They spend less time being repaired than any other automobile manufactured.

3. Read the following descriptions of the Keytronic and the Word-King, two business typewriters being considered for purchase by Peezio Company. Then write an argument for purchasing either one of the typewriters. Use the information in the descriptions, along with these criteria:

(1) Because Peezio Company contracts with the Hollywood film studios to supply thousands of copies of television and feature film scripts, its typewriters must have excellent word processing capabilities.

(2) Because Peezio Company also provides detailed budgets for the studios, numerical and spreadsheet capabilities of its typewriters are also essential.

The Keytronic is the state-of-the-art typewriter. Not only can it perform the usual word processing operations, but it also contains an interior calculator that can handle most businesses' financial operations and spreadsheets. It can add, subtract, multiply, and divide to the 18th decimal place as well as into the billions of dollars, something no other typewriter can do. It has a special function that allows review of accounting and budgeting, to determine where cost overruns can be minimized. Designed by a mathematician, this typewriter can use any of the existing computer budgeting software currently on the market.

The WordKing has been praised by screenwriters throughout the film industry for its remarkable ability to make typing scripts—commonly an arduous task—easy and, in fact, enjoyable. Built into this typewriter is a special format which automatically aligns text in proper columns and tabs. No longer does the typist have to work at positioning scene numbers, dialogue, stage directions, character directions, character names, and camera moves in their proper places on the page. With one touch of a key, WordKing does it automatically. In addition, WordKing can perform the simple functions found on most personal calculators.

4. Read the following descriptions of Block and Blitzer, two candidates for the position of Chief Referee for this year's Super Bowl football game. Then write an argument for hiring either Block or Blitzer. Use the information in the descriptions, along with these criteria:

(1) The Chief Referee must have a thorough working knowledge of professional football.

(2) Because the Super Bowl is the most important game of the year and is viewed by a national television audience of some 80 million fans, the Chief Referee must be able to work effectively under intensive pressure.

Block was recently honored by the Football Hall of Fame for writing the *New Official Rule Book of Football,* now currently used in all professional football games. Prior to his work, the two leagues used different rules. Now both leagues use his regulations. He also is a consultant for the Commissioner of Football on any questions about rulings, procedures, or protests that have occurred during the season. Though he has refereed only on the college level, the name Block is synonymous with the rules of the professional sport of football.

Blitzer has been a professional football referee for the past 20 years. Though occasionally his judgment has been questioned on certain calls, he has refereed most of the big games during the season and the playoffs. His clarity and quickness of thought as well as his fairness in assessing personal fouls are respected by most of the players in the game today. Blitzer is a former Marine Captain decorated for excellence under fire. Indeed, he has been known to calm rookie referees when teamed with them for big games.

ESSAY CHECKLISTS

A well written exam essay will always be successful in four important ways. It will:

1. address the assigned topic
2. be well organized
3. be well supported and developed
4. use correct written English

In addition, the essay paper will be readable—that is, neat enough and legible enough to be read.

Use the Essay Checklists on the following pages to evaluate your written work. Critical evaluation and practice can help you improve your ability to write essays.

ESSAY CHECKLIST

**HOW EFFECTIVELY DOES
YOUR ESSAY . . .**

EVALUATION

Address the Topic?	Excellent	Average	Poor
1. Does it focus on the assigned topic?	1.		
2. Does it complete all tasks set by the assignment?	2.		
3. Are such topic words as "either," "or," "and," etc., correctly addressed?	3.		

Organize Its Thoughts?	Excellent	Average	Poor
4. Is there an effective introduction?	4.		
5. Are the paragraphs logically arranged?	5.		
6. Does each paragraph focus on one main idea?	6.		
7. Are there smooth transitions between paragraphs?	7.		

Support Its Points?	Excellent	Average	Poor
8. Are there sufficient specific details for each point?	8.		
9. Are the examples given relevant to the issue?	9.		
10. Are the examples fully developed?	10.		
11. Are paragraphs full rather than skimpy?	11.		

Use Language Correctly?	Excellent	Average	Poor
12. Is language mature and varied?	12.		
13. Is punctuation correct?	13.		
14. Is spelling correct?	14.		
15. Are grammar and usage correct?	15.		

Present Itself?	Excellent	Average	Poor
16. Is the handwriting legible?	16.		
17. Is the paper neat?	17.		

CUT HERE

ESSAY CHECKLIST

**HOW EFFECTIVELY DOES
YOUR ESSAY . . .**

EVALUATION

Address the Topic?	Excellent	Average	Poor
1. Does it focus on the assigned topic?	1.		
2. Does it complete all tasks set by the assignment?	2.		
3. Are such topic words as "either," "or," "and," etc., correctly addressed?	3.		

Organize Its Thoughts?	Excellent	Average	Poor
4. Is there an effective introduction?	4.		
5. Are the paragraphs logically arranged?	5.		
6. Does each paragraph focus on one main idea?	6.		
7. Are there smooth transitions between paragraphs?	7.		

Support Its Points?	Excellent	Average	Poor
8. Are there sufficient specific details for each point?	8.		
9. Are the examples given relevant to the issue?	9.		
10. Are the examples fully developed?	10.		
11. Are paragraphs full rather than skimpy?	11.		

CUT HERE

Use Language Correctly?	Excellent	Average	Poor
12. Is language mature and varied?	12.		
13. Is punctuation correct?	13.		
14. Is spelling correct?	14.		
15. Are grammar and usage correct?	15.		

Present Itself?	Excellent	Average	Poor
16. Is the handwriting legible?	16.		
17. Is the paper neat?	17.		

CUT HERE

ESSAY CHECKLIST

HOW EFFECTIVELY DOES YOUR ESSAY . . .

EVALUATION

Address the Topic?	Excellent	Average	Poor
1. Does it focus on the assigned topic?	1.		
2. Does it complete all tasks set by the assignment?	2.		
3. Are such topic words as "either," "or," "and," etc., correctly addressed?	3.		

Organize Its Thoughts?	Excellent	Average	Poor
4. Is there an effective introduction?	4.		
5. Are the paragraphs logically arranged?	5.		
6. Does each paragraph focus on one main idea?	6.		
7. Are there smooth transitions between paragraphs?	7.		

Support Its Points?	Excellent	Average	Poor
8. Are there sufficient specific details for each point?	8.		
9. Are the examples given relevant to the issue?	9.		
10. Are the examples fully developed?	10.		
11. Are paragraphs full rather than skimpy?	11.		

CUT HERE

Use Language Correctly?	Excellent	Average	Poor
12. Is language mature and varied?	12.		
13. Is punctuation correct?	13.		
14. Is spelling correct?	14.		
15. Are grammar and usage correct?	15.		

Present Itself?	Excellent	Average	Poor
16. Is the handwriting legible?	16.		
17. Is the paper neat?	17.		

CUT HERE

ESSAY CHECKLIST

HOW EFFECTIVELY DOES
YOUR ESSAY . . .

EVALUATION

Address the Topic?	Excellent	Average	Poor
1. Does it focus on the assigned topic?	1.		
2. Does it complete all tasks set by the assignment?	2.		
3. Are such topic words as "either," "or," "and," etc., correctly addressed?	3.		

Organize Its Thoughts?	Excellent	Average	Poor
4. Is there an effective introduction?	4.		
5. Are the paragraphs logically arranged?	5.		
6. Does each paragraph focus on one main idea?	6.		
7. Are there smooth transitions between paragraphs?	7.		

Support Its Points?	Excellent	Average	Poor
8. Are there sufficient specific details for each point?	8.		
9. Are the examples given relevant to the issue?	9.		
10. Are the examples fully developed?	10.		
11. Are paragraphs full rather than skimpy?	11.		

CUT HERE

Use Language Correctly?	Excellent	Average	Poor
12. Is language mature and varied?	12.		
13. Is punctuation correct?	13.		
14. Is spelling correct?	14.		
15. Are grammar and usage correct?	15.		

Present Itself?	Excellent	Average	Poor
16. Is the handwriting legible?	16.		
17. Is the paper neat?	17.		

CUT HERE

Part IV: Verbal Ability Strategies and Practice

VERBAL ABILITY STRATEGIES

Verbal ability is equated with vocabulary skills on many standardized tests. You may be asked to (1) choose the antonym of a given word, (2) choose the synonym of a given word, (3) complete an analogy, or (4) complete a sentence by choosing the appropriate word(s).

The level of vocabulary, in each of these cases, is challenging. Although there is no way to quickly develop a strong vocabulary, you may increase your vocabulary gradually by reading widely, always checking the definitions of unfamiliar words, and by learning the meanings of common roots, prefixes, and suffixes. Before discussing the particular types of vocabulary skills tests you may encounter, we will suggest some general strategies that are useful in all cases.

PREFIXES

A prefix is the beginning section of a word and tells the *partial meaning* of the word. For instance, the *pre* in *prefix* means *before* and tells us that a prefix occurs before the rest of the word. Here are ten common prefixes.:

PREFIX	MEANING	EXAMPLE
anti-	against	*antibiotic*—against life (bacteria)
bi-	two	*bilingual*—capable of speaking two languages
co-, com-, con-	together, with	*cooperation*—joint effort
dia-	through, across, between	*dialogue*—conversation between two people
dis-	not, opposite of, un-	*disreputable*—not reputable, not respectable
equi-	equal, equally	*equinox*—when day and night are of equal length

217

PREFIX	MEANING	EXAMPLE
mis-	wrongly, bad, badly	*misinterpretation*—wrong interpretation
re-	again, over again	*repetend*—repeated sound or phrase in music
sub-	under, beneath, smaller than	*subdue*—to bring under control
trans-	across, over, beyond	*transcendental*—beyond human experience

If you are in doubt about the prefix of an unfamiliar word, try this:

1. Focus on the beginning section of the word. For instance, if you encounter *malevolence,* focus on *mal.*

2. Recall a word in your vocabulary that contains the same prefix. In this case, one such word might be *malfunction* or *malicious.*

3. Apply your knowledge of the word(s) you know to the word you do not know. In this case, *mal* seems to mean *bad,* so you might conclude that *malevolence* has a bad, or negative, connotation.

SUFFIXES

A suffix is a word ending that affects the meaning of the word. Here are ten common suffixes:

SUFFIX	MEANING	EXAMPLE
-able, -ible	capable of being	*combustible*—capable of burning
-ant, -ent	person who	*aspirant*—a person who aspires, seeks
-ful	full of, with qualities of	*remorseful*—full of remorse, or sadness
-fy	cause to be, make	*emulsify*—make into an emulsion, or milky fluid

SUFFIX	MEANING	EXAMPLE
-ism	condition of being	*pauperism*—the condition of being a pauper
-ive	having the quality of	*predictive*—having the quality of a prediction
-less	without	*relentless*—without relenting, or giving up
-ness	state of being	*vociferousness*—state of being vociferous, or loud
-ous, -ose	full of, like	*jocose*—full of humor or jokes
-tude	state of being	*lassitude*—state of being weary

To practice with common suffixes, try this. For every suffix, list at least five familiar words and define them. For instance, you might practice with *-less* as follows:

fearless	without fear
errorless	without error
hopeless	without hope, and so forth.

ROOTS

Take away prefixes and suffixes, and you are left with the root of a word, the part that holds its essential meaning. Here are ten common roots:

ROOT	MEANING	EXAMPLE
belli	war	*belligerent*—warlike
ben, bene	well, good	*benefit*—good result
fac, fic	to do or make	*facile*—easy to do

ROOT	MEANING	EXAMPLE
grad, gress	to go	*regression*—going or moving backwards
liber	book, free	*libretto*—words of an opera
meter	to measure	*asymmetry*—lack of equality in size, proportion
nov	new	*novel*—new
port	to carry	*deportation*—expulsion from a country
un, uni	one	*disunify*—break apart a unit
vid, vis	to see	*visage*—the face

Roots, prefixes, and suffixes work together to make up the meaning of a word. Take *disunify,* for instance: *dis* = *not, uni* = *one, fy* = *make.* Therefore, *disunify* means *make not one,* or as noted above, *breake apart a unit.*

Memorizing and identifying common roots, prefixes, and suffixes will strengthen your ability to recognize the unfamiliar words that occur in all vocabulary skills tests. Now we will survey specific skills and strategies related to each type of test question.

ANTONYMS AND SYNONYMS

Directions

Each word in CAPITAL LETTERS is followed by five words or phrases. The correct choice is the word or phrase whose meaning is most nearly *opposite* to the meaning of the word in capitals. You may be required to distinguish fine shades of meaning. Look at all the choices before marking your answer.

NOTE: If you are being asked to identify *synonyms,* the phrase *opposite to* in the directions above will be replaced by *similar to.*

Analysis

1. Remember that the "most nearly *opposite*" choice may not be a *perfect* opposite and that the "most nearly *similar*" choice may not be a *perfect* synonym. In all cases, you are looking for the best choice, not necessarily the perfect choice. Study the following examples:

Choose the *most nearly opposite.*

CONSEQUENTIAL
(A) indifferent   (D) resultant
(B) contradictory   (E) dismembered
(C) irrelevant

Consequential consists of *con* (with) and *sequential* (in a sequence). It literally means *with a sequence,* or more precisely, *following as an effect.* The "perfect" opposite of *consequential* is *inconsequential* (having no effect), which is not among the choices. So, in this case, the most nearly opposite of *consequential* is *irrelevant* (not related).

Choose the *most nearly similar.*

PITHY
(A) ambitious   (D) concise
(B) belligerent   (E) fated
(C) barbarous

Pithy means *full of substance;* so the "perfect" synonym is *substantial.* However, in this case, the most nearly similar term is *concise* because it means *stating much in few words,* referring to language that is *full of substance.*

2. The meaning of the word in capital letters will not necessarily be its most common meaning. Study the following example:

Choose the *most nearly opposite.*

CONSEQUENTIAL
(A) punctual   (D) angry
(B) irregular   (E) humble
(C) confused

In this case, because no opposite of the most common meaning appears, you must consider secondary meanings. A secondary meaning of *consequential* is *feeling important*. Given this meaning, the most nearly opposite is *humble*.

3. You may be faced with more than one possible choice. Be aware of *why* your choice is the *best* of all. Study the following example:

Choose the *most nearly opposite*.

PERNICIOUS
(A) lovely   (D) innocuous
(B) baneful   (E) meritorious
(C) philanthropic

Pernicious has a negative connotation. It means *causing injury or destruction*. Four of the choices have positive connotations: *lovely, philanthropic, innocuous,* and *meritorious*. However, only one of these choices denotes the *absence* of injury or destruction. *Innocuous* means *not harmful,* and so it is the most nearly opposite.

ANALOGIES

Directions

You are given a related pair of words or phrases. Select the lettered pair that *best* expresses a relationship similar to that in the original pair of words.

Analysis

1. Once you have identified the meaning of the words you are given, you should focus on the *relationship* between them. Study this example:

INITIATE : TERMINATE ::
(A) float : recoil   (D) allow : forbid
(B) unbalance : rebound   (E) succeed : control
(C) tie : revolve

First ask yourself, "What is the relationship between *initiate* and *terminate?*" To *initiate* is to *begin.* To *terminate* is to *end.* Therefore, they are opposites. Survey the answer choices for another pair of opposites. Choice (D), *allow : forbid,* is the correct answer because it expresses the same relationship (opposites) as the original pair.

With this example in mind, remember to first label the *relationship* of the original pair and then to locate an answer choice that corresponds most closely to that relationship.

2. Sometimes more than one choice will correspond to the relationship of the original choice. For example:

FLEET : SHIPS ::
(A) herd : elephants   (D) house : windows
(B) squadron : jets   (E) grass : lawn
(C) collection : stamps

What is the relationship here? It appears that the first word is a grouping of the second word. (A *fleet* is a group of *ships.*) Note that three answers—choices (A), (B), and (C)—correspond to this relationship. Therefore, now a *secondary* consideration is applied. Since *fleet : ships* has a military connotation, the best answer from the three choices—(A), (B), and (C)—would be (B), *squadron : jets,* since the military function applies here as well. Notice that the secondary "category," or "function," was applied only *after* the relationship was established.

3. Although the best choice might often be from the same subject area as the original pair (as in the preceding example), this need not be true. Study the following example:

PHYSIOGNOMY : CHEEKBONES ::
(A) geography : planet   (D) spirituality : virtue
(B) architecture : frame   (E) poetics : reading
(C) physiology : infection

Here the best choice is (B), *architecture : frame.* The relationship of *physiognomy* to *cheekbones* is that of *whole to part: physiognomy* refers to *facial features and expression,* and *cheekbones* comprise one of those features. Choice (B) is the only choice that presents a whole-to-part relationship. *Architecture* refers to the *design and construction of buildings,* and the *frame* is one feature of architecture.

Note that the correct choice in this case is in an entirely different subject area from the original pair.

4. The correct choice will always follow the same *order* as the original pair. One way to clarify the order of the relationship you are after is through this sentence: "A is to B in the same way as C is to D." Study the following example:

SCOLD : REVILE ::
(A) accelerate : progress   (D) shove : push
(B) portray : fictionalize   (E) wonder : question
(C) chuckle : guffaw

Note that the relationship between *scold* and *revile* is that of lesser to greater. To *revile* (to use abusive language against another) is a greater or more extreme form of *scolding.* To put it another way, *scolding* is a less extreme form of *reviling.* Using the structure "A is to B in the same way as C is to D," we have, "*Scold* is a lesser form of *revile* in the same way as _____ is a lesser form of _____." Surveying the answer choices, you should recognize (C) as the best choice. "*Scold* is a lesser form of *revile* in the same way as *chuckle* is a lesser form of *guffaw.*" Note that choice (D), *shove : push,* presents the correct relationship in the wrong order: *shove* is a greater (rather than lesser) form of *push.*

Some Common Relationships Expressed in Analogies

1. a broad category : one of its members—BIRD : SPARROW

2. a word : its extreme—WIND : TORNADO

3. a whole : a part—DINNER : DESSERT

4. an instrument or machine : its function—
   MICROSCOPE : MAGNIFY

5. a cause : its effect—STORM CLOUD : RAIN

6. a user : the user's tool—ARTIST : EASEL

7. something : its medium—DUCK : WATER

8. an object : its hindrance—CAR : RUT

Note that all of these relationships can also be expressed in the reverse order.

SENTENCE COMPLETION

Directions

Each sentence contains one or two blanks to indicate omitted words. Considering the lettered choices beneath each sentence, choose the word or set of words that best fits the whole sentence.

Analysis

1. As you read each sentence, first ask yourself (before looking at the answer choices) what words *you* would insert in the blank(s). Study the following sentence:

Public _____ for exercise has grown over the last ten years, so that now fitness is a top _____ for the majority of American adults.

How would you fill in the blanks? The positive associations with *fitness* in the second half of the sentence (particularly the word *top*) suggest that the first half contains a positive-attitude word in the blank—for instance, *liking* or *support*. Consequently, you might guess that those who like exercise make it a top *interest,* or *activity,* or *value,* perhaps. With such guesses in mind, consider the answer choices:

(A) fondness . . . drawer   (D) strength . . . achievement
(B) enthusiasm . . . priority   (E) substitution . . . evasion
(C) patience . . . concern

The terms closest to the guesses we have proposed are *enthusiasm* and *priority* from choice (B). None of the other choices suits the meaning, logic, and word choice of the original sentence so well.

2. Words surrounding the blank(s) can provide clues. Study the following example:

Modern U.S. Congress members who have discouraged _____ public money on social programs are identified with conservative politics, even though not all of them have been _____.

(A) voting . . . correct
(B) pushing . . . rightist
(C) ferreting . . . callous

(D) spending . . . Republicans
(E) squandering . . . chary

The clue words here are *public money* and *conservative politics*. Ask yourself, "What is an action on public money that conservatives would discourage?" *Spending* (D) and *squandering* (E) are both possible answers. However, considering the second blank, we must choose (D) because *Republicans* are often *identified with conservative politics*.

3. There are other special words in sentences that, although they may not necessarily surround the blanks, nevertheless may provide important clues to the meaning or connotation of the missing words. These words are commonly called *signal words*. They include words such as *but, although, nevertheless, despite, though, in spite of, however,* etc. Study the following example:

Although he was a friendly man, Bob continually _____ my sister.

(A) called
(B) surprised
(C) avoided

(D) complimented
(E) rewarded

Notice the word *although*. This signal word establishes that the first part of the sentence must contrast with (be opposite to) the second part of the sentence. Since *avoiding* someone contrasts with being *friendly,* answer choice (C) is correct. None of the other choices directly contrasts with *friendly.*

Look for these signal words because they commonly establish opposite connotations within sentences.

4. Consider whether the correct choice(s) should have positive or negative connotations. Study the following example:

Those who prefer Shakespeare's plays to his poems sometimes argue that many of the poems are _____ compositions.

(A) distinctive   (D) dramatic
(B) courtly   (E) mediocre
(C) lucid

Because the sentence presents the poems as less preferred, we expect the word describing them to have a *negative* connotation. The only word with a clearly negative connotation is (E), *mediocre.*

SUMMARY OF MAJOR STRATEGIES FOR SUCCESS ON VOCABULARY SKILLS TESTS

1. Look up unfamiliar words regularly.

2. Review and practice with common roots, prefixes, and suffixes.

3. On tests, look for the *best* choice rather than the *perfect* choice.

4. Always consider the *relationship* between the words you are considering. For instance, remember that antonyms must be *opposites,* analogies must represent *similar* relationships, and the fill-in words for sentence completion must fit the relationship suggested by the structure and content of the sentence.

ANTONYMS

CUT HERE

Set One

1	Ⓐ	Ⓑ	Ⓒ	Ⓓ	Ⓔ
2	Ⓐ	Ⓑ	Ⓒ	Ⓓ	Ⓔ
3	Ⓐ	Ⓑ	Ⓒ	Ⓓ	Ⓔ
4	Ⓐ	Ⓑ	Ⓒ	Ⓓ	Ⓔ
5	Ⓐ	Ⓑ	Ⓒ	Ⓓ	Ⓔ
6	Ⓐ	Ⓑ	Ⓒ	Ⓓ	Ⓔ
7	Ⓐ	Ⓑ	Ⓒ	Ⓓ	Ⓔ
8	Ⓐ	Ⓑ	Ⓒ	Ⓓ	Ⓔ
9	Ⓐ	Ⓑ	Ⓒ	Ⓓ	Ⓔ
10	Ⓐ	Ⓑ	Ⓒ	Ⓓ	Ⓔ
11	Ⓐ	Ⓑ	Ⓒ	Ⓓ	Ⓔ
12	Ⓐ	Ⓑ	Ⓒ	Ⓓ	Ⓔ
13	Ⓐ	Ⓑ	Ⓒ	Ⓓ	Ⓔ
14	Ⓐ	Ⓑ	Ⓒ	Ⓓ	Ⓔ
15	Ⓐ	Ⓑ	Ⓒ	Ⓓ	Ⓔ

Set Two

1	Ⓐ	Ⓑ	Ⓒ	Ⓓ	Ⓔ
2	Ⓐ	Ⓑ	Ⓒ	Ⓓ	Ⓔ
3	Ⓐ	Ⓑ	Ⓒ	Ⓓ	Ⓔ
4	Ⓐ	Ⓑ	Ⓒ	Ⓓ	Ⓔ
5	Ⓐ	Ⓑ	Ⓒ	Ⓓ	Ⓔ
6	Ⓐ	Ⓑ	Ⓒ	Ⓓ	Ⓔ
7	Ⓐ	Ⓑ	Ⓒ	Ⓓ	Ⓔ
8	Ⓐ	Ⓑ	Ⓒ	Ⓓ	Ⓔ
9	Ⓐ	Ⓑ	Ⓒ	Ⓓ	Ⓔ
10	Ⓐ	Ⓑ	Ⓒ	Ⓓ	Ⓔ
11	Ⓐ	Ⓑ	Ⓒ	Ⓓ	Ⓔ
12	Ⓐ	Ⓑ	Ⓒ	Ⓓ	Ⓔ
13	Ⓐ	Ⓑ	Ⓒ	Ⓓ	Ⓔ
14	Ⓐ	Ⓑ	Ⓒ	Ⓓ	Ⓔ
15	Ⓐ	Ⓑ	Ⓒ	Ⓓ	Ⓔ

Set Three

1	Ⓐ	Ⓑ	Ⓒ	Ⓓ	Ⓔ
2	Ⓐ	Ⓑ	Ⓒ	Ⓓ	Ⓔ
3	Ⓐ	Ⓑ	Ⓒ	Ⓓ	Ⓔ
4	Ⓐ	Ⓑ	Ⓒ	Ⓓ	Ⓔ
5	Ⓐ	Ⓑ	Ⓒ	Ⓓ	Ⓔ
6	Ⓐ	Ⓑ	Ⓒ	Ⓓ	Ⓔ
7	Ⓐ	Ⓑ	Ⓒ	Ⓓ	Ⓔ
8	Ⓐ	Ⓑ	Ⓒ	Ⓓ	Ⓔ
9	Ⓐ	Ⓑ	Ⓒ	Ⓓ	Ⓔ
10	Ⓐ	Ⓑ	Ⓒ	Ⓓ	Ⓔ
11	Ⓐ	Ⓑ	Ⓒ	Ⓓ	Ⓔ
12	Ⓐ	Ⓑ	Ⓒ	Ⓓ	Ⓔ
13	Ⓐ	Ⓑ	Ⓒ	Ⓓ	Ⓔ
14	Ⓐ	Ⓑ	Ⓒ	Ⓓ	Ⓔ
15	Ⓐ	Ⓑ	Ⓒ	Ⓓ	Ⓔ

Set Four

1	Ⓐ	Ⓑ	Ⓒ	Ⓓ	Ⓔ
2	Ⓐ	Ⓑ	Ⓒ	Ⓓ	Ⓔ
3	Ⓐ	Ⓑ	Ⓒ	Ⓓ	Ⓔ
4	Ⓐ	Ⓑ	Ⓒ	Ⓓ	Ⓔ
5	Ⓐ	Ⓑ	Ⓒ	Ⓓ	Ⓔ
6	Ⓐ	Ⓑ	Ⓒ	Ⓓ	Ⓔ
7	Ⓐ	Ⓑ	Ⓒ	Ⓓ	Ⓔ
8	Ⓐ	Ⓑ	Ⓒ	Ⓓ	Ⓔ
9	Ⓐ	Ⓑ	Ⓒ	Ⓓ	Ⓔ
10	Ⓐ	Ⓑ	Ⓒ	Ⓓ	Ⓔ
11	Ⓐ	Ⓑ	Ⓒ	Ⓓ	Ⓔ
12	Ⓐ	Ⓑ	Ⓒ	Ⓓ	Ⓔ
13	Ⓐ	Ⓑ	Ⓒ	Ⓓ	Ⓔ
14	Ⓐ	Ⓑ	Ⓒ	Ⓓ	Ⓔ
15	Ⓐ	Ⓑ	Ⓒ	Ⓓ	Ⓔ

Set Five

1	Ⓐ	Ⓑ	Ⓒ	Ⓓ	Ⓔ
2	Ⓐ	Ⓑ	Ⓒ	Ⓓ	Ⓔ
3	Ⓐ	Ⓑ	Ⓒ	Ⓓ	Ⓔ
4	Ⓐ	Ⓑ	Ⓒ	Ⓓ	Ⓔ
5	Ⓐ	Ⓑ	Ⓒ	Ⓓ	Ⓔ
6	Ⓐ	Ⓑ	Ⓒ	Ⓓ	Ⓔ
7	Ⓐ	Ⓑ	Ⓒ	Ⓓ	Ⓔ
8	Ⓐ	Ⓑ	Ⓒ	Ⓓ	Ⓔ
9	Ⓐ	Ⓑ	Ⓒ	Ⓓ	Ⓔ
10	Ⓐ	Ⓑ	Ⓒ	Ⓓ	Ⓔ
11	Ⓐ	Ⓑ	Ⓒ	Ⓓ	Ⓔ
12	Ⓐ	Ⓑ	Ⓒ	Ⓓ	Ⓔ
13	Ⓐ	Ⓑ	Ⓒ	Ⓓ	Ⓔ
14	Ⓐ	Ⓑ	Ⓒ	Ⓓ	Ⓔ
15	Ⓐ	Ⓑ	Ⓒ	Ⓓ	Ⓔ

ANSWER SHEET FOR VERBAL ABILITY PRACTICE
(Remove This Sheet and Use It to Mark Your Answers)

ANALOGIES

Set One

1 Ⓐ Ⓑ Ⓒ Ⓓ Ⓔ
2 Ⓐ Ⓑ Ⓒ Ⓓ Ⓔ
3 Ⓐ Ⓑ Ⓒ Ⓓ Ⓔ
4 Ⓐ Ⓑ Ⓒ Ⓓ Ⓔ
5 Ⓐ Ⓑ Ⓒ Ⓓ Ⓔ
6 Ⓐ Ⓑ Ⓒ Ⓓ Ⓔ
7 Ⓐ Ⓑ Ⓒ Ⓓ Ⓔ
8 Ⓐ Ⓑ Ⓒ Ⓓ Ⓔ
9 Ⓐ Ⓑ Ⓒ Ⓓ Ⓔ
10 Ⓐ Ⓑ Ⓒ Ⓓ Ⓔ
11 Ⓐ Ⓑ Ⓒ Ⓓ Ⓔ
12 Ⓐ Ⓑ Ⓒ Ⓓ Ⓔ
13 Ⓐ Ⓑ Ⓒ Ⓓ Ⓔ
14 Ⓐ Ⓑ Ⓒ Ⓓ Ⓔ
15 Ⓐ Ⓑ Ⓒ Ⓓ Ⓔ

Set Two

1 Ⓐ Ⓑ Ⓒ Ⓓ Ⓔ
2 Ⓐ Ⓑ Ⓒ Ⓓ Ⓔ
3 Ⓐ Ⓑ Ⓒ Ⓓ Ⓔ
4 Ⓐ Ⓑ Ⓒ Ⓓ Ⓔ
5 Ⓐ Ⓑ Ⓒ Ⓓ Ⓔ
6 Ⓐ Ⓑ Ⓒ Ⓓ Ⓔ
7 Ⓐ Ⓑ Ⓒ Ⓓ Ⓔ
8 Ⓐ Ⓑ Ⓒ Ⓓ Ⓔ
9 Ⓐ Ⓑ Ⓒ Ⓓ Ⓔ
10 Ⓐ Ⓑ Ⓒ Ⓓ Ⓔ
11 Ⓐ Ⓑ Ⓒ Ⓓ Ⓔ
12 Ⓐ Ⓑ Ⓒ Ⓓ Ⓔ
13 Ⓐ Ⓑ Ⓒ Ⓓ Ⓔ
14 Ⓐ Ⓑ Ⓒ Ⓓ Ⓔ
15 Ⓐ Ⓑ Ⓒ Ⓓ Ⓔ

Set Three

1 Ⓐ Ⓑ Ⓒ Ⓓ Ⓔ
2 Ⓐ Ⓑ Ⓒ Ⓓ Ⓔ
3 Ⓐ Ⓑ Ⓒ Ⓓ Ⓔ
4 Ⓐ Ⓑ Ⓒ Ⓓ Ⓔ
5 Ⓐ Ⓑ Ⓒ Ⓓ Ⓔ
6 Ⓐ Ⓑ Ⓒ Ⓓ Ⓔ
7 Ⓐ Ⓑ Ⓒ Ⓓ Ⓔ
8 Ⓐ Ⓑ Ⓒ Ⓓ Ⓔ
9 Ⓐ Ⓑ Ⓒ Ⓓ Ⓔ
10 Ⓐ Ⓑ Ⓒ Ⓓ Ⓔ
11 Ⓐ Ⓑ Ⓒ Ⓓ Ⓔ
12 Ⓐ Ⓑ Ⓒ Ⓓ Ⓔ
13 Ⓐ Ⓑ Ⓒ Ⓓ Ⓔ
14 Ⓐ Ⓑ Ⓒ Ⓓ Ⓔ
15 Ⓐ Ⓑ Ⓒ Ⓓ Ⓔ

Set Four

1 Ⓐ Ⓑ Ⓒ Ⓓ Ⓔ
2 Ⓐ Ⓑ Ⓒ Ⓓ Ⓔ
3 Ⓐ Ⓑ Ⓒ Ⓓ Ⓔ
4 Ⓐ Ⓑ Ⓒ Ⓓ Ⓔ
5 Ⓐ Ⓑ Ⓒ Ⓓ Ⓔ
6 Ⓐ Ⓑ Ⓒ Ⓓ Ⓔ
7 Ⓐ Ⓑ Ⓒ Ⓓ Ⓔ
8 Ⓐ Ⓑ Ⓒ Ⓓ Ⓔ
9 Ⓐ Ⓑ Ⓒ Ⓓ Ⓔ
10 Ⓐ Ⓑ Ⓒ Ⓓ Ⓔ
11 Ⓐ Ⓑ Ⓒ Ⓓ Ⓔ
12 Ⓐ Ⓑ Ⓒ Ⓓ Ⓔ
13 Ⓐ Ⓑ Ⓒ Ⓓ Ⓔ
14 Ⓐ Ⓑ Ⓒ Ⓓ Ⓔ
15 Ⓐ Ⓑ Ⓒ Ⓓ Ⓔ

Set Five

1 Ⓐ Ⓑ Ⓒ Ⓓ Ⓔ
2 Ⓐ Ⓑ Ⓒ Ⓓ Ⓔ
3 Ⓐ Ⓑ Ⓒ Ⓓ Ⓔ
4 Ⓐ Ⓑ Ⓒ Ⓓ Ⓔ
5 Ⓐ Ⓑ Ⓒ Ⓓ Ⓔ
6 Ⓐ Ⓑ Ⓒ Ⓓ Ⓔ
7 Ⓐ Ⓑ Ⓒ Ⓓ Ⓔ
8 Ⓐ Ⓑ Ⓒ Ⓓ Ⓔ
9 Ⓐ Ⓑ Ⓒ Ⓓ Ⓔ
10 Ⓐ Ⓑ Ⓒ Ⓓ Ⓔ
11 Ⓐ Ⓑ Ⓒ Ⓓ Ⓔ
12 Ⓐ Ⓑ Ⓒ Ⓓ Ⓔ
13 Ⓐ Ⓑ Ⓒ Ⓓ Ⓔ
14 Ⓐ Ⓑ Ⓒ Ⓓ Ⓔ
15 Ⓐ Ⓑ Ⓒ Ⓓ Ⓔ

CUT HERE

SENTENCE COMPLETION

Set One

1 Ⓐ Ⓑ Ⓒ Ⓓ Ⓔ
2 Ⓐ Ⓑ Ⓒ Ⓓ Ⓔ
3 Ⓐ Ⓑ Ⓒ Ⓓ Ⓔ
4 Ⓐ Ⓑ Ⓒ Ⓓ Ⓔ
5 Ⓐ Ⓑ Ⓒ Ⓓ Ⓔ
6 Ⓐ Ⓑ Ⓒ Ⓓ Ⓔ
7 Ⓐ Ⓑ Ⓒ Ⓓ Ⓔ
8 Ⓐ Ⓑ Ⓒ Ⓓ Ⓔ
9 Ⓐ Ⓑ Ⓒ Ⓓ Ⓔ
10 Ⓐ Ⓑ Ⓒ Ⓓ Ⓔ
11 Ⓐ Ⓑ Ⓒ Ⓓ Ⓔ
12 Ⓐ Ⓑ Ⓒ Ⓓ Ⓔ
13 Ⓐ Ⓑ Ⓒ Ⓓ Ⓔ
14 Ⓐ Ⓑ Ⓒ Ⓓ Ⓔ
15 Ⓐ Ⓑ Ⓒ Ⓓ Ⓔ

Set Two

1 Ⓐ Ⓑ Ⓒ Ⓓ Ⓔ
2 Ⓐ Ⓑ Ⓒ Ⓓ Ⓔ
3 Ⓐ Ⓑ Ⓒ Ⓓ Ⓔ
4 Ⓐ Ⓑ Ⓒ Ⓓ Ⓔ
5 Ⓐ Ⓑ Ⓒ Ⓓ Ⓔ
6 Ⓐ Ⓑ Ⓒ Ⓓ Ⓔ
7 Ⓐ Ⓑ Ⓒ Ⓓ Ⓔ
8 Ⓐ Ⓑ Ⓒ Ⓓ Ⓔ
9 Ⓐ Ⓑ Ⓒ Ⓓ Ⓔ
10 Ⓐ Ⓑ Ⓒ Ⓓ Ⓔ
11 Ⓐ Ⓑ Ⓒ Ⓓ Ⓔ
12 Ⓐ Ⓑ Ⓒ Ⓓ Ⓔ
13 Ⓐ Ⓑ Ⓒ Ⓓ Ⓔ
14 Ⓐ Ⓑ Ⓒ Ⓓ Ⓔ
15 Ⓐ Ⓑ Ⓒ Ⓓ Ⓔ

Set Three

1 Ⓐ Ⓑ Ⓒ Ⓓ Ⓔ
2 Ⓐ Ⓑ Ⓒ Ⓓ Ⓔ
3 Ⓐ Ⓑ Ⓒ Ⓓ Ⓔ
4 Ⓐ Ⓑ Ⓒ Ⓓ Ⓔ
5 Ⓐ Ⓑ Ⓒ Ⓓ Ⓔ
6 Ⓐ Ⓑ Ⓒ Ⓓ Ⓔ
7 Ⓐ Ⓑ Ⓒ Ⓓ Ⓔ
8 Ⓐ Ⓑ Ⓒ Ⓓ Ⓔ
9 Ⓐ Ⓑ Ⓒ Ⓓ Ⓔ
10 Ⓐ Ⓑ Ⓒ Ⓓ Ⓔ
11 Ⓐ Ⓑ Ⓒ Ⓓ Ⓔ
12 Ⓐ Ⓑ Ⓒ Ⓓ Ⓔ
13 Ⓐ Ⓑ Ⓒ Ⓓ Ⓔ
14 Ⓐ Ⓑ Ⓒ Ⓓ Ⓔ
15 Ⓐ Ⓑ Ⓒ Ⓓ Ⓔ

Set Four

1 Ⓐ Ⓑ Ⓒ Ⓓ Ⓔ
2 Ⓐ Ⓑ Ⓒ Ⓓ Ⓔ
3 Ⓐ Ⓑ Ⓒ Ⓓ Ⓔ
4 Ⓐ Ⓑ Ⓒ Ⓓ Ⓔ
5 Ⓐ Ⓑ Ⓒ Ⓓ Ⓔ
6 Ⓐ Ⓑ Ⓒ Ⓓ Ⓔ
7 Ⓐ Ⓑ Ⓒ Ⓓ Ⓔ
8 Ⓐ Ⓑ Ⓒ Ⓓ Ⓔ
9 Ⓐ Ⓑ Ⓒ Ⓓ Ⓔ
10 Ⓐ Ⓑ Ⓒ Ⓓ Ⓔ
11 Ⓐ Ⓑ Ⓒ Ⓓ Ⓔ
12 Ⓐ Ⓑ Ⓒ Ⓓ Ⓔ
13 Ⓐ Ⓑ Ⓒ Ⓓ Ⓔ
14 Ⓐ Ⓑ Ⓒ Ⓓ Ⓔ
15 Ⓐ Ⓑ Ⓒ Ⓓ Ⓔ

Set Five

1 Ⓐ Ⓑ Ⓒ Ⓓ Ⓔ
2 Ⓐ Ⓑ Ⓒ Ⓓ Ⓔ
3 Ⓐ Ⓑ Ⓒ Ⓓ Ⓔ
4 Ⓐ Ⓑ Ⓒ Ⓓ Ⓔ
5 Ⓐ Ⓑ Ⓒ Ⓓ Ⓔ
6 Ⓐ Ⓑ Ⓒ Ⓓ Ⓔ
7 Ⓐ Ⓑ Ⓒ Ⓓ Ⓔ
8 Ⓐ Ⓑ Ⓒ Ⓓ Ⓔ
9 Ⓐ Ⓑ Ⓒ Ⓓ Ⓔ
10 Ⓐ Ⓑ Ⓒ Ⓓ Ⓔ
11 Ⓐ Ⓑ Ⓒ Ⓓ Ⓔ
12 Ⓐ Ⓑ Ⓒ Ⓓ Ⓔ
13 Ⓐ Ⓑ Ⓒ Ⓓ Ⓔ
14 Ⓐ Ⓑ Ⓒ Ⓓ Ⓔ
15 Ⓐ Ⓑ Ⓒ Ⓓ Ⓔ

CUT HERE

231

VERBAL ABILITY PRACTICE

ANTONYMS

DIRECTIONS

Each word in CAPITAL LETTERS in Sets 1 through 5 is followed by five words or phrases whose meaning is most nearly *opposite* to the meaning of the word in capitals. You may be required to distinguish fine shades of meaning. Look at all the choices before marking your answer. The Answer Key for the Antonym section may be found on page 270, and the explanatory answers may be found beginning on page 272.

Set One

1. REPLACE
   - (A) dismiss
   - (B) locate
   - (C) remove
   - (D) package
   - (E) desire

2. DEPART
   - (A) part
   - (B) adopt
   - (C) evolve
   - (D) land
   - (E) exit

3. BLUNDER
   - (A) bluster
   - (B) miss often
   - (C) complete perfectly
   - (D) win
   - (E) accept

4. DETERIORATION
   - (A) improvement
   - (B) reformation
   - (C) promotion
   - (D) retrogression
   - (E) descent

5. GORY
   - (A) peaceful
   - (B) reasonable
   - (C) nosey
   - (D) sanitized
   - (E) marvelous

6. NETTED
   (A) changed
   (B) taxed
   (C) salaried
   (D) profitable
   (E) lost

7. RENUNCIATION
   (A) announcement
   (B) abandonment
   (C) adoption
   (D) partiality
   (E) majority opinion

8. INSUFFICIENCY
   (A) affluence
   (B) disinterestedness
   (C) benign
   (D) property
   (E) reputation

9. GREGARIOUS
   (A) unmarried
   (B) greedy
   (C) moody
   (D) lonely
   (E) hungry

10. PARALLEL
    (A) straight
    (B) meridian
    (C) long
    (D) direct
    (E) triangle

11. OBSTINATE
    (A) direct
    (B) abstaining
    (C) patient
    (D) unforgiving
    (E) whimsical

12. ACCLAIM
    (A) detract
    (B) deport
    (C) denounce
    (D) give way
    (E) revive

13. MARTIAL
    (A) pacifistic
    (B) plain
    (C) single
    (D) lawless
    (E) primitive

14. RECESS
    (A) admittance
    (B) cessation
    (C) mound
    (D) compartment
    (E) sac

15. TUMID
    (A) dry
    (B) contracted
    (C) long-winded
    (D) terse
    (E) massive

Set Two

1. VIRTUOUS
    (A) religious
    (B) disobedient
    (C) wicked
    (D) impious
    (E) slow

2. INFANCY
    (A) senility
    (B) maturity
    (C) ripeness
    (D) intelligence
    (E) well-being

3. EMIGRATE
    (A) transport
    (B) sail
    (C) migrate
    (D) arrive
    (E) send out

4. IMPERFECTIBILITY
    (A) indefectibility
    (B) irreproachability
    (C) uniformity
    (D) larger than life
    (E) strength

5. URBANE
    (A) suave
    (B) direct
    (C) behind the times
    (D) mannerless
    (E) so-called

6. RECTIFY
    (A) lower
    (B) naturalize
    (C) meddle with
    (D) damage
    (E) conform

7. TROPICAL
   (A) dark
   (B) pleasant
   (C) cloudy
   (D) wet
   (E) dry

8. PLATITUDINOUS
   (A) without passion
   (B) idealized
   (C) freshly conceived
   (D) risking ridicule
   (E) bestial

9. QUIESCENT
   (A) locomotive
   (B) impaired
   (C) maneuverable
   (D) frozen
   (E) putrid

10. PARADIGMATIC
    (A) standard
    (B) duplicated
    (C) atypical
    (D) classic
    (E) fascinating

11. RECTANGULAR
    (A) quadrilateral
    (B) meticulous
    (C) convex
    (D) circular
    (E) geometric

12. AMBLE
    (A) ramble
    (B) gallop
    (C) stop
    (D) converge
    (E) rout

13. EXCESSIVE
    (A) moderate
    (B) not fast
    (C) pleasant
    (D) understood
    (E) requisite

14. DISCLOSED
    (A) deregulated
    (B) infamous
    (C) fully explained
    (D) proper
    (E) not revealed

15. FRAZZLED
    (A) dazzled
    (B) darned
    (C) rested
    (D) safe
    (E) boiled

Set Three

1. REPULSE
   (A) reside
   (B) persuade
   (C) emphasize
   (D) motivate
   (E) attract

2. SCANT
   (A) moving slowly
   (B) sufficient
   (C) marvelous
   (D) major
   (E) obtuse

3. LITERACY
   (A) lack of schooling
   (B) mastery
   (C) stubbornness
   (D) deprivation
   (E) social grace

4. ENDEARING
   (A) resigned
   (B) quiet
   (C) makeshift
   (D) despicable
   (E) unequal

5. HAIL
   (A) continue
   (B) bid farewell
   (C) break
   (D) regress
   (E) sustain

6. PENCHANT
   (A) bias
   (B) distance
   (C) affection
   (D) remnant
   (E) dislike

7. PLACATED
   (A) angered
   (B) persuaded
   (C) cheated
   (D) strained
   (E) remembered

8. RETRACT
   (A) bring out
   (B) reel
   (C) stay in
   (D) go over
   (E) make safe

9. SAGACITY
   (A) pleasure
   (B) ignorance
   (C) youth
   (D) flexibility
   (E) mastery

10. DOGMATIC
    (A) serene
    (B) broad-minded
    (C) sloppy
    (D) tender
    (E) realistic

11. ISOLATION
    (A) repentance
    (B) persistence
    (C) mobilization
    (D) socialization
    (E) cure

12. RAZE
    (A) lower
    (B) construct
    (C) append
    (D) mull over
    (E) sink

13. DISPEL
    (A) call for
    (B) circulate
    (C) contract
    (D) collect
    (E) stop

14. PROFICIENT
    (A) undesirable
    (B) funny
    (C) amateur
    (D) incompetent
    (E) out of style

15. COMPELLING
    (A) unaffecting
    (B) distracting
    (C) slow
    (D) boring
    (E) undramatic

Set Four

1. COMPLACENCY
   - (A) excess of riches
   - (B) sense of evil
   - (C) lack of satisfaction
   - (D) lack of distance
   - (E) measure of success

2. PERSPICUOUS
   - (A) sufficient
   - (B) creative
   - (C) confusing
   - (D) derisive
   - (E) indiscrete

3. DECORUM
   - (A) malice
   - (B) desiccation
   - (C) egalitarianism
   - (D) impropriety
   - (E) serenity

4. MISOGYNY
   - (A) good humor
   - (B) love of learning
   - (C) love of women
   - (D) mistrust of government
   - (E) love of youth

5. LICENTIOUS
   - (A) regal
   - (B) esoteric
   - (C) beset
   - (D) virtuous
   - (E) straightforward

6. DISREGARD
   - (A) mark
   - (B) pay attention
   - (C) sell out
   - (D) make ready
   - (E) hold on

7. DOUBTLESS
   - (A) demanding
   - (B) curious
   - (C) older
   - (D) learned
   - (E) uncertain

8. CONFORMITY
   - (A) authority
   - (B) power
   - (C) immaturity
   - (D) indecision
   - (E) rebelliousness

9. PIDDLING
   - (A) important
   - (B) expensive
   - (C) majestic
   - (D) reliable
   - (E) sensitive

10. PERTINENT
    - (A) irrelevant
    - (B) thoughtless
    - (C) prejudiced
    - (D) regular
    - (E) unconventional

11. IRREPROACHABLE
    - (A) resentful
    - (B) ready for approach
    - (C) poor
    - (D) blameworthy
    - (E) praiseworthy

12. BANNER
    - (A) horizontal
    - (B) dejected
    - (C) manifest
    - (D) traitorous
    - (E) subsequent

13. PROTRUSION
    - (A) recess
    - (B) lie
    - (C) plane
    - (D) portion
    - (E) release

14. TURGID
    - (A) put simply
    - (B) easily overcome
    - (C) overprotective
    - (D) underrated
    - (E) on the mark

15. MALLEABLE
    - (A) pliable
    - (B) stubborn
    - (C) brittle
    - (D) mistaken
    - (E) driven

Set Five

1. VETO
   - (A) resist
   - (B) regret
   - (C) disagree
   - (D) accuse
   - (E) consent

2. ILLUMINATION
   - (A) disregard
   - (B) shrinking
   - (C) brilliance
   - (D) darkness
   - (E) healthful

3. PERSONABLE
   - (A) inhuman
   - (B) mechanical
   - (C) silly
   - (D) unattractive
   - (E) suave

4. VERMIN
   - (A) strong leader
   - (B) patient teacher
   - (C) bad actor
   - (D) good person
   - (E) fast worker

5. SPARE
   - (A) energetic
   - (B) rotund
   - (C) extra
   - (D) unending
   - (E) blank

6. DERAIL
   - (A) stay on track
   - (B) arrive on time
   - (C) keep quiet
   - (D) obey
   - (E) whisper

7. ONE-TRACK
   - (A) overrated
   - (B) thoughtless
   - (C) confused
   - (D) versatile
   - (E) complicated

8. IMPOTENT
   - (A) unstoppable
   - (B) virile
   - (C) native
   - (D) elated
   - (E) persistent

9. LIONIZE
   - (A) weaken
   - (B) injure
   - (C) recapture
   - (D) ignore
   - (E) hide

10. DESPOTISM
    - (A) fanaticism
    - (B) egalitarianism
    - (C) stoicism
    - (D) monotheism
    - (E) revisionism

11. VIRGINAL
    - (A) sore
    - (B) late
    - (C) mature
    - (D) hard
    - (E) sullied

12. TRANSACT
    - (A) carry over
    - (B) take back
    - (C) overdo
    - (D) stop short
    - (E) give way

13. BAMBOOZLED
    - (A) treated fairly
    - (B) revived
    - (C) muzzled
    - (D) cleaned
    - (E) recovered

14. PHLEGMATIC
    - (A) insufferable
    - (B) distracted
    - (C) clear
    - (D) excited
    - (E) lazy

15. CLOY
    - (A) repel
    - (B) liquefy
    - (C) separate
    - (D) deny
    - (E) expand

ANALOGIES

DIRECTIONS

You are given a related pair of words or phrases. Select the lettered pair that best expresses a relationship similar to that in the original pair of words. The Answer Key for the Analogy section may be found on page 270, and the explanatory answers may be found beginning on page 279.

Set One

1. SWEATER : CASHMERE ::
   - (A) gold : bracelet
   - (B) bee : honey
   - (C) apple : cider
   - (D) salad : lettuce
   - (E) palette : brush

2. AFRICA : CONTINENT ::
   - (A) Antarctica : northernmost
   - (B) Czechoslovakia : bloc
   - (C) Mississippi : ocean
   - (D) pyramids : wonder
   - (E) India : Hinduism

3. PAINTINGS : FRAME ::
   - (A) photographs : margin
   - (B) brooms : handle
   - (C) spectacles : rim
   - (D) faces : hair
   - (E) globe : universe

4. TAX : GOVERNMENT ::
   - (A) duty : exporter
   - (B) refund : product
   - (C) price : merchant
   - (D) profit : investor
   - (E) salary : employer

5. REDWOOD : DESERT ::
   - (A) pine : forest
   - (B) hurricane : ocean
   - (C) cactus : tropics
   - (D) tornado : city
   - (E) boulder : plains

6. ENERGETIC : OVERWORK ::
   - (A) trim : food
   - (B) playful : imagination
   - (C) intelligent : failure
   - (D) happy : catastrophe
   - (E) reasonable : logic

7. ANAEROBE : OXYGEN ::
    (A) animal : food   (D) candy : chocolate
    (B) Spanish moss : soil   (E) ingot : silver
    (C) fish : water

8. CAREFULNESS : PERFECTIONISM ::
    (A) complex : complicated (D) direct : plain
    (B) manual : simple   (E) praise : sycophancy
    (C) virtuousness : happiness

9. QUARANTINE : SMALLPOX ::
    (A) hide : clue   (D) hospitalize : surgery
    (B) shut : climate   (E) manipulate : rumor
    (C) imprison : larceny

10. PHOTOGRAVURE : PRINTER ::
    (A) dramaturgy : philosopher
    (B) salutation : soldier
    (C) fidelity : spouse
    (D) patience : saint
    (E) oration : speaker

11. HAND : ARM ::
    (A) sister : family   (D) throne : chair
    (B) dinner : dessert   (E) earth : sun
    (C) wristwatch : clock

12. BIOGRAPHY : HISTORIAN ::
    (A) photography : cinematographer
    (B) chemistry : humanist
    (C) politics : senator
    (D) sonata : musician
    (E) philanthropy : parent

13. LOSS : ROUT ::
    (A) sky : twilight   (D) colt : mare
    (B) misdemeanor : felony   (E) typhoon : blizzard
    (C) pencil : eraser

14. IGNORANCE : TEACHER ::
    (A) marriage : clergyman   (D) fire : blacksmith
    (B) challenge : athlete   (E) car trouble : mechanic
    (C) distress : physician

15. BELLICOSE : PEACE ::
    (A) infectious : health   (D) riotous : demonstration
    (B) distressful : patience   (E) cancerous : tobacco
    (C) corrective : error

Set Two

1. BOXED IN : CORRAL ::
    (A) up a creek : regret
    (B) overtly influenced : persuade
    (C) around the corner : indirect
    (D) after the fact : later
    (E) crowd pleaser : antagonize

2. VALIANT : TIMIDITY ::
    (A) revived : trouble   (D) instantaneous : express
    (B) undecided : pollster   (E) jubilant : dejection
    (C) pretentious : actor

3. CHANGE : TIRE ::
    (A) eat : starvation   (D) strike : match
    (B) replace : battery   (E) defeat : candidate
    (C) purchase : dress

4. THRIFTINESS : SALE ::
    (A) vitality : rest   (D) creativity : change
    (B) joyfulness : despair   (E) persistence : strength
    (C) curiosity : answer

5. AMENDMENT : CONSTITUTION ::
    (A) bibliography : essay   (D) overtime : game
    (B) credits : film   (E) codicil : will
    (C) chapter : novel

6. POLYTHEISM : GODS ::
   (A) polyandry : farms
   (B) multidimensional : activities
   (C) naturalism : zoology
   (D) polygamy : mates
   (E) imperialism : citizens

7. INSERT : THRUST ::
   (A) race : run
   (B) look : glance
   (C) purchase : steal
   (D) make : invent
   (E) dive : plunge

8. *WAR AND PEACE* : NOVEL ::
   (A) *Love Story* : book
   (B) Washington : place
   (C) Popeye : name
   (D) *Romeo and Juliet* : play
   (E) World War II : history

9. PIROUETTE : TURN ::
   (A) maneuver : run
   (B) follow : search
   (C) place : put
   (D) like : understand
   (E) soar : fly

10. LINE : GEOMETRY ::
    (A) interpretation : literature
    (B) answer : mathematics
    (C) date : history
    (D) brush : art
    (E) imagination : poetry

11. DIVORCE : PERSONS ::
    (A) damage : catastrophe
    (B) tear : paper
    (C) partition : rooms
    (D) reconsider : decision
    (E) skim : book

12. ACQUAINTANCE : FRIENDSHIP ::
    (A) meeting : intimacy
    (B) recline : sit
    (C) sensation : response
    (D) couple : group
    (E) shout : whisper

13. BENEDICTION : RELIGIOUS ::
    (A) revival : popular   (D) editorial : objective
    (B) imprecation : malicious   (E) drink : nutritious
    (C) impression : artistic

14. DISSERTATION : WRITER ::
    (A) equation : theory   (D) destruction : tornado
    (B) malfunction : wristwatch (E) brightness : light
    (C) touchdown : player

15. PHYSICS : SCIENCE
    (A) taste : aesthetics   (D) light : photography
    (B) testing : school   (E) management : business
    (C) sound : entertainment

Set Three

1. LEADER : QUARTERBACK ::
    (A) driver : adult   (D) healer : surgeon
    (B) drinker : distiller   (E) helper : husband
    (C) thinker : baboon

2. BLUR : CLARITY ::
    (A) wind : sound   (D) action : plan
    (B) rank : communication   (E) friction : motion
    (C) depth : distance

3. SORORITY : SOCIALIZING ::
    (A) playground : swinging   (D) clock : accuracy
    (B) desk : business   (E) legislature : debate
    (C) cup : drinking

4. GRATE : CHEESE ::
    (A) egg : separate   (D) fry : rice
    (B) boil : potato   (E) bake : oven
    (C) slice : bread

5. GRATITUDE : SATISFACTION ::
   (A) love : marriage   (D) celebration : victory
   (B) ridicule : humor   (E) entertainment : enthusiasm
   (C) persistence : fear

6. CADUCEUS : PHYSICIAN ::
   (A) peace : dove   (D) snake : danger
   (B) disease : cure   (E) fire : excitement
   (C) laurel wreath : victory

7. SHORE : WATER ::
   (A) molding : wall   (D) jamb : door
   (B) frame : glass   (E) curb : asphalt
   (C) cliff : air

8. WORDS : DICTIONARY
   (A) names : biography   (D) phrases : lexicon
   (B) places : atlas   (E) dishes : cabinet
   (C) lines : notebook

9. ORACLE : REVELATION ::
   (A) scholar : justice   (D) infant : cunning
   (B) athlete : health   (E) attorney : opinion
   (C) scientist : fact

10. SPURIOUS : VERACITY ::
    (A) abject : cowardly   (D) dense : gravity
    (B) lucid : lunacy   (E) psychic : testimony
    (C) partisan : piety

11. WEB : SPIDER ::
    (A) tree : monkey   (D) stable : horse
    (B) meadow : rabbit   (E) cave : bat
    (C) hill : ant

12. SPEED : ACCELERATED ::
    (A) light : magnified   (D) evil : gained
    (B) rage : tempered   (E) height : elevated
    (C) reason : sharpened

13. KNOB : DOOR ::
   (A) hook : picture
   (B) handle : drawer
   (C) rod : curtain
   (D) bulb : light
   (E) cover : pot

14. TESTIFY : WITNESS ::
   (A) divulge : spy
   (B) betray : patriot
   (C) reveal : minister
   (D) confess : sinner
   (E) forgive : friend

15. EXPENDABLE : SACRIFICE ::
   (A) palatable : meal
   (B) pretentious : intelligence
   (C) objectionable : profit
   (D) indispensable : demotion
   (E) convicted : punishment

Set Four

1. SPINNAKER : SAIL ::
   (A) child : mother
   (B) goldfinch : bird
   (C) boat : motion
   (D) car : driver
   (E) eagle : soar

2. PLACEBO : HYPOCHONDRIAC ::
   (A) deliberation : juror
   (B) vitamin : executive
   (C) permission : sailor
   (D) thesis : teacher
   (E) compliment : fop

3. WHEAT : CHAFF ::
   (A) butter : churn
   (B) gold : fool's gold
   (C) grain : bread
   (D) calorie : nutrient
   (E) blanket : bed

4. KILOGRAM : GRAM ::
   (A) whole : quarter
   (B) century : decade
   (C) meter : millimeter
   (D) pound : pence
   (E) sesquicentennial : centennial

5. FANATIC : ENTHUSIAST ::
   (A) traitor : dissenter   (D) command : proof
   (B) companion : rival   (E) patriot : advocate
   (C) employer : advisor

6. BORE : DRILL ::
   (A) fly : plane   (D) sharpen : knife
   (B) switch : lamp   (E) pound : hammer
   (C) whet : saw

7. GENERAL : REGIMENT ::
   (A) admiral : fleet
   (B) corporal : platoon
   (C) prime minister : congress
   (D) president : judiciary
   (E) captain : squad

8. BABBLE : TALK ::
   (A) jab : punch   (D) sonata : symphony
   (B) display : show   (E) doodle : draw
   (C) rock : cradle

9. PURSUE : CAPTURE ::
   (A) scavenge : food   (D) hire : profit
   (B) persuade : agreement   (E) command : respect
   (C) film : impression

10. PASSIONATE : FEELING ::
    (A) predisposed : analysis
    (B) fatuous : decency
    (C) imaginative : freedom
    (D) stoic : indifference
    (E) cantankerous : philosophy

11. CONSCRIPTION : ARMY ::
    (A) infiltration : business   (D) collision : vehicle
    (B) intrusion : home   (E) reception : wedding
    (C) baptism : religion

12. QUELL : REBELLION ::
    (A) replace : property   (D) soothe : pain
    (B) message : skin   (E) deplore : change
    (C) addle : brain

13. GIBE : SARCASM ::
    (A) image : narrative   (D) poem : comparison
    (B) portrait : metaphor   (E) blow : irony
    (C) caricature : satire

14. BRAINSTORMING : DECISION ::
    (A) victory : practice   (D) reasoning : premise
    (B) mulling : despair   (E) initiating : character
    (C) tinkering : repair

15. UNDERNOURISHED : HUNGRY
    (A) dying : languishing   (D) joyous : attractive
    (B) desperate : disaster   (E) insistent : curious
    (C) alert : ready

Set Five

1. PENICILLIN : INFECTION ::
    (A) lever : work   (D) oxygen : ventilation
    (B) song : harmony   (E) insult : anger
    (C) lamp : darkness

2. CENTAUR : HORSE ::
    (A) unicorn : maiden   (D) monster . Frankenstein
    (B) satyr : goat   (E) Pluto : dog
    (C) Pied Piper : rat

3. STAY : EXECUTION ..
    (A) tide : time   (D) speed : action
    (B) reserve : judgment   (E) sustain : decision
    (C) waive : arrival

4. CHARITY : STINGY ::
   (A) love : passionate
   (B) humor : distracted
   (C) optimism : cynical
   (D) penance : courageous
   (E) respect : admiring

5. SUGARY : SACCHARIN ::
   (A) tan : sun
   (B) clean : detergent
   (C) evil : character
   (D) curly : permanent
   (E) strength : exercise

6. PREMONITION : WARY ::
   (A) rejection : unsympathetic
   (B) realization : ignorant
   (C) recollection : uncertain
   (D) tension : relaxed
   (E) reward : jubilant

7. SLITHER : SNAKE ::
   (A) swing : monkey
   (B) gallop : horse
   (C) weave : spider
   (D) amble : bear
   (E) dig : ant

8. SUGGEST : INSIST ::
   (A) plague : protect
   (B) twist : rotate
   (C) survey : detour
   (D) mix : blend
   (E) hint : disclose

9. CONSTITUENT : REPRESENTATIVE ::
   (A) atom : molecule
   (B) investor : broker
   (C) populace : judiciary
   (D) speaker : investigator
   (E) goose : gaggle

10. INESTIMABLE : MEASURE ::
    (A) multiple : restrict
    (B) incessant : terminate
    (C) infrequent : regulate
    (D) disconnected : relate
    (E) voiceless : characterize

11. FILE CABINET : ARRANGE ::
    (A) bedroom : relax
    (B) mortgage : repossess
    (C) notebook : create
    (D) phone booth : communicate
    (E) incinerator : destroy

12. TWILIGHT : NIGHT ::
    (A) page : book
    (B) aging : death
    (C) second : minute
    (D) payment : wealth
    (E) plan : problem

13. PENCIL : HANDWRITING ::
    (A) legs : running
    (B) shoulders : lifting
    (C) words : talking
    (D) clock : watching
    (E) portrait : painting

14. ELITIST : SELECT ::
    (A) mechanic : scholarly
    (B) legislator : elected
    (C) criminal : permanent
    (D) orator : lucid
    (E) saint : skillful

15. ARREST : INFECTION ::
    (A) intermission : play
    (B) prevention : fire
    (C) suspension : crime
    (D) refund : purchase
    (E) halt : interruption

SENTENCE COMPLETION

DIRECTIONS

Each sentence in Sets 1 through 5 contains one or two blanks to indicate omitted words. Considering the lettered choices beneath each sentence, choose the word or set of words that best fits the whole sentence. The Answer Key for the Sentence Completion section may be found on page 271, and the explanatory answers may be found beginning on page 290.

Set One

1. Even though we buy most of our groceries weekly, we visit the market _____ to pick up an item or two.
   - (A) reluctantly
   - (B) daily
   - (C) hungrily
   - (D) locally
   - (E) together

2. Paradoxically, all the local residents demonstrating for world peace _____ gun control.
   - (A) need
   - (B) condone
   - (C) miss
   - (D) represent
   - (E) oppose

3. The panel leader was responsible for dividing the speaking time evenly among the participants, and so he _____ each one fifteen minutes.
   - (A) averaged
   - (B) matched
   - (C) performed
   - (D) allotted
   - (E) obtained

4. Most of the merchants have overstocked shelves and do not welcome the manufacture of new _____ .
   - (A) ideas
   - (B) necessities
   - (C) products
   - (D) stores
   - (E) policies

5. The local _____ is represented by the work of neighborhood _____ , whose creations are unique, beautiful, and useful.
   - (A) mood . . . businessmen
   - (B) renaissance . . . artisans
   - (C) traits . . . energy
   - (D) facility . . . afficionados
   - (E) consensus . . . dissenters

6. With a _____ hope that the erratic path of the economy would stabilize and begin moving along a(n) _____ course, the Prime Minister continued those government programs in effect since his election.
   - (A) squelched . . . unending
   - (B) persistent . . . steady
   - (C) high . . . better
   - (D) sincere . . . patriotic
   - (E) false . . . winning

7. Everyone at the PTA meeting was encouraged by the news that, although national test scores had fallen, local scores _____ even more sharply than officials had _____ .
   - (A) rose . . . predicted
   - (B) spoke . . . spoken
   - (C) spiked . . . explained
   - (D) remained . . . planned
   - (E) increased . . . feared

8. History has taught us that crises which seem _____ and portend ultimate _____ often end not in destruction but in an unforeseen technological advance.
   - (A) placid . . . deviation
   - (B) beneficial . . . chaos
   - (C) interesting . . . involvement
   - (D) minor . . . harm
   - (E) insoluble . . . doom

9. One's inclination to remain a _____ is often _____ by a hard economic fact: those without a specialized and thorough understanding of a subject will not find a good job.
   - (A) vagrant . . . repulsed
   - (B) martinet . . . distinguished
   - (C) worker . . . salted
   - (D) dilletante . . . thwarted
   - (E) thief . . . undercut

10. Nuclear technology has _____ the need for _____ human forces; now the power of many battalions can be activated with the touch of a button.
    (A) lessened . . . mobilized
    (B) bluffed . . . unusual
    (C) mitigated . . . supernatural
    (D) emphasized . . . irresponsible
    (E) dampened . . . decent

11. Although the most important factor causing World War II remains a matter of _____ , we can be certain that changing economic conditions _____ to the eventual conflict.
    (A) speculation . . . contributed
    (B) nationalism . . . added
    (C) power . . . proceeded
    (D) interpretation . . . speeded
    (E) obscurity . . . led

12. At its best, informative writing is clear, direct, and never _____ .
    (A) personalized
    (B) terse
    (C) esoteric
    (D) interesting
    (E) fresh

13. Maintaining one's psychological equilibrium may mean resisting both _____ emotion and _____ .
    (A) moderate . . . reason
    (B) calculated . . . rage
    (C) nullified . . . love
    (D) extreme . . . insensitivity
    (E) false . . . uncertainty

14. _____ becoming a star, Harold realized that he would not attain that goal unless all of his activities were _____ .
    (A) Tending toward . . . major
    (B) Looking at . . . limited
    (C) Asking about . . . curious
    (D) Intent upon . . . purposeful
    (E) Flirting with . . . calculated

15. His _____ was reflected by the books he chose to read;
    every author on his shelf advanced a sneering and _____
    view.
    (A) pretentiousness . . . peremptory
    (B) image . . . idealistic
    (C) generosity . . . parsimonious
    (D) literacy . . . licentious
    (E) cynicism . . . morose

Set Two

1. While a nuclear holocaust will never become _____ , we can
   help to make it less _____ by advising the superpowers to
   change their hawkish attitudes.
   (A) desperate . . . routine
   (B) serious . . . powerful
   (C) impossible . . . probable
   (D) inevitable . . . devastating
   (E) real . . . imaginary

2. Because he acted _____ whenever he was in public, most
   people concluded that he was a rather _____ adult.
   (A) in movies . . . famous
   (B) silly . . . immature
   (C) angry . . . secretive
   (D) in private . . . backwards
   (E) up . . . mysterious

3. Poetry is not the favorite study of most modern college students
   because they believe in the utilitarian function of education and
   do not think poetry has any _____ value.
   (A) literary
   (B) artistic
   (C) practical
   (D) timeless
   (E) imaginative

4. Because we had eaten turkey on Thanksgiving for so many years, we never wondered whether some other _____ might be an equally _____ alternative.
   (A) dish . . . tasty
   (B) bird . . . expensive
   (C) holiday . . . enjoyable
   (D) delicacy . . . exotic
   (E) pursuit . . . familiar

5. Responding to the _____ that he hoards a _____ share of the wealth of the community, Winterset described at length his charitable contributions.
   (A) question . . . questionable
   (B) charge . . . disproportionate
   (C) implication . . . marginal
   (D) threat . . . fractional
   (E) fact . . . growing

6. A memorial in Washington, D. C., _____ Vietnam War _____ by listing all who were killed in battle or missing in action.
   (A) protests . . . philosophy
   (B) portrays . . . heroes
   (C) predicts . . . intervention
   (D) immortalizes . . . casualties
   (E) describes . . . supporters

7. The singer's cynicism was disclosed by _____ lyrics that denied hope, and contrasted sharply with the _____ melody that accompanied them.
   (A) fragmentary . . . brief
   (B) standard . . . complex
   (C) garbled . . . clear
   (D) passionate . . . throbbing
   (E) bitter . . . pleasant

8. When _____ an unpopular viewpoint, one must expect that many will not listen and that an equal number will listen and _____ .
   (A) demonstrating . . . languish
   (B) propagating . . . sneer
   (C) disclaiming . . . leave
   (D) denying . . . applaud
   (E) crucifying . . . watch

9. Police science has advanced quickly over the past decade, but the incidence of crime has remained _____ .
   (A) unconsidered   (D) inconsequential
   (B) decreasing   (E) substantial
   (C) malevolent

10. Hume was the most _____ of the eighteenth-century philosophers; while others looked to God as the source of truth, he proposed that truth was a variable.
    (A) ornery   (D) learned
    (B) ignorant   (E) optimistic
    (C) skeptical

11. Utopian theories have been repeatedly _____ ; experimental communities eventually fail when the eternal human _____ enter the picture.
    (A) undervalued . . . spirit   (D) praised . . . graces
    (B) disproven . . . vices   (E) studied . scholars
    (C) attempted . . . beings

12. Although he was criticized by some for being overly _____ , those closest to Wilson insisted that his sense of humor was sharp and delightful.
    (A) authoritarian   (D) neat
    (B) somber   (E) foppish
    (C) proud

13. Recognizing once again that competition is the life blood of a capitalist society, the federal government has lifted restrictions placed on banks so that they are on a(n) _____ with thrift institutions.

(A) par
(B) basis
(C) era
(D) edge
(E) capacity

14. Those who _____ Byron's poetry as satanic have been replaced today by critics with less moral _____ and more appreciation for unorthodox viewpoints.

(A) minced . . . appetite
(B) bowdlerized . . . staunchness
(C) destroyed . . . turpitude
(D) condemned . . . inflexibility
(E) recited . . . knowledge

15. Rather than propose a budget that is both balanced and austere, the state legislators have opted to continue _____ spending.

(A) sharply curtailed
(B) red-ink
(C) makeshift
(D) voting
(E) over and above

Set Three

1. After observing that hurricanes move in a(n) _____ pattern, Benjamin Franklin was able to predict that such a storm coming from the east would not continue directly _____ .

(A) standard . . . seaward
(B) circular . . . west
(C) destructive . . . unseen
(D) unpredictable . . . north
(E) original . . . longitudinally

2. Any candidate for office, no matter how _____ , cannot win if he or she is discovered to have substituted _____ for truth.

(A) derogatory . . . praise
(B) eloquent . . . facts
(C) personable . . . artifice
(D) execrable . . . candor
(E) distracting . . . virtue

3. Some studies indicate that young children stop being _____
   as soon as they reach school age because the classroom is a place
   where facts rather than imagination predominate.
   (A) creative   (D) mischievous
   (B) understanding   (E) restive
   (C) cooperative

4. Socrates' seeming _____ _____ fooled many of his opponents, who
   mistook the wise man's hesitant stance for ignorance.
   (A) persistence   (D) diffidence
   (B) despair   (E) indifference
   (C) wit

5. Every incidence of social injustice sets Mack out on a
   _____ ; he cannot learn of any inequity without attempting
   to correct it.
   (A) crusade   (D) dilemma
   (B) tantrum   (E) lark
   (C) limb

6. Many business leaders complain that students graduating with
   business degrees have had a _____ education, and are
   urging college entrants to major in fields that __ _____ rather
   than focus their knowledge.
   (A) marketable . . . blur
   (B) conventional . . . change
   (C) useful . . . employ
   (D) dreadful . . . ridicule
   (E) narrow . . . broaden

7. An amateur athlete who becomes a professional gets more than
   _____ compensation; there are also the _____ rewards
   associated with representing American ideals.
   (A) fancy . . . questionable
   (B) monetary . . . intangible
   (C) extraordinary . . . fringe
   (D) over . . . possible
   (E) legendary . . . mythic

8. The professor's great learning _____ Bill while it also encouraged him; so he approached each class meeting both with _____ and the desire to enrich his own knowledge.
(A) threatened . . . understanding
(B) repulsed . . . zeal
(C) frightened . . . trepidation
(D) heartened . . . suspicion
(E) puzzled . . . clarity

9. By _____ all of the more difficult questions posed by the press, the senator aroused suspicion that he was not well informed on the issues.
(A) deflecting
(B) rehearsing
(C) considering
(D) answering
(E) requesting

10. Universities which previously had ignored students deficient in basic skills are now instituting _____ programs designed to _____ the mathematical and verbal literacy of entering freshmen.
(A) elitist . . . challenge
(B) experimental . . . eradicate
(C) pretentious . . . disguise
(D) remedial . . . ameliorate
(E) new . . . maintain

11. The keynote speaker's address can be dismissed as simply _____ ; some potentially interesting points were lost in a garble of _____ jargon.
(A) fascinating . . . short-lived
(B) basic . . . apt
(C) wonderful . . . delightful
(D) dull . . . esoteric
(E) brief . . . clipped

12. Although his pursuit of Sarah's love was _____ , Charles Smithson tried to remain _____ each time they met.
(A) forbidden . . . uninterested
(B) central . . . dignified
(C) magnified . . . troubled
(D) feeble . . . aloof
(E) desperate . . . calm

13. There are those who excuse their unwillingness to help the unfortunate by claiming that interfering in another's life is a violation of _____ .
   (A) selfishness
   (B) law
   (C) privacy
   (D) benevolence
   (E) human rights

14. Many poets have claimed that their work was the spontaneous product of _____ , but their original manuscripts reveal the close and painstaking attention paid to _____ .
   (A) chance . . . correctness
   (B) inspiration . . . revision
   (C) indifference . . . popularity
   (D) collaboration . . . isolation
   (E) education . . . rebellion

15. Leaving aside her _____ , the department chair responded objectively to the issues raised in the meeting.
   (A) authority   (D) knowledge
   (B) biases   (E) ability
   (C) facts

Set Four

1. One thing is sure—political power in this country is always _____ ; for every elected official the support of his constituents wanes all too soon.
   (A) short-lived   (D) also ran
   (B) overemphasized   (E) in question
   (C) underestimated

2. Rising unemployment is yet another symptom of progress toward a time when machines that are both "strong" and "smart" will make human labor _____ .
   (A) cerebral   (D) obsolete
   (B) renewable   (E) cheap
   (C) leisurely

3. In order to understand that _____ is inevitable, one need only listen to current high-school slang and _____ it to that spoken a generation ago.
   (A) behaviorism . . . adjust
   (B) learning . . . analogize
   (C) change . . . compare
   (D) sloppiness . . . measure
   (E) communication . . . couple

4. Those in the humanities hope that the popularity of business, computer science, and engineering is _____ and look toward a time when a love for art and literature will _____ itself.
   (A) mistaken . . . correct
   (B) transient . . . reassert
   (C) precipitate . . . bury
   (D) adaptable . . . declare
   (E) succinct . . . distend

5. When asked to _____ the oil industry, government responded _____ so that neither oil magnates nor consumer advocates could claim to have Uncle Sam on their side.
   (A) haze . . . stringently
   (B) penalize . . . favorably
   (C) review . . . slowly
   (D) deregulate . . . ambiguously
   (E) disavow . . . promptly

6. Any scientist who does not appreciate the conclusions of an empirical _____ must be one who does not believe in importance of _____ facts.
   (A) investigation . . . experiential
   (B) theory . . . speculative
   (C) colleague . . . careful
   (D) treatise . . . bald
   (E) datum . . . familiar

7. Many of the critics _____ the film, but their notices did not deter the movie-going public, who waited in long lines for every performance.

(A) cancelled   (D) ignored
(B) panned   (E) resurrected
(C) glossed

8. Without complete _____ consumer prices, each of us can only hope that the will of the majority will both _____ our own will and affect the price-setting activity of manufacturers.

(A) disclosure of . . . reward
(B) allegiance to . . . hold
(C) control over . . . reflect
(D) knowledge of . . . enrich
(E) evidence about . . . sense

9. Those who advocate nuclear _____ believe that strong American missile power will keep other countries from making a first strike.

(A) proliferation   (D) fission
(B) deterrence   (E) protract
(C) freeze

10. While the publication of new discoveries is desirable, we must not stop writing clear _____ of well-established information.

(A) refutations
(B) legends
(C) summaries
(D) reminiscences
(E) retorts

11. While extolling the virtue of _____ , we must also wonder whether donations to worthy causes would cease if contributions were no longer deductible.

(A) progress   (D) hope
(B) healing   (E) investing
(C) charity

12. Teachers who make _____ comments on students papers only succeed in _____ the students' desire for improvement and belief in their abilities.
(A) cryptic . . . sharpening
(B) tedious . . . fanning
(C) constructive . . . maintaining
(D) profuse . . . distracting
(E) derogatory . . . dulling

13. The resistance to Darwin's theory of evolution came mainly from those who believed that man was created almost _____ .
(A) perfectly   (D) wildly
(B) instantly   (E) demonically
(C) routinely

14. Some believe that the smarter students are those who _____ most frequently in class, but until it can be shown that intelligence is _____ only through the vocal cords, I must argue that silence and ignorance are not always partners.
(A) persist . . . insinuated   (D) speak . . . revealed
(B) laugh . . . captured   (E) interrupt . . . dispensed
(C) attend . . . formed

15. _____ his opponent's thrusts repeatedly, Blake seemed unwilling to make a(n) _____ move, even though the weapons were blunted and dangerous injury was impossible.
(A) Parrying . . . offensive   (D) Ridiculing . . . sophisticated
(B) Inviting . . . cowardly   (E) Calling . . . predictable
(C) Fending . . . notable

Set Five

1. Before _____ against consumer fraud were _____ during the 1970s, government seemed to have little interest in reducing unfair business practices.
(A) programs . . . overturned
(B) citizens . . . quelled
(C) sentiments . . . characterized
(D) opinions . . . challenged
(E) safeguards . . . legislated

2. Nan's reputation as a decisive business leader puzzled her family, because she often _____ about domestic decisions.

(A) laughed
(B) vacillated
(C) meandered
(D) angered
(E) foundered

3. Lenahan boasted to everyone about his accomplishments but secretly realized that his accomplishments were not _____ .

(A) public
(B) exceptional
(C) understood
(D) current
(E) intuitive

4. Mr. Lind's _____ knowledge dismays opponents who expect to find a chink in his intellectual armor.

(A) commendable
(B) personal
(C) thorough
(D) questionable
(E) lasting

5. Anthropologists have suggested that only those who can stand _____ a culture will ever recognize its flaws, and thus one _____ whether they can see the flaws in their own.

(A) against . . . knows
(B) for . . . argues
(C) before . . . postulates
(D) outside . . . wonders
(E) within . . . doubts

6. Many of his new coworkers greeted him cordially, even _____ , dispelling his suspicion that he would be unwelcome.

(A) enthusiastically
(B) tirelessly
(C) angrily
(D) subtly
(E) perfunctorily

7. The theorist and the practitioner cannot be entirely separated; after all, every theory refers to the _____ world and every practitioner bases his activity on an intellectual _____ of the task.

(A) unseen . . . sense
(B) modern . . . history
(C) whole . . . illusion
(D) mental . . . sampling
(E) practical . . . conception

8. Everyone else on the dais laced his remarks with humor, but
   Professor Dexter remained _____ , even _____ ,
   throughout his speech.
   (A) argumentative ... garrulous
   (B) stern ... solemn
   (C) detached ... malignant
   (D) indifferent ... droll
   (E) attentive ... crisp

9. In their attempt to attract _____ professionals to the
   corporation, the administrative officers have advertised that
   higher salaries will be paid to those whose past record shows an
   unwillingness to skirt professional obligations.
   (A) learned
   (B) aggressive
   (C) responsible
   (D) expensive
   (E) select

10. Many of those who argue against communism also advocate
    government _____ of the underprivileged, not realizing that
    this advocacy entails Communist principles.
    (A) protection
    (B) acknowledgment
    (C) denial
    (D) location
    (E) review

11. While national parks remain protected from the invasion of
    private industry, offshore drilling continues; obviously the pro-
    tection of the sea does not have the same _____ as the
    protection of the land.
    (A) signification
    (B) regard
    (C) priority
    (D) effects
    (E) penalty

12. Searching for a comprehensive introduction to mathematics, Lamont found courses that were limited in _____ , and decided that completing several of these would give him the _____ he desired.
    (A) explanations . . . participation
    (B) scope . . . breadth
    (C) practice . . . motivation
    (D) time . . . burden
    (E) difficulty . . . satisfaction

13. Although he revealed the _____ lives led by early immigrants in New York, Riis also betrayed his racial _____ by reinforcing the idea that foreigners are uncivilized and ignorant.
    (A) forsaken . . . charity
    (B) curious . . . approval
    (C) slavish . . . indifference
    (D) wretched . . . prejudice
    (E) improved . . . objectivity

14. If it is true that _____ and _____ are distinct characteristics in a piece of writing, then it might also be true that one's appearance is a quite different matter from one's identity.
    (A) form . . . arrangement   (D) spelling . . . imagination
    (B) style . . . content   (E) ideas . . . expression
    (C) grammar . . . usage

15. The _____ portrayal of Glenn in a motion picture will certainly strengthen his image in this age when _____ and nobility are rare.
    (A) controversial . . . virtue
    (B) unexceptional . . . folksiness
    (C) brief . . . fervor
    (D) glamorous . . . royalty
    (E) heroic . . . courage

ANSWER KEY FOR VERBAL ABILITY PRACTICE
ANTONYMS

Set One	Set Two	Set Three	Set Four	Set Five
1. C	1. C	1. E	1. C	1. E
2. D	2. B	2. B	2. C	2. D
3. C	3. D	3. A	3. D	3. D
4. A	4. A	4. D	4. C	4. D
5. D	5. D	5. B	5. D	5. B
6. E	6. D	6. E	6. B	6. A
7. C	7. E	7. A	7. E	7. D
8. A	8. C	8. A	8. E	8. B
9. D	9. A	9. B	9. A	9. D
10. B	10. C	10. B	10. A	10. B
11. E	11. D	11. D	11. D	11. E
12. C	12. B	12. B	12. E	12. D
13. A	13. A	13. D	13. A	13. A
14. C	14. E	14. D	14. A	14. D
15. B	15. C	15. A	15. C	15. D

ANALOGIES

Set One	Set Two	Set Three	Set Four	Set Five
1. D	1. B	1. D	1. B	1. C
2. D	2. E	2. E	2. E	2. B
3. C	3. B	3. E	3. B	3. B
4. C	4. C	4. C	4. C	4. C
5. C	5. E	5. D	5. A	5. D
6. D	6. D	6. C	6. E	6. E
7. B	7. E	7. C	7. A	7. B
8. E	8. D	8. B	8. E	8. E
9. C	9. E	9. C	9. B	9. B
10. E	10. C	10. B	10. D	10. B
11. A	11. C	11. C	11. C	11. E
12. D	12. A	12. E	12. D	12. B
13. B	13. B	13. B	13. C	13. A
14. E	14. C	14. D	14. C	14. B
15. A	15. E	15. E	15. A	15. A

ANSWER KEY FOR VERBAL ABILITY PRACTICE
SENTENCE COMPLETION

Set One	Set Two	Set Three	Set Four	Set Five
1. B	1. C	1. B	1. A	1. E
2. E	2. B	2. C	2. D	2. B
3. D	3. C	3. A	3. C	3. B
4. C	4. A	4. D	4. B	4. C
5. B	5. B	5. A	5. D	5. D
6. B	6. D	6. E	6. A	6. A
7. A	7. E	7. B	7. B	7. E
8. E	8. B	8. C	8. C	8. B
9. D	9. E	9. A	9. B	9. C
10. A	10. C	10. D	10. C	10. A
11. A	11. B	11. D	11. C	11. C
12. C	12. B	12. E	12. E	12. B
13. D	13. A	13. C	13. B	13. D
14. D	14. D	14. B	14. D	14. B
15. E	15. B	15. B	15. A	15. E

ANSWERS TO VERBAL ABILITY PRACTICE

ANTONYMS

Set One

1. (C) *Replace* (put back) is the opposite of *remove* (take away).

2. (D) *Depart* (leave) is the opposite of *land* (to arrive at a particular place). *Land* here is a verb rather than a noun.

3. (C) *Blunder* (make a careless or foolish mistake) is the opposite of *complete perfectly*. Note that *blunder* is a decidedly negative word, so its antonym must be positive. The only other positive term is *win*, an inappropriate choice.

4. (A) *Deterioration* (becoming worse) is the opposite of *improvement*. The only other positive choice, *promotion*, refers to advancement but not necessarily to betterment.

5. (D) *Gory* (bloody and dirty) is most nearly opposite to *sanitized* (made clean).

6. (E) *Netted* (gained) is the opposite of *lost*.

7. (C) *Renunciation* (a giving up or disowning) is the opposite of *adoption* (taking in or accepting).

8. (A) *Insufficiency* (lack of enough) is the opposite of *affluence* (great plenty).

9. (D) *Gregarious* (sociable) is most nearly the opposite of *lonely*. Other choices may suggest unsociability, but only choice (D) is an explicit and direct opposite.

10. (B) *Parallel* (an imaginary line of latitude, parallel to the equator, on the earth's surface) is the opposite of *meridian* (an imaginary line of longitude on the earth's surface).

11. (E) *Obstinate* (stubbornly single-minded) is the opposite of *whimsical* (prone to change one's mind fancifully).

12. (C) *Acclaim* (to approve or applaud loudly) is the opposite of *denounce* (to condemn strongly). Note that *acclaim* is a positive term and that *denounce* is strongly negative (as indicated by the prefix *de-*).

13. (A) *Martial* (warlike) is the opposite of *pacifistic* (advocating peace, opposed to war). Note that Mars is the Roman god of war and that *pacify* means *to make peaceful*.

14. (C) *Recess* (a hollow indentation) is the opposite of *mound*. It is important to recognize that *recess* is not being used here in its school-related sense.

15. (B) *Tumid* (swollen or inflated) is the opposite of *contracted* (reduced in size, shrunken). *Terse* (brief) is not as direct an opposite.

Set Two

1. (C) *Virtuous* is the opposite of *wicked*. Note that both are broad, general terms. Choices (B), *disobedient*, and (D), *impious*, are also negative terms that contrast with *virtuous*, but they are not the best choices because they are more specific and narrow.

2. (B) *Infancy* is the opposite of *maturity*. *Senility* is not the best choice here because it refers to a *condition* associated with aging rather than a *stage* of life.

3. (D) *Emigrate* (to depart from a place) is the opposite of *arrive*. Several other choices suggest arrival, but choice (D) is the most explicit opposite.

4. (A) *Imperfectibility* (inability to be or become perfect) is the opposite of *indefectibility* (inability to be or become defective). Note that the root words, *perfect* and *defect*, are strong opposites.

5. (D) *Urbane* (polite) is the opposite of *mannerless*. Note the root word *urban*, which refers to city-associated, or civilized, characteristics.

6. (D) *Rectify* (to set right or correct) is the opposite of *damage.* Note the root, *recti,* which means *right* or *straight* and indicates that *rectify* is a positive word with a negative antonym.

7. (E) *Tropical,* which refers to a hot and humid climate, is most nearly opposite to *dry.* Answering (B), *pleasant,* requires a subjective judgment and is therefore not the best choice.

8. (C) *Platitudinous* (full of platitudes, or commonplaces) is the opposite of *freshly conceived.*

9. (A) *Quiescent* (inactive or quiet) is the opposite of *locomotive* (moving from one place to another). Note that *quie* suggests *quiet.* and gives you a strong clue about the meaning of *quiescent.*

10. (C) *Paradigmatic* (representative, exemplary) is the opposite of *atypical* (not typical).

11. (D) *Rectangular* is the opposite of *circular.* The rectangle, a four-sided figure, is most nearly opposite to a no-sided figure, the circle.

12. (B) *Amble* is the opposite of *gallop.* An amble is a leisurely walk, quite the opposite of a gallop.

13. (A) *Excessive* is the opposite of *moderate.* Choice (B), *not fast,* is not best because it refers to speed only; whereas *excessive* may refer to any characteristic.

14. (E) *Disclosed* is the opposite of *not revealed.* To disclose is to reveal.

15. (C) *Frazzled* is the opposite of *rested.* To be frazzled is to be worn or exhausted.

Set Three

1. (E) *Repulse* (to drive away) is the opposite of *attract.*

2. (B) *Scant* is the opposite of *sufficient. Scant* means *not enough,* and *sufficient* means *enough.* Choice (D), *major,* connotes prominence but is not so directly opposite as choice (B).

3. (A) *Literacy* is the opposite of *lack of schooling*. Choice (B), *mastery*, is not best because it might refer to any number of skills that don't entail literacy—sports skills for example.

4. (D) *Endearing* (dear or well liked) is the opposite of *despicable* (something strongly disliked).

5. (B) *To hail* is the opposite of *to bid farewell*. *Hail* is a greeting and therefore directly opposite to *farewell*.

6. (E) *Penchant* (a strong affection or liking) is the opposite of *dislike*.

7. (A) *Placated* is the opposite of *angered*. To placate someone is to stop that person from being angry.

8. (A) *Retract* is the opposite of *bring out*. To retract is to draw something back or in; therefore, the most nearly opposite is *bring out*.

9. (B) *Sagacity* (wisdom—*sage* = *wise*) is the opposite of *ignorance*.

10. (B) *Dogmatic* is the opposite of *broad-minded*. To be dogmatic is to hold a positive, absolute, and sometimes arrogant belief; the word suggests inflexiblity and therefore contrasts with *broad-minded* (which suggests a capacity or inclination to entertain more than one opinion or belief).

11. (D) *Isolation* is the opposite of *socialization*. Isolation involves being along, and socialization involves being part of a group.

12. (B) *Raze* is the opposite of *construct*. To raze is to tear down or level to the ground (that meaning is the basis for the word *razor*). This negative meaning contrasts with the positive choice (B).

13. (D) *Dispel* is the opposite of *collect*. To dispel is to scatter (*dis* = *apart*). *Collect* is most nearly opposite because it is associated with pulling things together.

14. (D) *Proficient* (highly competent, skilled) is the opposite of *incompetent*.

15. (A) *Compelling* is the opposite of *unaffecting*. Something compelling is forceful and moving, quite different from something that does not affect one at all.

Set Four

1. (C) *Complacency* is the opposite of *lack of satisfaction*. *Complacency* means *passive satisfaction* and therefore contrasts somewhat with both choices (A) and (B) as well.

2. (C) *Perspicuous* is the opposite of *confusing*. *Perspicuous* refers most often to writing which is simple, clear, and not at all confusing. Less directly, *perspicuous* might contrast with *creative* if we realize that creativity does not always entail simplicity and clarity.

3. (D) *Decorum* is the opposite of *impropriety*. The term *decorum* means *proper behavior* or *politeness*. The term *impropriety* refers to behavior which is *improper*.

4. (C) *Misognyny* (hatred of women) is the opposite of *love of women*.

5. (D) *Licentious* is the opposite of *virtuous*. Someone who is licentious acts with great license, with a lack of moral restraint. Someone who is virtuous is morally restrained.

6. (B) *Disregard* is the opposite of *pay attention*. To disregard is to not regard, that is, to pay no attention.

7. (E) *Doubtless* (free from doubt, certain) is the opposite of *uncertain*.

8. (E) *Conformity* is the opposite of *rebelliousness*. One who conforms accepts the prevailing way of life without question. One who is rebellious rebels against, or protests, the prevailing way of life.

9. (A) *Piddling* (unimportant, insignificant) is the opposite of *important*.

10. (A) *Pertinent* is the opposite of *irrelevant*. *Pertinent* means *relevant*, referring to something which *pertains*.

11. (D) *Irreproachable* is the opposite of *blameworthy*. *Irreproach-*

able means *not reproachable* or *not blamable*. Someone who *is* reproachable is worthy of blame.

12. (E) *Banner* is the opposite of *subsequent*. Here *banner* is used as adjective (note that all the answer choices are adjectives) meaning *leading* or *foremost*. The most nearly opposite is the word which suggests following rather than leading—*subsequent*.

13. (A) *Protrusion* is the opposite of *recess*. A protrusion is something which protrudes, or sticks out; whereas a recess is an inner or hidden place.

14. (A) *Turgid* is the opposite of *put simply*. *Turgid* usually refers to writing which is exaggerated or overstated, in contrast to writing which is put simply.

15. (C) *Malleable* is the opposite of *brittle*. Something malleable can be reshaped without breaking; something brittle is easily breakable.

Set Five

1. (E) *Veto* is the opposite of *consent*. A veto is a denial or rejection. Because *veto* is a negative term, its antonym must be positive, and the only such choice is *consent*.

2. (D) *Illumination* is the opposite of *darkness*. *Illumination* is synonymous with *light*.

3. (D) *Personable* is the opposite of *unattractive*. Someone personable is pleasing in both appearance and personality—that is, he or she is attractive rather than unattractive.

4. (D) *Vermin* is the opposite of *good person*. The answer choices indicate that *vermin* is to be considered in its "human" sense, and in that sense it means a *vile* or *loathsome person*. Because this term is so highly negative, its opposite should be the most generally positive of the choices, (D).

5. (B) *Spare* is the opposite of *rotund*. *Spare* here means *thin*, or *lean*, and contrasts with *rotund* (plump). *Spare* may also mean *extra*, but only the synonym, not the antonym, is listed here.

6. (A) *Derail* is the opposite of *stay on track*. *Derail* usually applies to trains and refers to their going off the rail, or track.

7. (D) *One-track* is the opposite of *versatile*. *One-track* refers to the ability to do or think about only one thing at a time, and *versatile* refers to the ability to move easily among different thoughts or tasks.

8. (B) *Impotent* is the opposite of *virile*. To be impotent is to be lacking "manly" strength and ability; to be virile is to possess these characteristics. *Impotent* can, in a more general sense, mean *helpless*. However, no antonym for this meaning is given.

9. (D) *Lionize* is the opposite of *ignore*. To treat someone as a celebrity or of importance is to lionize him or her. Choice (D) is an obvious and direct opposite of this.

10. (B) *Despotism* is the opposite of *egalitarianism*. A despot is a (usually evil) ruler with absolute power. Egalitarianism directly opposes despotism. It refers to equal rights (equality, or in French, *egalite*) for all.

11. (E) *Virginal* (fresh and pure) is the opposite of *sullied* (soiled or tarnished).

12. (D) *Transact* is the opposite of *stop short*. Usually referring to business, *transact* means to *carry through* or *complete* (*trans = through*). The choice which denotes an incomplete action is (D).

13. (A) *Bamboozled* (cheated or tricked) is the opposite of *treated fairly*.

14. (D) *Phlegmatic* is the opposite of *excited*. About 500 years ago, phlegm was believed to be a bodily fluid that caused sluggishness or dullness. From this we get *phlegmatic,* which describes a sluggish, dull person. The direct opposite is *excited.*

15. (D) *Cloy* (oversatisfy by supplying too much of something, usually food) is the opposite of *deny* (supply too little or none of something).

ANALOGIES

Set One

1. (D) *Sweater* is to *cashmere* in the same way as *salad* is to *lettuce*. The relationship is one between a thing and the material of which it is sometimes made. Choices (A) and (C) would be correct only if they were in the reverse order.

2. (D) *Africa* is to *continent* in the same way as *pyramids* are to *wonder*. The relationship is between the particular and the general. Africa is a particular continent among several just as pyramids are a particular wonder of the world among several.

3. (C) *Paintings* are to *frame* in the same way as *spectacles* are to *rim*. The relationship is between a thing and its perimeter or border. A frame surrounds a painting in the same way as a rim surrounds a lens of a pair of spectacles. The margin of a photograph is a part of the print rather than a separate piece such as a frame or a rim. Consequently, (A) would not be the best choice.

4. (C) *Tax* is to *government* in the same way as *price* is to *merchant*. The relationship is between an expenditure and its recipient. A tax is received by the government just as the price of an item is received by the merchant.

5. (C) *Redwood* is to *desert* in the same way as *cactus* is to *tropics*. The relationship is between a plant and an inappropriate locale. A redwood does not grow in the desert just as a cactus does not grow in the tropics.

6. (D) *Energetic* is to *overwork* in the same way as *happy* is to *catastrophe*. The relationship is between a positive state of being and its negation. Overwork makes one less energetic just as a catastrophe makes one less happy.

7. (B) *Anaerobe* is to *oxygen* as *Spanish moss* is to *soil*. The relationship is that between an organism and something *not* required to sustain life. The anaerobe can exist without the presence of free oxygen, and Spanish moss does not require soil in which to root as do most plants.

8. (E) *Carefulness* is to *perfectionism* in the same way as *praise* is to *sycophancy*. The relationship is between a desirable characteristic and its less desirable extreme. Perfectionism is extreme and often compulsive carefulness just as sycophancy is extreme and obsequious flattery or praise.

9. (C) *Quarantine* is to *smallpox* in the same way as *imprison* is to *larceny*. The relationship is between an isolating treatment and a social problem. Those with smallpox are quarantined to protect others from the effects of the disease just as those convicted of larceny are imprisoned to protect others from the crime. While it is true that one is hospitalized to have surgery performed, the protection of others is not involved, and consequently, this is not the best choice.

10. (E) *Photogravure* is to *printer* in the same way as *oration* is to *speaker*. The relationship is between a product and its producer. Printers make photogravures (reproduction on a printing plate) just as speakers make speeches (orations).

11. (A) *Hand* is to *arm* in the same way as *sister* is to *family*. The relationship is between a part and a whole. A hand is part of an arm just as a sister is part of a family.

12. (D) *Biography* is to *historian* in the same way as *sonata* is to *musician*. The relationship is between a subgroup and a specialist. Biography is a subgroup of history, which is the specialty of historians, and the sonata is a subgroup of musical compositions/performances, which are the specialties of musicians. Choices (A) and (C) are weak choices because the first term in each is not a subgroup.

13. (B) *Loss* is to *rout* as *misdemeanor* is to *felony*. The relationship is of a less serious matter to a more serious matter. A loss is a defeat; a rout is a disasterous or major defeat. A misdemeanor is a crime; a felony is a major crime.

14. (E) *Ignorance* is to *teacher* in the same way as *car trouble* is to *mechanic*. The relationship is between a problem and the professional who attempts to eliminate it. A teacher attempts to eliminate ignorance, and a mechanic attempts to eliminate car trouble. Choice (C) is weak because distress is not the exclusive

concern of the physician, whereas the teacher is exclusively concerned with ignorance and the mechanic with car trouble.

15. (A) *Bellicose* is to *peace* in the same way as *infectious* is to *health*. The relationship is between opposites. A bellicose (warlike) condition opposes peace just as an infectious condition opposes health.

Set Two

1. (B) *Boxed in* is to *corral* in the same way as *overtly influenced* is to *persuade*. The relationship is between a result and the action which causes it. Becoming boxed in is the result of being corralled just as being overtly (openly) influenced is the result of persuasion.

2. (E) *Valiant* is to *timidity* in the same way as *jubilant* is to *dejection*. The relationship is between opposites. Being valiant (courageous) is the opposite of timidity (being timid) just as being jubilant (very happy) is the opposite of dejection (being very sad).

3. (B) *Change* is to *tire* in the same way as *replace* is to *battery*. The relationship is between a remedy and an object which may, in its defective state, require the remedy. A defective tire requires changing in the same way that a defective battery requires replacement.

4. (C) *Thriftiness* is to *sale* in the same way as *curiosity* is to *answer*. The relationship is between a quality and what appeals to that quality. A sale appeals to thriftiness just as an answer appeals to curiosity.

5. (E) *Amendment* is to *constitution* in the same way as *codicil* is to *will*. The relationship is between an addition and the original text, *which it alters*. An amendment, added to a constitution alters that constitution just as a codicil is an addition to a will which alters the will.

6. (D) *Polytheism* is to *gods* as *polygamy* is to *mates*. The relationship is that of practices involving multiple objects and the multiple objects they involve. Polytheism refers to a religion

recognizing multiple gods. Polygamy refers to the practice of an individual's having multiple husbands or wives (mates).

7. (E) *Insert* is to *thrust* in the same way as *dive* is to *plunge*. The relationship is between an action and a more "forceful" form of that action. Thrusting is a more forceful act of inserting just as plunging is a more forceful act of diving.

8. (D) *War and Peace* is to *novel* in the same way as *Romeo and Juliet* is to *play*. The relationship is between a literary work and its type, or genre. *War and Peace* is a novel just as *Romeo and Juliet* is a play. In choice (B), *place* is too general a term, and so this choice is not the best.

9. (E) *Pirouette* is to *turn* in the same way as *soar* is to *fly*. The relationship is between a graceful action and its more ordinary counterpart. To pirouette is to turn gracefully just as to soar is to fly gracefully.

10. (C) *Line* is to *geometry* in the same way as *date* is to *history*. The relationship is between a basic unit and the subject it is basic to. A line is a basic unit of geometry just as a date is a basic unit of history.

11. (C) *Divorce* is to *persons* in the same way as *partition* is to *rooms*. The relationship is between a division and what is affected by the division. Divorce divides persons in the same way as a partition divides rooms.

12. (A) *Acquaintance* is to *friendship* in the same way as *meeting* is to *intimacy*. The relationship is between lesser and greater. Acquaintance is a lesser form of friendship just as a meeting is a lesser, or less personal, form of intimacy.

13. (B) *Benediction* is to *religious* in the same way as *imprecation* is to *malicious*. The relationship is between an utterance and its basic characteristic. A benediction is a religious utterance, a blessing, just as an imprecation is a malicious (evil) utterance, a curse.

14. (C) *Dissertation* is to *writer* in the same way as *touchdown* is to *player*. The relationship is between a product and a human

producer. Dissertations are produced by writers just as touch-downs are produced by players.

15. (E) *Physics* is to *science* in the same way as *management* is to *business*. The relationship is between specific and general. Physics is a specific subarea of science just as management is a specific subarea of business.

Set Three

1. (D) *Leader* is to *quarterback* is the same way as *healer* is to *surgeon*. The relationship is between a general characteristic and a specific practitioner of that characteristic. A quarterback is a leader (of a team) just as a surgeon is a healer. Choice (E) presents a relationship that is less necessarily true than (D).

2. (E) *Blur* is to *clarity* in the same way as *friction* is to *motion*. The relationship is between an impediment and a characteristic. A blur impedes clarity just as friction impedes motion.

3. (E) *Sorority* is to *socializing* in the same way as *legislature* is to *debate*. The relationship is between an organization and a characteristic activity. Socializing is characteristic of a sorority just as debate is characteristic of a legislature. Other choices include similar relationships but do not include an organization.

4. (C) *Grate* is to *cheese* in the same way as *slice* is to *bread*. The relationship is between a kitchen activity and the food to which it is appropriate. Each activity involves the cutting of food items, and thus they are closer in their relationship than either choice (B) or choice (D) is to the original pair.

5. (D) *Gratitude* is to *satisfaction* in the same way as *celebration* is to *victory*. The relationship is between a likely effect and its cause. Gratitude is a likely effect of satisfaction just as celebration is a likely effect of victory.

6. (C) *Caduceus* is to *physician* in the same way as *laurel wreath* is to *victory*. The relationship is between a symbol and that which is symbolized. The caduceus (a staff with entwined snakes) symbolizes the physician just as the laurel wreath symbolizes victory, particularly in athletic competition.

7. (C) *Shore* is to *water* in the same way as *cliff* is to *air*. The relationship is between a border and what always lies beyond it. A shore borders water just as a cliff borders air. None of the other choices presents a relationship that is always true.

8. (B) *Words* are to *dictionary* in the same way as *places* are to *atlas*. The relationship is between something referenced and the reference book used. Words are listed in a dictionary just as places (cities, states, countries, etc.) are shown on the maps of the atlas.

9. (C) *Oracle* is to *revelation* in the same way as *scientist* is to *fact*. The relationship is between a person and his usual mode of expression. An oracle (divine fortune-teller) is associated with revelation (revealing mysteries or secrets) just as a scientist is associated with facts. None of the second words in the other choices is a mode of expression as it is in the original.

10. (B) *Spurious* is to *veracity* in the same way as *lucid* is to *lunacy*. The relationship is between opposites. Spurious (not true) is the opposite of veracity (truth) just as lucid (clear or clear-headed) is the opposite of lunacy (madness).

11. (C) *Web* is to *spider* in the same way as *hill* is to *ant*. The relationship is between a dwelling and its inhabitant/builder. A spider builds and lives in a web just as ants build and live in a hill.

12. (E) *Speed* is to *accelerated* in the same way as *height* is to *elevated*. The relationship is between a characteristic and the term for increasing it. To accelerate is to increase speed just as to elevate is to increase height.

13. (B) *Knob* is to *door* in the same way as *handle* is to *drawer*. The relationship is between an opening device and the object which it opens. A knob opens a door just as a handle opens a drawer.

14. (D) *Testify* is to *witness* in the same way as *confess* is to *sinner*. The relationship is between an expression and the type of person normally associated with it. Witnesses testify just as sinners confess. Note that this is a usual but not a necessary relationship.

15. (E) *Expendable* is to *sacrifice* in the same way as *convicted* is to *punishment*. The relationship is cause/effect. Being expendable (worth sacrificing) can lead to being sacrificed just as being convicted can lead to punishment.

Set Four

1. (B) *Spinnaker* is to *sail* in the same way as *goldfinch* is to *bird*. The relationship is between a specific item and the group to which that item belongs. A spinnaker is a type of sail just as a goldfinch is a type of bird.

2. (E) *Placebo* is to *hypochondriac* in the same way as *compliment* is to *fop*. The relationship is between an object and the type of person it humors. A placebo (ineffective and harmless "medication") humors a hypochondriac (someone who always thinks he or she is ill) just as a compliment humors a fop (a vain person obsessed with personal appearance).

3. (B) *Wheat* is to *chaff* in the same way as *gold* is to *fool's gold*. The relationship is between something of value and something of comparatively little value. Wheat (a food grain) is of value and the chaff (seed coverings separated from the grain while threshing) is of comparatively little value just as gold is of value and fool's gold (pyrite) is of comparatively little value.

4. (C) *Kilogram* is to *gram* in the same way as *meter* is to *millimeter*. The relationship is between larger and smaller in equal ratio. A kilogram equals 1,000 grams just as a meter equals 1,000 millimeters. While the other choices give a larger and a smaller unit, the ratio is not equal to the original pair.

5. (A) *Fanatic* is to *enthusiast* in the same way as *traitor* is to *dissenter*. The relationship is between an extreme, negative term and its less extreme, less negative counterpart. A fanatic is an extreme type of enthusiast just as a traitor is a more extreme type of dissenter (one who disagrees with the way things are).

6. (E) *Bore* is to *drill* in the same way as *pound* is to *hammer*. The relationship is between an action and the tool which produces it. A drill bores holes just as a hammer pounds nails.

7. (A) *General* is to *regiment* in the same way as *admiral* is to *fleet*. The relationship is between a top commander and a large military force. A general commands a regiment just as an admiral commands a fleet. Choices (B) and (E) contain forces too small to be the best analogies.

8. (E) *Babble* is to *talk* in the same way as *doodle* is to *draw*. The relationship is between a disorganized activity and its more organized counterpart. Babbling is a disorganized and usually unclear form of talking just as doodling is a disorganized, random form of drawing.

9. (B) *Pursue* is to *capture* in the same way as *persuade* is to *agreement*. The relationship is between an action and an outcome. Capture is the outcome of pursuit just as agreement is the outcome of persuasion.

10. (D) *Passionate* is to *feeling* in the same way as *stoic* is to *indifference*. The relationship is between two associated characteristics. To be passionate is to display feeling just as to be stoic is to display indifference.

11. (C) *Conscription* is to *army* in the same way as *baptism* is to *religion*. The relationship is between a rite of membership and its associated organization. Conscription ushers one into the army just as baptism ushers one into a religion.

12. (D) *Quell* is to *rebellion* in the same way as *soothe* is to *pain*. The relationship is between a calming action and its object. To quell a rebellion is to calm it down just as to soothe pain is to calm it down.

13. (C) *Gibe* is to *sarcasm* in the same way as *caricature* is to *satire*. The relationship is between specific and general. A gibe is a specific form of sarcasm just as a caricature is a specific form of satire.

14. (C) *Brainstorming* is to *decision* in the same way as *tinkering* is to *repair*. The relationship is between an activity and its desired result. The desired result of brainstorming is a decision or solution just as the desired result of tinkering with something is its repair.

15. (A) *Undernourished* is to *hungry* in the same way as *dying* is to *languishing*. The relationship is between more extreme and less extreme. Undernourishment is an extreme form of hunger just as dying is an extreme form of languishing (becoming weak, lacking vitality).

Set Five

1. (C) *Penicillin* is to *infection* in the same way as *lamp* is to *darkness*. The relationship is between a solution and a problem. Penicillin is a solution to infection just as a lamp is the solution to darkness.

2. (B) *Centaur* is to *horse* in the same way as *satyr* is to *goat*. The relationship is between a mythic creature and a portion of its body. The centaur was said to be part man and part horse just as the satyr was said to be part man and part goat.

3. (B) *Stay* is to *execution* in the same way as *reserve* is to *judgment*. The relationship is between a postponing action and its object. To stay an execution is to postpone it just as to reserve judgment is to delay or postpone it.

4. (C) *Charity* is to *stingy* in the same way as *optimism* is to *cynical*. The relationship is between opposites. Charity is the opposite of stinginess in the same way as optimism is the opposite of cynicism (believing that human action is motivated by selfishness and insincerity).

5. (D) *Sugary* is to *saccharin* in the same way as *curly* is to *permanent*. The relationship is between a quality and an agent which artificially produces that quality. Saccharin produces artificial sugary taste just as a permanent produces artificially curly hair.

6. (E) *Premonition* is to *wary* in the same way as *reward* is to *jubilant*. The relationship is between a cause and one likely effect. A premonition (foreshadowing of evil) may cause one to be wary just as a reward may cause one to be jubilant (extremely happy).

7. (B) *Slither* is to *snake* in the same way as *gallop* is to *horse*. The relationship is between a forward motion over land and the animal with which it is associated. Snakes slither just as horses gallop.

8. (E) *Suggest* is to *insist* in the same way as *hint* is to *disclose*. The relationship is between a less absolute and more absolute form of expression. Suggesting is a less absolute form of communicating a viewpoint than insisting just as hinting is a less absolute form of communication than disclosing.

9. (B) *Constituent* is to *representative* in the same way as *investor* is to *broker*. The relationship is between the person represented and the selected representative. A representative represents a constituency (those who elected or appointed the person) just as a broker represents investors.

10. (B) *Inestimable* is to *measure* in the same way as *incessant* is to *terminate*. The relationship is between an infinite quality and a limited quality. Inestimable means too large or numerous to count or measure just as incessant means unceasing (with no termination).

11. (E) *File cabinet* is to *arrange* in the same way as *incinerator* is to *destroy*. The relationship is between a container and its use. A file cabinet is a container for arranging materials just as an incinerator is a container for destroying materials.

12. (B) *Twilight* is to *night* in the same way as *aging* is to *death*. The relationship is between a stage of progress and a final outcome. Twilight leads to night in the same way as aging leads to death.

13. (A) *Pencil* is to *handwriting* in the same way as *legs* are to *running*. The relationship is between an instrument and the action it performs. A pencil is the instrument of handwriting just as legs are the instruments of running. Choice (C) would be a stronger answer if *words* were replaced with *voice*.

14. (B) *Elitist* is to *select* in the same way as *legislator* is to *elected*. The relationship is between a type of person and a characteristic of the group to which he or she belongs. An elitist is a member of a select (preferred, exclusive, elite) group just as a legislator is a member of an elected group.

15. (A) *Arrest* is to *infection* in the same way as *intermission* is to *play*. The relationship is between a halting action and the activity it halts. To arrest an infection is to halt its progress just as the intermission of a play halts *its* progress.

SENTENCE COMPLETION

Set One

1. **(B)** *daily.* The phrase *even though* indicates that the blank will contrast with a term in the first half of the sentence—in this case, *weekly.* None of the other terms supplies a contrast.

2. **(E)** *oppose.* Opposing gun control seems to be an action that contradicts the desire for world peace. Therefore, these two attitudes have a paradoxical relationship.

3. **(D)** *allotted.* To allot is to give a part of something. This choice is consistent with the term *dividing* earlier in the sentence.

4. **(C)** *products.* Logically, if shelves are overstocked (presumably with products), merchants will not welcome the existence of even more products.

5. **(B)** *renaissance ... artisans.* A renaissance is a revival, especially of art, and is therefore consistent with the second term, *artisans.* Terms such as *creations, unique,* and *beautiful* suggest the appropriateness of *artisans* (skilled and artistic craftspeople).

6. **(B)** *persistent ... steady.* In this sentence, the correct choices have commonplace associations with the words that follow them: *persistent hope, steady course.* The other choices are either inconsistent or not as appropriate to the meaning of the sentence.

7. **(A)** *rose ... predicted.* The sentence contrasts national scores with local scores, so *rose* is the indicated choice, and *predicted* is its logical partner.

8. **(E)** *insoluble ... doom.* Terms such as *crises* and *destruction* signal two negative blanks, and only choice (E) supplies them.

9. **(D)** *dilletante ... thwarted.* The first blank describes someone *without a specialized and thorough understanding of a subject.* This definition fits *dilletante,* and *thwarted* (hindered or obstructed) also fits the sentence.

10. (A) *lessened . . . mobilized.* The sentence stresses technology, and so we expect that the first blank will be a term that weakens the value of human forces. *Mobilized human forces* seems the logical equivalent to *power of many battalions.*

11. (A) *speculation . . . contributed.* The first blank contrasts with *certain,* and *contributed* is also logically and meaningfully related to the sentence as a whole.

12. (C) *esoteric* (understandable by only a chosen few). This term contrasts with *clear* and *direct* and is therefore the best choice.

13. (D) *extreme . . . insensitivity.* Each blank should be a threat to psychological equilibrium. Choice (D) is best because it contains the most extreme and negative terms.

14. (D) *Intent upon . . . purposeful.* Harold has a goal, and this term signals the equivalent term, *intent,* and the phrase *intent upon.* The term *purposeful* is also appropriate to his goal-oriented attitude.

15. (E) *cynicism . . . morose. Sneering* indicates that both blanks are similar negative terms.

Set Two

1. (C) *impossible . . . probable.* Working from the second blank first, note that *less probable* is a logical result of changing hawkish attitudes and that *impossible* makes sense also.

2. (B) *silly . . . immature.* The sentence points toward human characteristics as appropriate for the blanks, and they should be characteristics that are consistent with each other—his behavior in public is consistent with the assessment of most people. For these reasons, *silly . . . immature* is the best answer choice.

3. (C) *practical.* The sentence suggests that poetry is not utilitarian—in other words, that it has no practical value.

4. (A) *dish . . . tasty. Some other* suggests an alternative to turkey. The alternative offered in choice (B) is too narrow, and those offered in choices (C), (D), and (E) are inappropriate.

5. (B) *charge . . . disproportionate.* The term *hoards* suggests that the blanks surrounding it are negative terms, terms consistent with hoarding. The only choice that offers two negative choices is (B).

6. (D) *immortalizes . . . casualties.* Working from the second blank first, note that *casualties* is the only term appropriate to *all who were killed.* Also, *immortalizes* appropriately describes the function of a memorial.

7. (E) *bitter . . . pleasant.* The sentence suggests a negative/positive contrast between the blanks—a term consistent with *cynicism* along with one that contrasts with it. The most striking and fitting negative/positive contrast is offered by choice (E).

8. (B) *propagating . . . sneer.* Working from the second blank first, note that *sneer* is a fitting response to an unpopular viewpoint. *Propagating* is another word for *transmitting* or *communicating.*

9. (E) *substantial. But* signals that the blank contrasts in meaning with the advance of police science. The idea of substantial crime fits that contrast.

10. (C) *skeptical.* The blank is defined in the second half of the sentence. One who views truth as a variable is a skeptic.

11. (B) *disproven . . . vices.* Working from the second blank first, note that the correct term must be one consistent with or causing the failure of communities. The only strongly negative term is *vices.*

12. (B) *somber. Although* signals a contrast, and *somber* (overly serious) contrasts well with *sense of humor.*

13. (A) *par. Par* means equal status, and noting that equal status makes competition possible, we see that this term is an appropriate choice. Note that *basis* is a more ambiguous term and therefore not the best choice.

14. (D) *condemned . . . inflexibility.* The first blank contrasts with the *appreciation* noted in the second half of the sentence, and the term which is in contrast to the positive attitude of appreciation is the one expressing a negative attitude—*condemned.* The second

term, *inflexibility,* appropriately describes this condemning attitude.

15. (B) *red-ink.* *Red-ink* is a standard coloquial term to indicate spending beyond one's budget.

Set Three

1. (B) *circular . . . west.* The sentence suggests that hurricanes do not move directly, and the term which best expresses indirect movement is *circular;* and a hurricane moving in a circle would not move linearly, from east to west.

2. (C) *personable . . . artifice.* Working from the second blank first, note that *artifice* (falsehood) is the only term that is a substitute for *truth. Personable* means appealing and attractive.

3. (A) *creative.* The sentence suggests that young children stop something which is inconsistent with facts and consistent with imagination. *Creative* best fits that description.

4. (D) *diffidence.* To be diffident is to be hesitant and unsure. Thus, *diffidence* describes the *stance* expressed in the sentence.

5. (A) *crusade.* A crusade is action taken against some injustice or abuse and is therefore a fitting term to describe Mack's action.

6. (E) *narrow . . . broaden.* Working from the second blank first, note that it requires a contrast to *focus.* Both choices (A) and (E) provide this contrast, but the second term offered by choice (A), *blur,* is illogical.

7. (B) *monetary . . . intangible.* The sentence describes two different types of reward. Therefore, the blanks should be filled with contrasting terms.

8. (C) *frightened . . . trepidation.* The blanks should be filled by terms which are somewhat synonymous with one another, both describing the negative aspect of Bill's response to the professor. Only choice (C) offers synonymous negative terms; *trepidation* is synonymous with *fear.*

9. (A) *deflecting.* To arouse suspicion, the senator would have to give an unacceptable response. *Deflecting* (turning away) is the only choice which suggests such a response.

10. (D) *remedial . . . ameliorate. Remedial* (providing a remedy) is a term appropriate to programs that address a deficiency, and *ameliorate* (make better) is consistent with the purpose of such programs.

11. (D) *dull . . . esoteric.* A speech in which interesting points were lost may best be described as *dull. Esoteric* means understandable only by a few.

12. (E) *desperate . . . calm. Although* suggests that the correct choices are contrasting terms. The most direct and meaningful contrast is provided by choice (E).

13. (C) *privacy.* Interfering in another's life is logically equivalent to a violation of *privacy.*

14. (B) *inspiration . . . revision.* Both choices (A) and (B) offer terms consistent with *spontaneous,* but (B) is the better choice because its second term, *revision,* directly contrasts with the idea of spontaneous writing.

15. (B) *biases.* The term *biases* contrasts with *objectivity* and fits the meaning of the sentence.

Set Four

1. (A) *short-lived.* The term *short-lived* is consistent with the description of a political career that wanes all too soon. *Wanes* means lessens or weakens.

2. (D) *obsolete.* The sentence suggests that machines will replace humans, and *obsolete* refers to something that is no longer useful or necessary.

3. (C) *change . . . compare.* Working from the second blank first, note that a comparison between two generations is suggested; so the term *compare* fits well, and *change* is also appropriate.

4. (B) *transient . . . reassert.* Working from the second blank first, note that those in the humanities, which includes the study of art and literature, would have a positive regard for these subjects. The most positive second term offered in the choices is *reassert. Transient* (not permanent) correctly describes the hope of those in the humanities concerning the other subjects mentioned.

5. (D) *deregulate ... ambiguously.* Working from the second blank first, note that the sentence suggests that the government response was not clearly for one side or the other. A response that is not clear and decisive may be termed *ambiguous. Deregulate* is an appropriate term for describing the lifting of restrictions and is often used in connection with the oil industry.

6. (A) *investigation ... experiential.* Working from the second blank first, note that *empirical* refers to conclusions based upon experience and is therefore a term consistent with *experiential. Empirical* also can denote the nature of an investigation.

7. (B) *panned.* The action of the public contrasts with that of the critics; so we are looking for a term that describes a negative critical response. *Panned* does just that.

8. (C) *control over ... reflect.* That we must hope for some influence on price-setting activity suggests that we have no control and pinpoints choice (C).

9. (B) *deterrence.* The portion of the sentence following the blank defines *deterrence* as applied to the nuclear issue.

10. (C) *summaries.* This term is consistent both with the positive attitude toward well-established information and with the form (summary) such information might logically take.

11. (C) *charity.* The sentence discusses donations to worthy causes, and *charity* is the term most consistent with that subject.

12. (E) *derogatory ... dulling.* The sentence suggests that the teachers' comments have a negative effect on the students, and the term which most logically expresses such an effect is *dulling. Derogatory* means insulting or belittling and also fits the overall negative assessment of teacher comments.

13. (B) *instantly.* The term that contrasts most clearly with *evolution* (slow development) is *instantly.*

14. (D) *speak ... revealed.* The sentence does not accept the idea that silence means ignorance, and both *speak* and *reveal* are appropriate terms in this discussion of the issue.

15. (A) *parrying . . . offensive.* The term *parrying* means warding off or deflecting and contrasts with an offensive (attacking) movement.

Set Five

1. (E) *safeguards . . . legislated.* Working from the second blank first, note that the term *government* suggests a verb that describes government action. Therefore, *legislated* is a fitting choice, and its partner, *safeguards,* also fits the meaning of the sentence.

2. (B) *vacillated.* Those who vacillate can't make up their minds. The term *vacillated* contrasts appropriately with *decisive.*

3. (B) *exceptional.* The word *but* indicates that Lanahan's accomplishments were nothing to boast about—that is, they were not exceptional (special, out of the ordinary).

4. (C) *thorough.* To find a chink in someone's intellectual armor is a figurative way of saying to find a weakness in that person's knowledge. Lind's opponents are dismayed because they can find no weakness because his knowledge is thorough.

5. (D) *within . . . doubts.* The only term that distinguishes between anthropologists' study of other cultures and the study of their own is *outside.* They are inside their own cultures but outside others. *Wonders* also fits the meaning of the sentence.

6. (A) *enthusiastically.* The sentence requires a positive term consistent with the meaning of *cordially. Enthusiastically* is the only appropriate choice.

7. (E) *practical . . . conception.* The sentence first says that theory and practice cannot be separated, suggesting that the blank referring to theory should indicate its practical nature and the blank referring to practice should include its theoretical nature. In short, we require a "practice" synonym for the first blank and a "theory" synonym for the second blank. Only choice (E) satisfies this requirement.

8. (B) *stern . . . solemn.* The word *but* tells us that the sentence requires terms that contrast with *humor,* and only choice (B) provides two such terms.

9. (C) *responsible.* An unwillingness to skirt professional obligations indicates responsibility, and therefore choice (C), *responsible,* is the best choice.

10. (A) *protection.* The blank should contain a term that makes the advocacy mentioned involve Communist principles (those reflecting increased government control). *Protection* of the underprivileged suggests government intervention and control more strongly than any of the other terms.

11. (C) *priority.* The term *priority* (importance) best fits the sense of the sentence.

12. (B) *scope . . . breadth.* Working from the second blank first, note that we are looking for a term consistent with *comprehensive* (including much) and that *breadth* (broadness) fits this requirement. Also, *limited in scope* appropriately contrasts with *comprehensive.*

13. (D) *wretched . . . prejudice.* Working from the second blank first, note that we are looking for a racial attitude that reinforces a negative view of foreigners—that is, a negative racial *prejudice.* The term *wretched* (miserable and unfortunate) also fits, describing the kind of lives led by early immigrants.

14. (B) *style . . . content.* We are looking for two terms that are comparable to *appearance* and *identity.* Appearance is comparable to *style* (outer characteristics of writing), and identity (the "substance" of a person) is comparable to *content* (the "substance" of writing).

15. (E) *heroic . . . courage.* The terms *heroic* and *courage* are consistent with the term *nobility,* and further, *courage* and *nobility* define the characteristics of someone who is heroic.

Part V: Reading Comprehension Strategies and Practice

READING COMPREHENSION STRATEGIES

Reading Comprehension is a common section on many standardized tests: the SAT, GRE, LSAT, GMAT, and CBEST, among others. On each of these tests, you will encounter a section that asks you to answer multiple-choice questions based on reading passages. On some tests, the CBEST in particular, many of the reading passages are relatively brief and followed by one or two questions. On other tests (the GRE, LSAT, and GMAT, for example), challenging reading passages of about 500 words appear, each followed by approximately six or seven questions. Passages nearly this long but somewhat less difficult appear on the SAT and other exams. Be sure to check the official bulletin for your exam to determine the length of passages and difficulty level of questions.

Following is an analysis, with examples, of techniques and strategies useful for attacking each variety of reading comprehension test. Some general procedures, which we will illustrate, apply in all cases.

- Read the directions carefully.
- Estimate and allot your time if possible.
- Sample the questions before reading each passage.
- Mark each passage as you read.
- Answer each question based only on information in the passage.
- Eliminate answer choices that are irrelevant, contradictory, or unreasonable.

The following directions are typical.

Directions

Each statement or passage in this test is followed by a question or questions based on its content. After reading a statement or passage, choose the best answer to each question from among the five choices given. Answer all questions following a statement or passage on the basis of what is *stated* or *implied* in that statement or passage.

Analysis

Notice that you are to choose the *best* answer given five choices; in some instances, the best answer may not be the ideal answer. Also, realize that your choice must be based only on stated (explicit) or implied (implicit) information. People who get low scores on reading comprehension often "read into" a passage, using their outside knowledge.

BRIEF PASSAGES

Consider the following brief passage of the type that may appear on the CBEST and other tests.

Passage

Norms serve the function of standardizing behavior, of bringing order to what otherwise would be a chaotic situation. If some of us drove on the left side of the road and others on the right side, or if some of us stopped for red lights while others did not, there would be much confusion and danger. In other words, social life as we know it would not be possible without norms. All cultures have a system of norms to provide such social control for a society.

Question

The author's primary purpose in this passage is to
(A) explain the function of norms for social control
(B) refute the belief that norms are unimportant
(C) instruct readers about which norms are appropriate in some cultures
(D) establish social norms that are especially popular in the United States
(E) warn drivers who are reckless to be more careful

Analysis

Typically, a brief passage such as this will be followed by one or two questions. By quickly reading the question here before reading the passage, you realize that you should keep in mind the author's primary purpose as you read. Usually, the primary purpose of any reading passage is not explicitly stated but becomes evident as you become aware, while reading, of *what* the author is trying to do.

After sampling the question, read the passage *steadily* and *carefully,* marking key words and phrases as you read. Keep the question or questions in mind as you mark, and mark places in the passage that either *address the question* or *stand out as interesting or important.* A sample of a fully marked, longer passage will be given later in this section.

Once you have carefully read and marked the passage, you must consider each answer choice and pick the best one. *Always read every choice before making a decision, even if one of the early choices seems obviously correct.* As you consider each choice, ask yourself whether it is *irrelevant, contradictory,* or *unreasonable.* A choice that falls into any of these categories should be eliminated.

When considering a "primary purpose" question, pay special attention to the first word of every answer choice and eliminate choices if the first word *obviously contradicts* the purpose of the passage. In this case, choice (B), refute, and choice (E), warn, do not seem consistent with the general and objective nature of the passage. Considering the remaining choices more fully, you should recognize choice (A) as a possibly correct answer and move on to consider choices (C) and (D). Choice (C) is *irrelevant* to the information in the passage, which does not address *which norms are appropriate* and does not focus on *some cultures* only. Choice (D) is not altogether irrelevant because it does mention norms that may possibly be popular in the United States (although note that the United States is never mentioned explicitly). Also, the description of driving norms is not the *primary* purpose, or *overall* purpose, of the author. If you answered (D), you would be mistaking a *secondary* purpose for a *primary* purpose. The best choice is (A).

On reading comprehension tests which combine many brief passages, such as the last one, with some longer passages, it is difficult to allot your time for each passage because of the irregular structure of the test. However, when your encounter a reading test with passages of approximately equal length, each followed by about the same number of questions, you can estimate the time you should spend on each passage. It is possible to do this on the LSAT and the GMAT and other similar exams. For example, on the LSAT the reading comprehension section usually consists of four passages of about 500 words each, with each passage followed by six or seven questions. You have a total of 35 minutes to complete the section. With all this information in mind, you should realize that no more than about eight minutes should be spent on each reading passage and questions. You should "subdivide" your time and pace yourself so that you are able to attempt all the questions before time is called.

LONGER PASSAGES—CHALLENGING

Following is one of the longer, more challenging passages of the sort that may show up on the LSAT, GMAT, or GRE.

Passage

A chemical formula consists of a single symbol or a group of symbols with number subscripts representing the composition of a substance whether it is a free element or a compound. The formula may represent 1 molecule of the substance if it exists in the molecular form. For ionic compounds—which exist in the form of charged ions rather than neutral molecules—the formula represents the atomic composition in terms of the simplest ratio of atoms.

A subscript is a small whole number in a formula, following a symbol and below it, indicating the relative number of atoms of a given element. We omit using the subscript when only 1 atom is present. A coefficient is a number placed before a formula, which multiplies every constituent in the formula. For example the formula I_2 represents 1 molecule of the element iodine, consisting of 2 iodine atoms chemically combined. The expression 2 I indicates 2 separate atoms of iodine not in combination. The formula HNO_3 represents 1 molecule of nitric acid, containing 1 atom of hydrogen, 1 atom of nitrogen, and 3 atoms of oxygen. The expression 3 HNO_3 represents 3 molecules of nitric acid. The total number of atoms represented by 3 HNO_3 would be 3 atoms of hydrogen, 3 atoms of nitrogen, and 9 atoms of oxygen. The formula KNO_3 represents 1 potassium ion (K^+) and 1 nitrate ion (NO_3^-), which is the simplest ratio of these ions forming a neutral entity. Only a knowledge of the chemistry of the various elements would allow us to know whether a certain compound exists in ionic or molecular form.

If we would perform a chemical analysis of a pure sample of the element sulfur, we would, of course, find that it was 100% sulfur. The symbol for sulfur is S and we may be tempted to write the formula for sulfur as S, which would indicate that elemental sulfur—that occurring in nature—consisted of sulfur atoms. However, various experiments show that sulfur at room temperature consists of molecules, each containing 8 sulfur atoms in a puckered-ring structure. The formula for sulfur is S_8. Twenty-five sulfur molecules would be represented by the expression 25 S_8.

According to the Law of Definite Proportions, pure compounds contain the same elements in the same proportion by weight, regardless of when and where the compound is found. A pure sample of aluminum sulfate (formula $Al_2(SO_4)_3$, an ionic compound containing 2 Al^{+3} ions for every 3($SO_4)_3$ $^{-2}$ ions, the simplest ratio of ions forming a neutral entity) contains by weight 15.8% Al, 28.1% S, and 56.1% O. That is, whenever or wherever a 100 gram sample of aluminum sulfate is decomposed to the elements, the products would be 15.8 g of Al, 28.1 g of S, and 56.1 g of O. From percent composition by weight data, we can readily determine the "simplest" or "empirical" formulas of compounds.

Questions

1. The primary purpose of the passage is to
   (A) combine elements to produce new chemical compounds
   (B) compare the weights of several chemical substances
   (C) eliminate misconceptions concerning chemical notation
   (D) invent representations of natural elements
   (E) explain methods of chemical notation

2. According to the passage, the Law of Definite Proportions can lead a chemist to
   (A) estimations of weight which apply only to 100-gram samples
   (B) decompose chemicals into free ions
   (C) apply other chemical laws that simplify complex compounds
   (D) determination of the relative weight of the elements in a compound
   (E) formulas for performing "simple" chemical experiments

3. The author of the passage assumes that the reader knows the meaning of which of the following terms?
   (A) molecule
   (B) chemical formula
   (C) subscript
   (D) coefficient
   (E) Law of Definite Proportions

4. Which of the following conclusions is supported by the passage?
   (A) Elemental sulfur is the most unusual of all chemical compounds.
   (B) The chemical formula for a pure element may contain a subscript.
   (C) The ratio of atoms in a compound is disregarded by a chemical formula.
   (D) The 3 in the expression 3H indicates the number of combined atoms.
   (E) The total number of atoms in a chemical compound is not represented by a chemical formula.

5. We may infer which of the following about the atomic composition of any molecule?
   (A) It yields a configuration that resembles a type of ring.
   (B) It most likely exists in ionic form.
   (C) It can be represented by a chemical formula if it consists of known elements.
   (D) It is unknown to scientists until molecules are studied at room temperature.
   (E) It is the same as a pure sample of an element.

6. The passage provides answers to which of the following questions?
   (A) Why do the elements in aluminum sulfate occur in a particular proportion?
   (B) Can any chemicals besides sulfur be represented by a puckered-ring structure?
   (C) Are ions charged differently than molecules?
   (D) Does potassium occur in compounds other than potassium nitrate?
   (E) Do changes in temperature alter all chemicals in a particular way?

Analysis

Sampling the questions first, you see that you must pay special attention, for question 1, to the primary purpose; for question 2, to the discussion of the Law of Definite Proportions; for question 3, to the meaning of scientific terms, and for question 5, to the discussion of atomic composition. Note that question 4 gives you no particular clue to what to look for in the passage.

Keeping in mind the questions you must answer and paying attention to any sections of the passage that stand out as *important or interesting,* you should read and *mark* the passage. A marked version of the chemistry passage follows.

Marked Passage

A chemical formula consists of a single symbol or a group of symbols with number(subscripts)representing the composition of a substance whether it is a free element or a compound. The formula may represent 1 molecule of the substance if it exists in the molecular form. For(ionic compounds)—which exist in the form of charged ions rather than neutral molecules—the formula represents the atomic composition in terms of the simplest ratio of atoms.

A subscript is a small whole number in a formula, following a symbol and below it, indicating the relative number of atoms of a given element. We omit using the subscript when only 1 atom is present. A coefficient is a number placed before a formula, which multiplies every constituent in the formula. For example the formula I_2 represents 1 molecule of the element iodine, consisting of 2 iodine atoms chemically combined. The expression 2 I indicates 2 separate atoms of iodine not in combination. The formula HNO_3 represents 1 molecule of nitric acid, containing 1 atom of hydrogen, 1 atom of nitrogen, and 3 atoms of oxygen. The expression 3 HNO_3 represents 3 molecules of nitric acid. The total number of atoms represented by 3 HNO_3 would be 3 atoms of hydrogen, 3 atoms of nitrogen, and 9 atoms of oxygen. The formula KNO_3 represents 1 potassium ion (K^+) and 1 nitrate ion (NO_3^-), which is the simplest ratio of these ions forming a neutral entity. Only a knowledge of the chemistry of the various elements would allow us to know whether a certain compound exists in ionic or molecular form.

If we would perform a chemical analysis of a pure sample of the element sulfur, we would, of course, find that it was 100% sulfur. The symbol for sulfur is S and we may be tempted to write the formula for sulfur as S, which would indicate that elemental sulfur—that occurring in nature—consisted of sulfur atoms. However, various experiments show that sulfur at room temperature consists of molecules, each containing 8 sulfur atoms in a puckered-ring structure. The formula for sulfur is S_8. Twenty-five sulfur molecules would be represented by the expression 25 S_8.

According to the Law of Definite Proportions, pure com- *
pounds contain the same elements in the same proportion by weight, regardless of when and where the compound is found. A pure sample of aluminum sulfate (formula $Al_2(SO_4)_3$, an ionic compound containing 2 Al^{+3} ions for every 3 $(SO_4)_3^{-2}$ ions, the simplest ratio of ions forming a neutral entity) contains by weight 15.8% Al, 28.1% S, and 56.1% O. That is, whenever or wherever a 100 gram sample of aluminum sulfate is decomposed to the elements, the products would be 15.8 g of Al, 28.1 g of S, and 56.1 g of O. From percent composition by weight data, we can readily determine the "simplest" or "empirical" formulas of compounds.

Answers and Explanations

1. (E) The first word of each answer choice is a clue to eliminating incorrect choices. *Combine, compare, eliminate,* and *invent* are not relevant to the obvious, overall purpose of the passage, which is to explain.

2. (D) Using the example of aluminum sulfate, the passage illustrates determination of the relative weight of the elements, using the Law of Definite Proportions. Choice (A) is contradictory. Choices (B), (C), and (E) are irrelevant to the information given in the passage.

3. (A) *Molecule* is the only term that is not explicitly defined or explained in the passage.

4. (B) Only this choice is explicitly supported in the passage. Each of the other choices contradicts information in the passage.

5. (C) A question that asks for information that is *implied* or *inferred* is asking you to derive conclusions or information that is suggested rather than explicitly stated. The correct choice here is (C), a choice you may arrive at through the process of elimination. Choices (A) and (D) are true about sulfur but irrelevant to molecular composition in general; choices (B) and (E) contradict the passage, which explains that a molecule is not the same as an ion or a pure element.

6. (C) This type of question is time consuming because you must locate the section of the passage relevant to each answer choice/question as you survey the answer choices. The question stated by choice (C) is answered in the third sentence of the first paragraph.

LONGER PASSAGES—INTERMEDIATE DIFFICULTY

Now try the following passage, which is lengthy but not as challenging as the chemistry passage we just examined. This type of passage might appear on the SAT or as one of the few long passages found on the CBEST and similar exams.

Passage

Woodrow Wilson is usually ranked among the country's great presidents in spite of his failure to win Senate approval of the League of Nations. Wilson had yearned for a political career all his life; he won his first office in 1910 when he was elected governor of New Jersey. Two years later he was elected president in one of the most rapid political rises in our history. For a while Wilson had practiced law but found it both boring and unprofitable; then he became a political scientist of great renown and finally president of Princeton University. He did an outstanding job at Princeton but lost out in a battle with Dean Andrew West for control of the graduate school. When he was asked by the Democratic boss of New Jersey, Jim Smith, to run for governor, Wilson readily accepted because his position at Princeton was becoming untenable.

Until 1910 Wilson seemed to be a conservative Democrat in the Grover Cleveland tradition. He had denounced Bryan in 1896 and had voted for the National Democratic candidate who supported gold. In fact, when the Democratic machine first pushed Wilson's nomination in 1912, the young New Jersey progressives wanted no part of him. Wilson later assured them that he would champion the progressive cause, and so they decided to work for his election. It is easy to accuse Wilson of political expendiency, but it is entirely possible that by 1912 he had changed his views as had countless other Americans. While governor of New Jersey, he carried out his election pledges by enacting an impressive list of reforms.

Wilson secured the Democratic nomination on the forty-sixth ballot after a fierce battle with Champ Clark of Missouri and Oscar W. Underwood of Alabama. Clark actually had a majority of votes but was unable to attract the necessary two-thirds. In the campaign, Wilson emerged as the middle-of-the road candidate—between the conservative William H. Taft and the more radical Theodore Roosevelt. Wilson called his program the New Freedom, which he said was the restoration of free competition as it had existed before the growth of the trusts. In contrast, Theodore Roosevelt was advocating a New Nationalism, which seemed to call for massive federal intervention in the economic life of the nation. Wilson felt that the trusts should be destroyed, but he made a distinction between a trust and a legitimately successful big business. Theodore Roosevelt, on the other hand, accepted the trusts as inevitable but said that the government should regulate them by establishing a new regulatory agency. The former president also felt that a distinction should be made between the "good" trusts and the "bad" trusts.

Questions

1. The author's main purpose in writing this passage is to
   (A) argue that Wilson is one of the great U.S. presidents
   (B) survey the differences between Wilson, Taft, and Roosevelt
   (C) explain Wilson's concept of the New Freedom
   (D) discuss some major events of Wilson's career
   (E) suggest reasons that Wilson's presidency may have started World War I

2. The author implies which of the following about the New Jersey progressives?
   (A) They did not support Wilson after he was governor.
   (B) They were not conservative Democrats.
   (C) They were more interested in political expediency than in political causes or reforms.
   (D) Along with Wilson, they were supporters of Bryan in 1896.
   (E) They particularly admired Wilson's experience as president of Princeton University.

3. The passage supports which of the following conclusions about the progress of Wilson's political career?
   (A) Few politicians have progressed so rapidly toward the attainment of higher office.
   (B) Failures late in his career cause him to be regarded as a president who regressed instead of progressed.
   (C) Wilson encountered little opposition once he determined to seek the presidency.
   (D) The League of Nations marked the end of Wilson's reputation as a strong leader.
   (E) Wilson's political progress was aided by Champ Clark and Oscar Underwood.

4. In the statement "Wilson readily accepted because his position at Princeton was becoming untenable," the meaning of *untenable* is probably which of the following?
   (A) unlikely to last for ten years
   (B) filled with considerably less tension
   (C) difficult to maintain or continue
   (D) filled with achievements that would appeal to voters
   (E) something he did not have a tenacious desire to continue

5. According to the passage, which of the following was probably true about the presidential campaign of 1912?

(A) Woodrow Wilson won the election by an overwhelming majority.

(B) The inexperience of Theodore Roosevelt accounted for his radical position.

(C) Wilson was unable to attract two-thirds of the votes but won anyway.

(D) There were three nominated candidates for the presidency.

(E) Wilson's New Freedom did not represent Democratic interests.

Answers and Explanations

1. (D) Choices (A) and (E) are irrelevant to the information in the passage, and choices (B) and (C) mention *secondary* purposes rather than the primary one.

2. (B) In the second paragraph, Wilson's decision to *champion the progressive cause* after 1912 is contrasted with his earlier career, when *he seemed to be a conservative Democrat.* Thus, we may conclude that the progressives, whom Wilson finally joined, were not conservative Democrats, as was Wilson earlier in his career. Choices (A) and (D) contradict information in the paragraph, while choices (C) and (E) are not suggested by any information given in the passage.

3. (A) This choice is explicitly supported by the third sentence in paragraph one in which we are told that Wilson was *elected president in one of the most rapid political rises in our history.*

4. (C) On any reading comprehension test, it is best to be alert to the positive and negative connotations of words and phrases in each passage as well as in the questions themselves. In the case of *untenable,* the prefix *un-* suggests that the word has a negative connotation. The context in which the word occurs does so as well. Wilson *left* his position at Princeton; therefore, we may conclude that the position was somehow unappealing. Only two of the answer choices, (C) and (E), provide a negative definition. Although choice (E) may attract your attention because *tenacious* looks similar to *tenable,* the correct choice is (C), which is the conventional definition of *untenable.*

5. (D) Choices (A), (B), and (C) contain information that is not addressed in the passage. We may eliminate them as irrelevant. Choice (E) contradicts the fact that Wilson was a Democratic candidate. The discussion of Taft and Roosevelt as the candidates who finally ran against Wilson for the presidency supports choice (D).

ANSWER SHEET FOR READING COMPREHENSION PRACTICE
(Remove This Sheet and Use It to Mark Your Answers)

CUT HERE

BRIEF PASSAGES

1 Ⓐ Ⓑ Ⓒ Ⓓ Ⓔ
2 Ⓐ Ⓑ Ⓒ Ⓓ Ⓔ
3 Ⓐ Ⓑ Ⓒ Ⓓ Ⓔ
4 Ⓐ Ⓑ Ⓒ Ⓓ Ⓔ
5 Ⓐ Ⓑ Ⓒ Ⓓ Ⓔ
6 Ⓐ Ⓑ Ⓒ Ⓓ Ⓔ
7 Ⓐ Ⓑ Ⓒ Ⓓ Ⓔ
8 Ⓐ Ⓑ Ⓒ Ⓓ Ⓔ
9 Ⓐ Ⓑ Ⓒ Ⓓ Ⓔ
10 Ⓐ Ⓑ Ⓒ Ⓓ Ⓔ
11 Ⓐ Ⓑ Ⓒ Ⓓ Ⓔ
12 Ⓐ Ⓑ Ⓒ Ⓓ Ⓔ
13 Ⓐ Ⓑ Ⓒ Ⓓ Ⓔ
14 Ⓐ Ⓑ Ⓒ Ⓓ Ⓔ
15 Ⓐ Ⓑ Ⓒ Ⓓ Ⓔ

LONGER PASSAGES INTERMEDIATE DIFFICULTY

1 Ⓐ Ⓑ Ⓒ Ⓓ Ⓔ
2 Ⓐ Ⓑ Ⓒ Ⓓ Ⓔ
3 Ⓐ Ⓑ Ⓒ Ⓓ Ⓔ
4 Ⓐ Ⓑ Ⓒ Ⓓ Ⓔ
5 Ⓐ Ⓑ Ⓒ Ⓓ Ⓔ
6 Ⓐ Ⓑ Ⓒ Ⓓ Ⓔ
7 Ⓐ Ⓑ Ⓒ Ⓓ Ⓔ
8 Ⓐ Ⓑ Ⓒ Ⓓ Ⓔ
9 Ⓐ Ⓑ Ⓒ Ⓓ Ⓔ
10 Ⓐ Ⓑ Ⓒ Ⓓ Ⓔ
11 Ⓐ Ⓑ Ⓒ Ⓓ Ⓔ
12 Ⓐ Ⓑ Ⓒ Ⓓ Ⓔ
13 Ⓐ Ⓑ Ⓒ Ⓓ Ⓔ
14 Ⓐ Ⓑ Ⓒ Ⓓ Ⓔ
15 Ⓐ Ⓑ Ⓒ Ⓓ Ⓔ
16 Ⓐ Ⓑ Ⓒ Ⓓ Ⓔ
17 Ⓐ Ⓑ Ⓒ Ⓓ Ⓔ
18 Ⓐ Ⓑ Ⓒ Ⓓ Ⓔ
19 Ⓐ Ⓑ Ⓒ Ⓓ Ⓔ
20 Ⓐ Ⓑ Ⓒ Ⓓ Ⓔ

21 Ⓐ Ⓑ Ⓒ Ⓓ Ⓔ
22 Ⓐ Ⓑ Ⓒ Ⓓ Ⓔ
23 Ⓐ Ⓑ Ⓒ Ⓓ Ⓔ
24 Ⓐ Ⓑ Ⓒ Ⓓ Ⓔ
25 Ⓐ Ⓑ Ⓒ Ⓓ Ⓔ
26 Ⓐ Ⓑ Ⓒ Ⓓ Ⓔ
27 Ⓐ Ⓑ Ⓒ Ⓓ Ⓔ
28 Ⓐ Ⓑ Ⓒ Ⓓ Ⓔ
29 Ⓐ Ⓑ Ⓒ Ⓓ Ⓔ
30 Ⓐ Ⓑ Ⓒ Ⓓ Ⓔ
31 Ⓐ Ⓑ Ⓒ Ⓓ Ⓔ
32 Ⓐ Ⓑ Ⓒ Ⓓ Ⓔ
33 Ⓐ Ⓑ Ⓒ Ⓓ Ⓔ
34 Ⓐ Ⓑ Ⓒ Ⓓ Ⓔ
35 Ⓐ Ⓑ Ⓒ Ⓓ Ⓔ
36 Ⓐ Ⓑ Ⓒ Ⓓ Ⓔ
37 Ⓐ Ⓑ Ⓒ Ⓓ Ⓔ
38 Ⓐ Ⓑ Ⓒ Ⓓ Ⓔ
39 Ⓐ Ⓑ Ⓒ Ⓓ Ⓔ

LONGER PASSAGES CHALLENGING

1 Ⓐ Ⓑ Ⓒ Ⓓ Ⓔ
2 Ⓐ Ⓑ Ⓒ Ⓓ Ⓔ
3 Ⓐ Ⓑ Ⓒ Ⓓ Ⓔ
4 Ⓐ Ⓑ Ⓒ Ⓓ Ⓔ
5 Ⓐ Ⓑ Ⓒ Ⓓ Ⓔ
6 Ⓐ Ⓑ Ⓒ Ⓓ Ⓔ
7 Ⓐ Ⓑ Ⓒ Ⓓ Ⓔ
8 Ⓐ Ⓑ Ⓒ Ⓓ Ⓔ
9 Ⓐ Ⓑ Ⓒ Ⓓ Ⓔ
10 Ⓐ Ⓑ Ⓒ Ⓓ Ⓔ
11 Ⓐ Ⓑ Ⓒ Ⓓ Ⓔ
12 Ⓐ Ⓑ Ⓒ Ⓓ Ⓔ
13 Ⓐ Ⓑ Ⓒ Ⓓ Ⓔ
14 Ⓐ Ⓑ Ⓒ Ⓓ Ⓔ
15 Ⓐ Ⓑ Ⓒ Ⓓ Ⓔ
16 Ⓐ Ⓑ Ⓒ Ⓓ Ⓔ
17 Ⓐ Ⓑ Ⓒ Ⓓ Ⓔ
18 Ⓐ Ⓑ Ⓒ Ⓓ Ⓔ
19 Ⓐ Ⓑ Ⓒ Ⓓ Ⓔ
20 Ⓐ Ⓑ Ⓒ Ⓓ Ⓔ
21 Ⓐ Ⓑ Ⓒ Ⓓ Ⓔ
22 Ⓐ Ⓑ Ⓒ Ⓓ Ⓔ
23 Ⓐ Ⓑ Ⓒ Ⓓ Ⓔ
24 Ⓐ Ⓑ Ⓒ Ⓓ Ⓔ
25 Ⓐ Ⓑ Ⓒ Ⓓ Ⓔ
26 Ⓐ Ⓑ Ⓒ Ⓓ Ⓔ
27 Ⓐ Ⓑ Ⓒ Ⓓ Ⓔ
28 Ⓐ Ⓑ Ⓒ Ⓓ Ⓔ
29 Ⓐ Ⓑ Ⓒ Ⓓ Ⓔ
30 Ⓐ Ⓑ Ⓒ Ⓓ Ⓔ
31 Ⓐ Ⓑ Ⓒ Ⓓ Ⓔ

READING COMPREHENSION PRACTICE

Following are sets of reading comprehension questions based on passages that are brief, passages of intermediate difficulty, and passages that are challenging. While you should concentrate on those sections which approximate your test in length and difficulty level, answering the questions from all difficulty levels is excellent practice for developing basic reading comprehension skills. The Answer Key for these practice units may be found on page 366, and the complete explanatory answers begin on page 367.

DIRECTIONS

Each statement or passage in this test is followed by a question or questions based on its content. After reading a statement or passage, choose the best answer to each question from among the five choices given. Answer all questions following a statement or passage on the basis of what is *stated* or *implied* in that statement or passage.

BRIEF PASSAGES

Religious groups, such as Catholics or lesser Protestant sects, have at one time or another borne the yoke of discrimination. Around the world and in the United States, persecution of religious minorities has considerably decreased in the twentieth century—the exceptions being the conflict between Protestant and Catholic factions in Northern Ireland and between Hindu and Moslem groups in India.

1. We may infer which of the following conclusions from this passage?
    (A) Only Catholics and Protestants have borne the yoke of discrimination.
    (B) Religious persecution was more widespread in the sixteenth century than it is today.
    (C) Northern Ireland and India are very similar regions.
    (D) Religious persecution in the United States is more of a problem than elsewhere in the world.
    (E) Hindus hold beliefs similar to those of Protestants, and Moslems hold beliefs similar to those of Catholics.

317

2. Which of the following best expresses the point of the passage?
   (A) Although religious persecution is less widespread now than it had been, it is no less repulsive.
   (B) Catholics and Protestants have not been persecuted for some time.
   (C) Only those groups which have been persecuted can call themselves religious.
   (D) Becoming a member of any religious group entails the risk of persecution.
   (E) Although religious discrimination has affected a number of religious groups, it is not so widespread now as it has been.

   The size of the American family has gradually grown smaller. One major reason for diminished size may have been growth in urbanization; whereas a large family may be practical on the farm, since it means more hands to help in the work, child-labor laws and relatively high living expenses make more than a few children prohibitive in the city. Evidence to support this is seen in the fact that the proportion of childless couples has actually declined; shrinkage in the average size of families has come mainly from the dramatic decrease in the percentage of families having more than four children.

3. The passage supports all of the following statements *except* which of the following?
   (A) The size of the American family is related to the growth of cities.
   (B) The nature of farmwork favors a large family.
   (C) The size of families in other countries has also increased.
   (D) The percentage of families with more than four children was once higher than it is now.
   (E) The cost of living in the city affects the size of families.

   A number of special psychotherapeutic techniques have been developed. In psychodrama people are placed in a staged situation involving one of their real-life conflicts and work out their problems there. In group therapy a number of persons and a therapist meet to interact about the problems of all the participants. Sharing their feelings and problems helps each of them. Play therapy, usually done with children, utilizes dolls, playhouses, etc., to permit children to release, on these inanimate objects, the reactions they are otherwise forbidden to use.

4. The author would probably agree that psychodrama, group therapy, and play therapy all encourage which of the following?
   (A) strange behavior
   (B) contact with the unconscious
   (C) theatrical techniques
   (D) introversion
   (E) self-expression

5. In the last sentence, the author assumes which of the following?
   (A) Some children hide their true reactions.
   (B) Dolls are most useful to the therapist when they are set in a playhouse.
   (C) Children love to do violence to inanimate objects.
   (D) Play therapy is the only type of therapy that is appropriate for children.
   (E) Most children do not have dolls and playhouses in their own homes.

Brainwashing refers to techniques employed during the Korean War to extract war crimes confessions from American soldiers. The goal of these techniques was to reeducate the prisoners to think in ways acceptable to their captors. This involved "unfreezing" old beliefs by an intensive propaganda campaign, under conditions of social isolation; changing beliefs by forcing prisoners to develop "confessions" acceptable to themselves and their captors; and reinforcing ("refreezing") new beliefs by requiring active participation in the brainwashing of others.

6. According to the passage, each of the following is true about brainwashing *except* that
   (A) it was employed during the Korean War
   (B) it was practiced on all those captured during the Korean War
   (C) it attempted to destroy old beliefs
   (D) it forced prisoners to confess to war crimes
   (E) the victims of brainwashing were socially isolated

In successive IQ tests on the same person, the score may vary. The test has some inherent variability as a measuring instrument. From one test to another, even if given under very similar conditions, variations in the person would produce score variations on identical tests.

7. The passage supports which of the following conclusions?
   (A) There are other tests that are more reliable than IQ tests.
   (B) Many educators no longer consider IQ test scores to be important.
   (C) People usually take the same IQ test a number of times.
   (D) A person who takes the same IQ test three times may get three different scores.
   (E) IQ test scores are infallible indicators of intelligence.

There are three major sources of frustration. The physical environment provides many instances in which persons are blocked from goals—for example, fences around swimming pools and washed-out bridges across roads. The social environment is frustrating—for example, being blackballed from a fraternity or turned down by a highly desirable dating partner. Personal limitations are also frustrating, as is witnessed by the fact that most adolescents desire but cannot achieve some radical change in their bodily attributes to meet a social norm.

8. The author of the passage above would probably agree that
   (A) dating partners are not often highly desirable
   (B) situations that occur in everyday life can cause frustration
   (C) the frustration of personal limitations is the worst frustration of all
   (D) frustration is a problem that can be eliminated
   (E) adolescents are usually less frustrated than are adults

9. Which of the following is one implication of the last sentence of the paragraph?
   (A) Personal limitations are no longer frustrating once one has passed adolescence.
   (B) A number of social norms are simply not fair.
   (C) Some adolescents desire a more socially acceptable appearance.
   (D) Personal limitations are not related to the social environment.
   (E) Adolescence is the most frustrating period of one's life.

There are about 14,500 commercial banks in the United States that accept checking deposits. About one-third of these are national banks that received their corporate charters from the federal government and must belong to the Federal Reserve System (hereafter called the Fed). The remaining two-thirds are state banks that need not, but may, belong to the Fed. About 60 percent of the banks do not belong to the Fed, but their deposits represent only about one-seventh of the total of all bank deposits.

10. The passage above supports which of the following conclusions?
    (A) National banks are not required to belong to the Fed.
    (B) The banks that do not belong to the Fed are located outside the United States.
    (C) More than 14,500 commercial banks are state banks.
    (D) National banks have no relationship to the federal government.
    (E) Banks that belong to the Federal Reserve System account for 6/7 of the total of all bank deposits.

"Vote! Vote! Regardless of how you vote, get out and vote!" All mature Americans are accustomed to being besieged by such pleas. And convincing statistics are advanced which indicate that a smaller proportion of Americans vote than citizens of most European countries. And yet, voting remains a considerable chore in most states.

11. According to the passage, the response of most Americans to the message "get out and vote" is
    (A) loud complaining about the real difficulty of getting to the polls
    (B) not as strong as it used to be
    (C) attention to statistics, which keeps them away from the polls
    (D) not as strong as the response of many Europeans
    (E) looked upon with the suspicion that their votes are being "bought"

12. Which of the following best summarizes the passage?
    (A) Americans have become too accustomed to hearing pleas that they vote.
    (B) As voting participation grows, democracy in America will rival that in Europe.
    (C) Although Americans are urged to vote, a large proportion of them do not.
    (D) It is much easier to get out and vote in European countries.
    (E) Voters in Europe rarely need encouragement.

Working behind closed doors during the hot summer of 1787, a group of distinguished representatives from twelve of the American states debated, contended, espoused, and compromised until they had produced a proposed new Constitution of the United States of America. When the doors were thrown open and the results of their handiwork revealed to the world, a mixed response followed.

13. Which of the following best describes the content of this passage?
    (A) hints of why the new Constitution was not immediately welcomed by all
    (B) account of the problems that challenged the writers of the Constitution
    (C) explanation of the reason that the writers of the Constitution met behind closed doors
    (D) list of reasons that the Constitution received a mixed response
    (E) brief summary of the writing of the U.S. Constitution

There is an expression, "Let the facts speak for themselves." But facts do not speak; people do. Facts are meaningless without interpretation. When people ask the question, "Why?" or "What does it mean?" they want an interpretation or evaluation. Thus, it seems inevitable that people will require philosophies.

14. The author of this passage implies which of the following?
    (A) Most people are full of questions.
    (B) Facts are not meaningful if they are independent of people.
    (C) Some facts *do* speak for themselves.
    (D) Some expressions are more correct than others.
    (E) Philosophies are more numerous than facts.

15. The author suggests that *philosophies* consist of
    (A) interpretation or evaluation
    (B) facts speaking for themselves
    (C) persons asking constant questions
    (D) belief in common expressions
    (E) belief in meaningless facts

LONGER PASSAGES—INTERMEDIATE DIFFICULTY

It is characteristic of human beings to make moral judgments with reference to conduct. Some actions are called right or good and others are said to be bad or wrong. These judgments are made concerning one's own conduct as well as that of other people. They may apply to individuals, to groups of people, or even to society as a whole. Moral philosophy is an attempt to understand this kind of experience. It is not an easy task, for it involves many questions that are highly controversial and these cannot be settled by using the same type of procedure that is employed in the natural sciences. Some of the questions which must be given careful consideration include the following. What is the basis for making any distinction between right and wrong? Is morality merely a matter of custom? Is the right identical with what people think is right or is it possible for people to be mistaken in their judgments? What is the role of conscience in matters of right and wrong? From what source or sources can knowledge about morals be obtained? Is it the function of ethics to describe how people act or should it attempt to indicate how they ought to act? If it is the latter what constitutes the standard by which their conduct can be judged to be right or wrong? Should morality be based on motive, consequences, intelligence, or a combination of these? To what extent is morality based on one's feelings? These and other questions of a similar nature are bound to arise in any serious discussion of morality and its problems. The fact that they cannot be answered by means of observation and experiment does not mean we can know nothing about them or that no other method is available for making an intelligent decision with reference to them. One can discover the implications involved in alternative answers and in the light of these select that answer which makes the most reasonable interpretation of one's experiences.

Intuition is a way of knowing through the feelings. In the field of ethics it means that one is made aware of what is right and good by direct and immediate experience rather than by means of thinking or sense perception. Sometimes it has been identified with the voice of conscience, which is interpreted to mean that the will of God is revealed directly to the human soul. Some intuitionists have maintained that we have a special sense for knowing right and wrong just as we have a sense of sight which reveals colors or a sense of hearing which reveals sounds. Others have recognized that only certain elements of one's moral consciousness are known intuitively. For example, some have taught that while the general principles of morality are known this way, their application to particular situations is the work of reason. All intuitionists agree that there are at least some elements included in anyone's consciousness of morals that can be known only in this way.

1. The author of this passage states that questions about morals
   (A) are too numerous to be answered
   (B) cannot be answered by scientific experiments
   (C) can only be answered through the feelings
   (D) do not usually provoke arguments between moral philosophers
   (E) are more relevant to individuals than to society

2. According to the passage, moral action in a particular situation
   (A) does not usually consider general principles of morality
   (B) is never detached from our intuitive sense of scientific principles
   (C) is a concern addressed by ethics rather than by moral philosophy
   (D) involves neither our sense of sight nor sense of learning
   (E) may involve both intuition and reason

3. With reference to the passage, moral philosophy may be summarized in which of the following ways?
   (A) a body of knowledge primarily concerned with intuition
   (B) the production of a series of questions about moral decisions
   (C) the study of moral judgments that influence human conduct
   (D) the study of the role of conscience in human behavior
   (E) the explanation of human ways of knowing

4. As defined in the passage, intuition is distinguished from
   (A) feelings   (D) conscience
   (B) reason   (E) morality
   (C) knowledge

Probably no concept is more difficult to define or describe in sociology than that of social change, for many reasons. Its causes are often attributable to a variety of social variables, all interacting with one another in a complex pattern. Change can be analytically distinguished in two separate spheres: social and cultural. Social change focuses primarily upon the alterations taking place in the society (such as social relationships, forms of interaction, etc.), while cultural change emphasizes the on-going transition within the social heritage as various traits and patterns are added or disappear. Change in one of these areas is likely to bring about change in the other area. In reality, it is often impossible to separate the overlap between the two.

Until recently, most sociological research was conducted at one point in time. The result was a "snap-shot" of social phenomena. By controlling for or excluding the intervention of time, it has been impossible to delineate subtle shifts occurring in the subject under study. In the past, a concentration upon discovering the social structure or social order has led to an unconscious bias regarding the importance of change. Another result has been the relative lack of knowledge sociologists have concerning change, although this is being rectified today.

A necessary cause of social change is the behavior of individuals. Other variables, such as receptivity of the society toward a particular change, must also be present. In this sense, individual behavior is not a sufficient cause, since it cannot produce change alone. Social deviants have been in the vanguard of social change; if everyone conformed completely life would be static.

Relative conformists can contribute to change as well. Studies of leaders suggest that those who closely adhere to the group norms will occupy such positions where they can initiate action and most effectively "get things done." It is then possible for those who "play the game by the rules" to be as, or possibly more, effective than the "rebel" who chooses to accomplish it by disapproved means.

But whether the person attempting to introduce change is deviant or conformist, to be most successful that person must:

1. Cloak the change so that it appears innocent and harmless.
2. Attain a position of relative prestige so that he or she will not be regarded as a "crack-pot."

3. Be aware of the culture into which the change is to be introduced so that the person will not needlessly offend anyone who can prevent the change or cause unintended but disastrous changes in other areas.

It remains true, however, that change is an inescapable, ever-present fact of life. All societies and cultures are continuously changing, although the rate and direction will be different (it is often claimed that the United States has a very high rate of change). The uniqueness of the individual personality, the "imperfections" of all societies and cultures, the desire to be creative, have new experiences, escape boredom, realize unmet needs, etc., all combine to guarantee modifications in the pattern of social life.

No society is an "island unto itself." Outside forces occasionally act upon a country in such a way as to produce strong reactions such as a declaration of war. Such outside forces can be so overwhelming as to virtually destroy a given society (the North American Indians were once in danger of complete eradication because of wars, disease, alcoholism, etc., introduced to them by European colonists). A more subtle but equally change-producing result of culture contact is the borrowing of material technology or social ideas (many Asian, African, and Latin American countries have changed radically under the influence of Westernization).

5. The author's primary purpose in this passage is to
   (A) survey familiar examples of social change
   (B) argue that the elimination of change is impossible
   (C) define and describe social change
   (D) criticize sociological research
   (E) compare the value of rebels and conformists

6. Which of the following does the passage mention as evidence that a society cannot insulate itself from the forces of change?
   (A) the near-elimination of the Indians
   (B) the number of wars that have occurred in this century
   (C) the threat of interference by social deviants
   (D) the efforts of researchers to influence the cultures they study
   (E) the high rate of change in the United States

7. The criticism of *most sociological research* may be stated in which of the following ways?
   (A) By studying a society at a particular moment in time, researchers do not detect social changes that occur over time.
   (B) Sociologists tend to be unaware of the histories of societies.
   (C) Most sociologists prefer slow rather than rapid social change.
   (D) Sociologists' knowledge of change is very weak at present.
   (E) Sociologists would like to pretend that time stands still.

8. The passage allows us to conclude that change will not occur if
   (A) it is perceived to be dangerous
   (B) it is introduced by a social deviant
   (C) it includes a respect of group norms
   (D) a majority does not agree that change is necessary
   (E) it requires the approval of conformists

9. We may characterize the author's attitude toward social change as
   (A) occasional suspicion   (D) lack of interest
   (B) stiff resistance   (E) unbridled anger
   (C) informed acceptance

The term "Industrial Revolution" describes the process of economic change from a stable agricultural and commercial society to the modern industrial society which is dependent on the use of machinery rather than hand tools. While the process was historically a gradual one and not the sudden change which the word "revolution" suggests, the economic, social, and political results were indeed revolutionary.

Basically, it meant the change from hand work to machine power—made possible by the use of steam for power through the perfection of the improved steam engine of James Watt in 1769, which made Thomas Newcomen's invention of 1708 practical for industrial use. The domestic system of production (goods produced in many homes and gathered for sale by a middleman)

was replaced by the factory system. Coupled with the technological advances which first affected the cotton textile industry and
the iron and coal industries in England, were the equally
significant technological improvements in agriculture.

Historically, the first stage of the Industrial Revolution began
slowly about 1760, gathered momentum after 1815, and
extended into the 1870s, with the main source of power being the
steam engine. Profits for the capitalists came from the manufacturing process itself, in contrast to the Commercial Revolution
when profits had come chiefly from the transportation of goods.
Coal replaced wood as fuel, and iron machines replaced wooden
machines.

Later, the second stage of the Industrial Revolution set in
during the 1870s and extended to 1914—brought about by a new
source of power, electricity, from Michael Faraday's dynamo of
1831. Characteristic of this stage was the adoption of mass
production techniques and the development of finance capitalism, with profits derived from the investment of finance capital
rather than from the manufacturing process alone, as in the
formation of the United States Steel Corporation in 1901. It was
in this second stage that the swift industrialization and urbanization of western Europe and the United States took place.

The Industrial Revolution soon carried the middle class to
political and economic power—and at the same time created the
greatest threat to capitalism, the rise of the proletariat.

10. We may infer which of the following from the author's discussion
    of economic change?
    (A) Previous to 1760 no significant economic changes had
        occurred in England.
    (B) It is difficult to name the type of change associated with the
        Industrial Revolution.
    (C) Economic change in this century constitutes the third stage
        of the Industrial Revolution.
    (D) The term *revolution* may refer to the results rather than the
        suddenness of change.
    (E) Social and political change is a separate phenomenon from
        economic change.

11. The author would probably agree that a "revolutionary" eco-
    nomic change
    (A) replaces one dominant system of production with another
    (B) is not recognizeable until long after it has occurred
    (C) is not likely to occur in the near future
    (D) is presently threatened by the rise of the proletariat
    (E) must now include regions besides western Europe and the
        United States

12. According to the passage, the United States Steel Corporation is
    an example of which of the following?
    (A) a company whose mass production techniques are an exten-
        sion of Faraday's dynamo
    (B) a company of the type that no one could have predicted
        during the first stage of the Industrial Revolution
    (C) a company which profited not only by selling what it
        manufactured but by investments as well
    (D) a company that represents at its most advanced the modern
        factory system
    (E) a company that set its sights on the industrialization of
        western Europe

13. Which of the following is a generalization supported by informa-
    tion in the passage?
    (A) Since the eighteenth century, economic change has been
        characterized by the development of new sources of profit.
    (B) The Industrial Revolution did not significantly affect social
        life until the twentieth century.
    (C) At the end of the first stage of the Industrial Revolution, the
        American standard of living was remarkably high.
    (D) Unlike steam power and electric power, atomic power has
        not had economic effects.
    (E) The Industrial Revolution contributed to the wretched
        condition of the lower class.

    No one individual has influenced the course of public educa-
tion in the United States during the first half of the twentieth
century more than John Dewey. The founder of what has
become known as "progressive education," his views have been

widely acclaimed as coming from one of the greatest educators of modern times. To be sure, his ideas have never been universally accepted, and there have been critics who were bitterly opposed to his position. Nevertheless, his influence has been tremendous. For many years two of the best known institutions for teacher training in this country were dominated by his philosophy. His high standing as an educator has been recognized throughout the world, and many countries have sought his counsel and advice. His views were illustrated in the Experimental School at Chicago, which was under his direction, and they have been stated in his book *Democracy and Education,* one of his most popular publications.

Philosophy and education have been so closely related in Dewey's thought that it is scarcely possible to consider one apart from the other. The spirit of instrumentalism is the guiding factor in both, and the goal for each of them is the betterment of human society. Both repudiate the idea of authoritarian control and provide encouragement for creative thinking on the part of each individual. Both are democratic in the sense that they advocate equal opportunity for all people to develop the talents and capacities which are peculiar to them.

Dewey was critical of many of the ideas and practices that were recurrent in the schools of his day. One of these in particular was the "transmissive" concept of education. It conceived of education as a process of transmitting to the new generation of students the ideas and customs of the older generation. It employed the use of textbooks, the contents of which were to be memorized at least to the extent that the substance of the materials could be reproduced in an examination. This kind of procudure was, in Dewey's opinion, more of a hindrance than a help to the real purpose of an education, which was to enable students to think creatively for themselves.

Recognizing that intellectual interests were not the predominant ones that usually prevail among typical American students, Dewey believed that the schools should begin with the interests that they do have. People learn primarily by doing things and, therefore, students should be given projects on which to work. This will stimulate a desire to find out more about the objects with which they have been working, and the more they find out the greater will be their desire to extend their knowledge still further. It will lead them into new fields that are related to their original subject, and because of the organic relationship of different fields of knowledge to one another, the scope of their inquiries will be practically boundless. The information which they have gained in this manner will be in response to their own sense of inquiry rather than something that has been forced upon them by pressures from without.

The relationship between facts and their uses will be brought to light through this kind of an educational process. Students will be anxious to discover the uses that can be made of the objects about which they have studied for the satisfaction of human needs. They will observe, too, that information on any topic is never complete in the sense that the last or final word has been spoken concerning it. This should encourage them to keep an open mind, ever ready to change their views whenever it is necessary to do so in order to bring those views into harmony with newly discovered facts.

14. Which of the following is the most appropriate title for this passage?
    (A) Theories of Progressive Education in the Twentieth Century
    (B) John Dewey and the Experimental School at Chicago
    (C) Creative Thinking and Transmissive Teaching
    (D) Dewey's Philosophy of Education
    (E) Twentieth-Century Progress in Intellectual History

15. According to the passage, John Dewey would probably agree with which of the following statements?
    (A) Learning is not a result of obedient listening.
    (B) Students must memorize facts before they can put them to use.
    (C) Students should be writing textbooks rather than reading them.
    (D) Authoritarian control and creative thinking both have as their goal the betterment of human society.
    (E) The real purpose of education is difficult to determine.

16. We may conclude which of the following about the educational theories and practice that prevailed before Dewey's views became popular?
    (A) They accounted for the weaknesses in Dewey's own education.
    (B) They accounted for the large number of incompetent teachers at the time.
    (C) They were especially well known in Chicago.
    (D) They were consistent with the transmissive concept of education.
    (E) They helped to undermine American democracy.

17. The passage implies that a human characteristic which Dewey found absolutely essential to learning was
    (A) love   (D) memory
    (B) curiosity   (E) obedience
    (C) humor

In the life and works of Plato, Greek philosophy reached one of its highest points of achievement. He was one of the greatest minds of all ages, and the influence of his thinking can be seen throughout the entire history of the western world. Philosophers of every succeeding generation have studied and interpreted the content of his teachings. People from many different nations and races have written accounts and evaluations of his works, and they will continue to do so for generations yet to come. He was not only a great thinker but a prolific writer, and for this reason it is impossible within a brief amount of space to give more than a bare outline of a few major events in his life and writings.

He was born in 427 B.C. He came from an aristocratic family that had for a long time been identified with leadership in the city of Athens. He was named Aristocles, but because of his broad shoulders, high forehead, and success as an athlete, he was given the nickname "Plato," and it is by this name that he has become known to posterity.

His early education began under the supervision of well

chosen tutors who guided his instruction in the elementary disciplines, including gymnastics, music, reading, writing, and the study of numbers. After reaching the age of eighteen or thereabouts, he spent two years in military training, during which time special emphasis was given to the development and proper care of the body. This was followed by a more advanced period of study in which he gained familiarity with the earlier schools of Greek philosophy. He received instruction also from several of the more prominent Sophists, who were especially active at that time. Finally, he spent several years as a pupil of Socrates, whose influence on his own thinking outweighed that obtained from any other source.

Plato was ill at the time of Socrates' death, and this prevented him from being present when a group of close friends made their last visit to the prison. Because Socrates had been put to death under the auspices of the Athenian government and Plato was known as one of his most devoted disciples, he felt that it was expedient to leave Athens for a time. He went at first to Megara, where he carried on conversations with Euclid. He then made extensive journeys to Egypt, Cyrene, Crete, and southern Italy, thus obtaining direct contact with Pythagorean, Heraclitian, and Eleatic philosophies.

About 390 B.C., when Plato was approximately forty years old, he undertook an experiment in government. From his early youth he had always been interested in political affairs, and his observations had convinced him that only persons who are well educated should be entrusted with the power to rule over others. At Syracuse, on the coast of the island of Sicily, a friend and pupil by the name of Dion urged him to undertake the education of Dionysius, the tyrant of Syracuse. Dionysius appeared willing to take instruction from Plato, and this made it possible for Plato's theory of government to be tried out under actual conditions. The experiment was unsuccessful. Dionysius was not an apt pupil, and when Plato rebuked him for his stupidity, the tyrant retaliated by having Plato put in chains and sentenced to death. Dion used his influence to get the sentence changed, and Plato was made a slave. Soon afterward Anniceris purchased his freedom, and Plato was allowed to return to Athens.

18. The author of the passage would probably agree that Plato's *experiment in government* in Syracuse was
    (A) an unwise project from the start
    (B) more appropriate to the exploits of a youth than to a forty-year-old
    (C) an act of great courage but not great wisdom
    (D) unsuccessful only because Plato was a tactless teacher
    (E) a major event in the life of the Greek philosopher

19. We may conclude that Plato's decision to leave Athens after the death of Socrates was probably a result of
    (A) his anger at the Athenian government for their treatment of his teacher
    (B) his need to learn philosophies other than that of Socrates
    (C) his fear that the government might seek to imprison him as well
    (D) his love for exploring unknown regions
    (E) his shame at not being present when Socrates was put to death

20. The passage creates which of the following impressions of Plato's education and intellectual interests?
    (A) that his instruction as a youth was limited, but the interests he developed later were broad and varied
    (B) that his education provided a rich and comprehensive background, and his later intellectual pursuits were extensive
    (C) that deficiencies in his early education were counterbalanced by his extensive travel to intellectual centers of the ancient world
    (D) that he was too heavily influenced by Socrates in his youth, and he became a mature philosopher only because of Socrates' death
    (E) that despite his lack of traditional education, he was able to create a philosophy that stands as one of the greatest of all time

21. Which of the following statements strengthens the conclusion that Plato was a unique individual?
   (A) He was a philosopher in the ancient world.
   (B) He was born before the birth of Christ.
   (C) During his life, he was both an aristocrat and a slave.
   (D) He traveled widely.
   (E) He had a great interest in politics.

   No event in modern history so completely shocked the world as did the French Revolution—a revolution in which the radical cry of *Liberty! Equality! Fraternity!* for the masses challenged the protected interests of the privileged few. The effects were profound, for Europe and the world would never be the same.

   It began as an attempt by the leaders of the industrial and commercial classes to sweep aside the injustices and abuses of the Old Regime, but it soon swept away the French monarchy and allied all of Europe against the rising tide of French republicanism. In the process of fighting the coalitions of foreign armies, the newly formed citizen armies of France—the first in modern history—inaugurated modern warfare. As against the cautious maneuvering of small professional armies, transporting hundreds of tents and baggage for their officers, along with bread wagons and flour wagons to supplement the full ration of the soldier, the new warfare was a rapid movement of large armies carrying small supplies and living off the land.

   A great wave of enthusiasm for France and the Republic swept the French people. There was to be no compromising of republican principles at home or abroad. At home the hated royalists were to be stamped out, and abroad France would become the protector and backer of all revolutionaries, for all Europe, and all the world would become republican. These citizen armies gave the common man—formerly a "nobody" among the despised lowly masses—the opportunity to take to the battlefield on the side of justice, and the youth of France poured into the Republican armies—spurred on by the stirring "Marseillaise." Before that chant, and the columns of bayonet-wielding French infantrymen supported by massive artillery, the foreign professional armies were rolled back, and French armies penetrated far beyond the farthest advance of Louis XIV's troops.

Then, with the excesses of the Reign of Terror at home and a lack of capable and responsible leadership, French national morale faltered. The monarchical powers formed new coalitions to suppress the upstart Republic, and French armies were rolled back, their momentum stopped as they were placed on the defensive. The cause of republicanism seemed lost. It was at this crucial period of time that Napoleon Bonaparte—acknowledged by both critics and idolizers as the world's greatest military genius—appeared. Calling himself the "Son of the Revolution," he relentlessly sought fame on the battlefield and through the formation of the First French Empire. While being accused of the betrayal of the Republic, he in fact saved France from the forces of monarchical reaction for some twenty years, and in the process the revolutionary theme of the French Revolution was carried to all corners of Europe.

22. We may infer which of the following statements from the passage?
    (A) Military strategy in this century is modeled on Napoleonic principles.
    (B) Before the Revolution, the citizen armies of Europe were less powerful.
    (C) The circumstances of the modern world were influenced by the French Revolution.
    (D) Professional armies are never a match for citizen armies.
    (E) Kindness was a virtue much practiced during the French Revolution.

23. The passage suggests that if Napoleon had not taken over the leadership of France,
    (A) the Reign of Terror would not have occurred
    (B) the concept of "military genius" might still be foreign to us
    (C) a leader would have arisen out of the citizen armies of France
    (D) the causes of the Revolution, in their weakened state, would have failed
    (E) liberty and equality would never have become strong national virtues in countries outside of France

24. According to the passage, which of the following is true about French republicanism during the Revolution?
    (A) It began as an effort by the nobility to strengthen the forces of the Old Regime.
    (B) It was introduced by Napoleon at a time when the causes of the Revolution were faltering badly.
    (C) It stood in opposition not only to monarchical forces inside of France but also to armies from other European countries.
    (D) It provided the foundation for beliefs which are associated today with the Republican Party of the United States.
    (E) It depended upon the services of professional armies because citizens were occupied with political demonstrations rather than military activities.

25. Which of the following was one of the effects of the French Revolution?
    (A) The lower classes comprised the power structure of the French government.
    (B) The power of professional armies was established for generations to come.
    (C) Fast-moving and resourceful soldiers engaged in successful, repeated attacks on the French forces.
    (D) The royalists reemerged as a powerful force for stability in France and throughout Europe.
    (E) The First French Empire was replaced by a citizen government.

What is history? Is it a record of what has actually happened, or is it merely what someone thinks has happened? Does it include all that has happened or only those events that are relevant to some particular purpose? Does history change from time to time, or is it something that remains fixed for all time to come? What are historical facts? Do they exist in the mind of historians at the time when they are writing, or do historical facts belong to past events? Does the historical process as understood at the present time have a central or essential meaning? If it does, what is that meaning? Philosophy of history is a serious attempt to provide satisfactory answers to these questions, along with many others that are closely related to them. Obviously, the answers given to each of these questions will vary with the different philosophers who have written concerning them. No one is in possession of the final or absolute truth about history, and it is impossible for anyone to do more than formulate the particular view which seems at the time to be most nearly satisfactory. While there seems to be general agreement about what is meant when one speaks of the historical process as a whole, there is a great deal of disagreement about any possible meaning that it may have. There are some well-known thinkers who deny that history has any meaning. For them history is only a succession of events "full of sound and fury, signifying nothing." Other writers on the subject are convinced that history does have a meaning, although there is a wide difference of opinion about what that meaning is.

Skepticism concerning any meaningful interpretation of history has appeared at various times and places in the history of Western thought. It has not always taken the same form, for there are several different ways in which the essential idea may be expressed. One of these forms, known as historical nihilism, is an outright denial of any meaningful pattern or purpose in the historical process. Another form, frequently referred to as historical skepticism, neither affirms nor denies that history has a meaning but insists that it is impossible for anyone to know whether or not it has a meaning. A third form, which has been called historical subjectivism, asserts that any meaningful interpretation of history is something that exists only in the mind of the historian and does not refer to anything external to the human mind. All of these forms are opposed to the idea that there is any cosmic force or power that is directing the course of events.

26. The author introduces which of the following possibilities in the passage?
    (A) Not all of the events recorded in historical documents may actually have happened.
    (B) Although historians and philosophers may not be able to agree upon which particular facts are true, they find it relatively easy to agree upon the meaning of a particular series of events.
    (C) Responsible history is never influenced by the historian's imagination.
    (D) Those with the absolute truth about history find that it is a meaningless subject.
    (E) Meaningful events in an individual's everyday life are unlikely to ever be regarded as "historical."

27. Which statement below might have come from a historical nihilist, as defined in the passage?
    (A) We cannot claim that the events that preceded the Civil War *caused* it or even *might have caused* it.
    (B) The victory of the Northern armies in 1865 really began with events that occurred as early as 1863.
    (C) As a Confederate sympathizer, I view the conclusion of the Civil War as a victory for the South rather than a defeat.
    (D) There are three clear reasons that General Lee's forces were eventually overcome.
    (E) The defect of the South is analogous in some ways to the defeat of the British during the American Revolution.

28. One of the characteristics that historical nihilism, historical skepticism, and historical subjectivism share in common is
    (A) their concern for the importance of meaningful historical interpretation
    (B) their respect for the power of the human mind to make experience meaningful
    (C) their proposal that although facts may be controversial, we must accept the most reasonable ones
    (D) their claim that all historical reporting must be scrutinized carefully for truth value
    (E) their disbelief in the power of some superhuman force or "fate" to influence history

29. Which of the following is one purpose that the passage fulfills?
   (A) to argue for historical skepticism as the most reasonable view of historical events
   (B) to raise more questions than it answers
   (C) to repeat the same question in many different ways
   (D) to introduce some famous historical skeptics
   (E) to propose that a general agreement about the historical process is in order

The railroads played a key role in the settlement of the West. They provided relatively easy access to the region for the first time, and they also actively recruited farmers to settle there (the Santa Fe Railroad, for example, brought 10.000 German Mennonites to Kansas). The railroads are criticized for their part in settling the West too rapidly, with its resultant economic unrest. (After the Civil War the vast Great Plains area was settled all at once.) Of course there were abuses connected with building and operating the railroads, but it must be pointed out that they performed a useful service in extending the frontier and helping to achieve national unity.

The real tragedy of the rapid settlement of the Great Plains was the shameful way in which the American Indians were treated. Threatened with the destruction of their whole mode of life, the Indians fought back savagely against the white man's final thrust. Justice was almost entirely on the Indians' side. The land was clearly theirs; frequently their title was legally certified by a treaty negotiated with the federal government. The Indians, however, lacked the military force and the political power to protect this right. Not only did white men encroach upon the Indians' hunting grounds, but they rapidly destroyed the Indians' principal means of subsistence—the buffalo. It has been estimated that some 15 million buffalo roamed the plains in the 1860s. By 1869 the railroads had cut the herd in half, and by 1875 the southern herd was all but eliminated. By the middle of the 1880s the northern herd was also a thing of the past. Particularly galling to the Indians was the fact that the white man frequently killed the buffalo merely for sport, leaving the valuable carcass to rot in the sun.

The plains Indians were considered different from the Indians encountered by the English colonists on the Atlantic coast. Mounted on horses descended from those brought by the Spanish to Mexico many years before, typical plains Indians were fierce warriors who could shoot arrows with surprising accuracy while galloping at top speed. Although they quickly adapted themselves to the use of the rifle, the Indians were not equal to the firepower of the United States army and thus were doomed to defeat.

Theoretically, at least, the government tried to be fair to the Indians, but all too often the Indian agents were either too indifferent or corrupt to carry out the government's promises conscientiously. The army frequently ignored the Indian Bureau and failed to coordinate its policies with the civilians who were nominally in charge of Indian affairs. The settlers hated and feared the Indians and wanted them exterminated. This barbaric attitude is certainly not excusable, but it is understandable in the context of the times.

30. The author's attitude toward the treatment of American Indians by whites is one of
    (A) qualified regret
    (B) violent anger
    (C) strong disapproval
    (D) objective indifference
    (E) unfair bias

31. The author implies which of the following about the forces at work during the settlement of the Great Plains?
    (A) The federal government represented the moral use of law.
    (B) Justice was overcome by military firepower.
    (C) Attempts by the government to be fair were rejected by the Indians
    (D) The settlers' hatred and fear was offset by the Indians' attempts at kindness.
    (E) The Indians and the white settlers shared a sporting interest in the hunting of buffalo

32. Which of the following is concrete evidence that the white settlers did not need the buffalo for their own subsistence, as did the Indians?
    (A) More than half of the great buffalo herd had disappeared by 1869.
    (B) Nearly fifteen million buffalo were killed within twenty years.
    (C) Buffalo carcasses were left rotting in the sun by whites.
    (D) The railroad brought necessary food and supplies to the white settlers from the East.
    (E) The white settlers had their own hunting grounds separate from the Indians'.

33. What is the point of the comparison between plains Indians and the Indians encountered on the Atlantic coast?
    (A) The Atlantic coast Indians were not as abused by white settlers.
    (B) Because they were considerably better warriors than the Atlantic coast Indians, the plains Indians were a match for the United States military.
    (C) If Indians such as those on the Atlantic coast had populated the plains, the bloodshed of the white settlement would have been lessened.
    (D) The Indians encountered by English colonists posed no violent threat to the colonists.
    (E) The Atlantic coast Indians were unfamiliar with horses.

34. Which of the following characteristics of the passage suggests that the abuse of the Indians is a more significant topic for the author than the beneficial role of the railroads?
    (A) the statement that the railroads *are criticized for their part in settling the West too rapidly*
    (B) the amount of discussion devoted to the abuse of the Indians
    (C) the reliance on statistical details in both the first and second paragraphs
    (D) the very brief mention of the migration of German Mennonites
    (E) the perception that the achievement of national unity was one of the services that the railroad performed

The study of human population is known as demography. Demography, as a branch of sociology, concerns itself with the three variables of fertility, mortality, and migration. It is also focused upon the composition and distribution of population and its allied characteristics. At a larger level, it encompasses the relationships of nations with regard to important population variables; for instance, most nations are concerned with the rapid increase (and the potential military superiority this may give) of population in other countries.

Above all, the study of population must invariably involve social and cultural factors as an integral part of its analysis. Many population experts prior to World War II learned from bitter experience that it was not sufficient to construct future population estimates from antecedent trends. A host of very low estimates (some of which actually predicted a decline in population by 1970) were proffered in the late 1930s, which proved to be very far from the mark. The subsequent "baby-boom" in the years after the war proved long lasting and pervasive—it was not until 1957 that fertility began to decline again.

Fertility is generally measured by crude birth rates, which is simply the number of births occurring in a given year per 1,000 people. As an overall figure and a quick synopsis of the general fertility in a population, the crude birth rate is an acceptable concept to use. It can be misleading, however, when comparisons are made from one country to another. It is entirely possible for country A to have a higher crude birth rate in comparison to country B, but at the same time have a *lower* rate of actual births than country B. In essence, country A could have a larger proportion of its population in the childbearing ages, while country B does not have; yet, the women of country A in the childbearing ages may have a *lower* rate of childbirth in comparison to the women of childbearing ages in country B, who make up a smaller proportion of the country's population.

Mortality is also measured by a crude rate, termed the death rate. As with crude birth rates, there is room for error in interpretation of such statistics. One country can be healthier than another but have a higher crude death rate, since a greater proportion of its population is in the advanced ages. To rectify such ambiguities, age-specific birth and death rates have been introduced, especially when comparisons between countries are being made. For example, a comparative age-specific birth rate would be the number of births per 1,000 women aged fifteen to forty-four (in the childbearing ages). Such considerations control for the effect of differential age distributions from one society to the next.

35. The passage implies which of the following general conclusions about demography?
    (A) Although demographers are concerned with the variables of fertility, mortality, and migration, other variables are irrelevant.
    (B) For a demographer, the terms *birth rate* or *death rate* require further definition that specifies the methods of measurement and analysis.
    (C) Population estimates being prepared now are likely to be absolutely reliable predictors of population change.
    (D) Demography was a crude science prior to World War II.
    (E) Sociologists are not, as a rule, interested in demography.

36. A demographer who wishes to correct for possible inaccuracies that result when measuring crude birth rates may do which of the following?
    (A) compare the birth rate with the death rate
    (B) check the estimates of population prepared by earlier analysts
    (C) use a sample of larger than 1,000 people
    (D) specify a particular age group in the population being measured
    (E) first perform a "quick synopsis of the general fertility" in the population

37. Which of the following is the most appropriate substitute for the use of the term *rectify* in the fourth paragraph?
    (A) correct   (D) advance
    (B) revise   (E) question
    (C) help

38. We may infer from the passage that a nation wishing to eventually increase the size of its armed forces might do which of the following?
    (A) commission a demographic study of enemy nations
    (B) calculate the age-specific death rate that occurs in its armed forces
    (C) encourage an increase in its population
    (D) look skeptically upon demographic predictions of population growth
    (E) offer greater financial benefits to those who join the armed forces

39. According to the passage, the future rate of population growth may not be reliably calculated with reference only to
    (A) the crude birth rate
    (B) the military interests of a country
    (C) the past
    (D) patterns of migration
    (E) a present decline in fertility

LONGER PASSAGES—CHALLENGING

Gnosticism was both a religious and a philosophical movement. It did not have its origin in Christian times nor were its teachings confined to Christian circles. In many respects it resembled the mystery religions, inasmuch as its main concern was salvation from this present world, which was regarded as essentially evil. This salvation could not be accomplished by efforts on the part of human beings alone but only through the aid of supernatural powers that would interfere on humans' behalf. Because the Pauline interpretation of Christianity resembled the mystery cults in so many ways some of the Gnostics found it congenial to their way of thinking and came to regard themselves as Christians. Two of the more prominent members of this group were Valentinus and Marcion, both of whom lived in the city of Rome. Among the beliefs that were generally accepted by the Gnostics we may mention the following.

(1) The universe was conceived as a thoroughgoing dualistic affair in which matter and spirit, good and evil, light and darkness were not only opposite in nature but forever at war with one another. The dualism went somewhat beyond that of Plato and was more like that which characterized Persian Zoroastrianism.

(2) The Gnostics were pessimistic with reference to this present world. There was no hope for its becoming any better, and salvation meant an escape from it. Salvation was not for the flesh but only for the spirit.

(3) Like the neo-Platonists they could not accept the idea of the supreme God coming into direct contact with matter, which is evil. They therefore developed the idea of a series of emanations which they called *aeons* coming forth from the deity but decreasing in potentiality the farther they were removed from the deity. Eventually one of them was far enough away to endure contact with matter, and it was this one that was responsible for bringing the world into existence.

(4) Into this world, which is a combination of matter and spirit, there entered into some souls sparks of divinity which produce a longing for return to the spiritual realm from which they came. These souls do not feel at home in an earthly abode. They are pilgrims and strangers waiting for a better kind of existence in a life to come.

(5) *Gnosis,* which is the Greek word for *knowledge* and from which the term *gnosticism* is derived, stands for a special kind of knowledge which is essential for salvation. This knowledge is not obtained by a thinking process nor is it derived directly from the senses. It is a kind of intuitive knowledge which is imparted to the believer from a supernatural source.

(6) The Gnostics were not in complete agreement among themselves concerning the proper methods to be followed in preparation for salvation. Some of them advocated a strict type of asceticism in order to overcome the demands of the flesh. Others advocated an opposite course yielding completely to the demands of the flesh on the grounds that the flesh was unimportant and the only thing that mattered was the life of the spirit.

1. According to the passage, the Gnostics' concept of the universe in terms of dualisms is represented by each of the following pairs of terms *except*
   (A) matter/spirit
   (B) good/evil
   (C) faith/reason
   (D) light/darkness
   (E) earthly life/afterlife

2. The author implies which of the following about the relationship of Gnosticism to other philosophies and religions?
   (A) Gnosticism stands apart as a unique system of beliefs.
   (B) Christianity and Gnosticism are not easily compared.
   (C) Gnosticism is comparable in some respects to both Greek philosophy and Persian Zoroastrianism.
   (D) Roman mythology was the basis of beliefs of some of the early Gnostics, especially Valentinus and Marcion.
   (E) Modern religions have ignored Gnosticism completely.

3. Which of the following examples from the passage best illustrates the tendency of some Gnostics to prepare for salvation in a different manner from others?
   (A) different attitudes toward the demands of the flesh
   (B) adaptation of the Pauline interpretation of Christianity
   (C) disagreements between Valentinus and Marcion
   (D) disagreements among the Gnostics about the definition of knowledge
   (E) the tendency of some Gnostics to prefer earthly existence to spiritual salvation

4. The Gnostic version of the creation of the world may be summarized as follows:
   (A) God created matter immediately and directly, but this was his only direct contact with matter.
   (B) Enduring contact with matter was impossible for the deity, so the creation of the world was done by his representative.
   (C) An emanation from God rather than God himself created the matter of our earthly abode.
   (D) In a duel between matter and spirit, matter was victorious and the earth was thus created.
   (E) The world was created by the forces of evil and remains completely separate from the supreme deity.

5. The passage supplies information that would answer which of the following questions?
   (A) What was the attitude of the Gnostics toward the earthly world?
   (B) What were the practices of the mystery cults?
   (C) To what extent were Gnostic beliefs approved by early Christians?
   (D) Are there any traces of Gnosticism in the modern world?
   (E) Why did Christianity become a more popular religion than Gnosticism?

6. Which of the following characteristics of Gnosticism is most
   emphasized in the passage?
   (A) the Gnostics' adaptation of neo-Platonism
   (B) the concern of the Gnostics with salvation
   (C) the definition and origin of *gnosis*
   (D) the Gnostic distinction between three types of knowledge
   (E) the influence of the more prominent members of the Gnostic
   religion

   The function of a manager in a large corporation is to handle
unplanned-for problems. The manager must define the problem,
generate some possible solutions, come to a decision, and take
the appropriate action. Some of these steps may be delegated to
other executive personnel, but the manager always remains in a
position of power within the organizational structure. Manager
training usually begins with job rotation through the key depart-
ments of the company, providing an overview of company
functions and an assessment of where the management trainee
might best fit in. Problem-centered group training develops
managerial skills by the case-work method. The experience of
senior management may be extended by problem-solving inter-
views with personnel psychologists and also by role-playing and
group training, which are designed to make managers more
sensitive to the problems and feelings of the company's personnel.
   For both managers and workers, fatigue effects show up in
either decreased output or increased errors or both. Decreased
output occurs where the job consists of physical effort or requires
sustained accuracy, in which case it takes longer to do as much
work. Increased errors occur where workers have no control over
the rate at which they work. Fatigue manifests itself physiologi-
cally or as a change in motivation to perform. Fatigue effects can
best be overcome by limiting the periods of time of work through
breaks and a shortened work day.
   A modern company may be regarded as a human-machine
system. In human-machine systems, three functions must be
assigned to either humans or machines. Sensing is best done by
people if the signals are within the range of the human senses,

but must, of course, be done by machines if the signals are in ranges outside of human detectability. Data processing is superior by machine if it involves handling large amounts of routine information, but it is better done by people if there is a need for flexibility in information processing. Control systems are best left to machines except at short, critical intervals for which advance programming is difficult or impossible.

The design of displays must take into account the rate at which information can be absorbed in any one sense modality. Overloading may be avoided by presenting information in more than one modality—for example, by presenting warning signals by means of buzzers while simultaneously giving quantitative information by a series of dials. Display systems may be either pictorial or symbolic. Pictorial displays are quickly interpreted and require no training for use; symbolic displays are simple, flexible, and more accurate. Indicators in symbolic displays may be qualitative, quantitative, or of the check-reading (on-off) type. Dials as quantitative indicators may be displayed as round, semicircular, open-window, vertical, or horizontal; the open-window type has been shown to be most accurately read. Where many dials are to be read rapidly, the display is patterned so that information is given as deviation from a standard position that all dials have in normal setting.

Control devices parallel indicator devices. Some are on-off, some are position controls, and some are continuous controls, in which changes in what is controlled are proportional to the changes in the control device—for example, a car's steering wheel. Controls should be placed so that there is minimal chance for error, particularly in the context of the operator's prior training (negative transfer of a motor skill). Control handles may be coded by shape so that operators can distinguish between them by touch.

7. Which of the following is the best title for this passage?
    (A) Varieties of Fatigue in the Corporate Workplace
    (B) The Manager's Overview of Company Functions
    (C) The Corporate Functions of People and Machines
    (D) Managerial Control Over Machine Systems
    (E) The Function of Machines and Their Management

8. With reference to the passage, we may conclude that an American driver who experiences difficulty operating a British automobile, with a steering wheel on the right, is illustrating which of the following problems?

(A) inability to properly interpret dials on the dashboard
(B) lack of control over the speed of operation
(C) negative prior experience with the effective use of motor skills
(D) control placement inconsistent with the operator's prior training
(E) the challenge of a control handle with an unfamiliar shape

9. We may infer which of the following about the skills that a senior manager may possess?

(A) They are instrumental in the prevention of the fatigue that workers suffer.
(B) They are identical to the skills required of personnel psychologists.
(C) They are restricted to expertise within a single department in the company.
(D) They include sensitivity to the problems and feelings of individuals.
(E) They are usually not acquired through group instruction.

10. According to the passage, people are superior to machines when performing which functions?

(A) sounding warning signals when a situation becomes hazardous
(B) processing large quantities of routine information
(C) detecting unusual signals and serving as individual "control systems"
(D) sensing signals within a human range and processing certain types of data
(E) adapting to a rapidly increasing demand for output

11. The author's primary purpose is to
    (A) present information that any manager with experience would be expected to know
    (B) suggest that workers are treated with less respect than managers
    (C) survey a number of aspects relevant to working in a company
    (D) contrast the problems of managers with those of workers
    (E) argue that display design is a crucial factor in any company

12. The author's attitude toward this subject may be described as
    (A) uneasy skepticism   (D) violent objection
    (B) subtle annoyance   (E) plain objectivity
    (C) consistent caution

In most societies, culture is transmitted through the kin group. The supposedly voluntary associations are dependent on kin groups for most of their membership. For example, a young man joins an association to which a close relative of his belongs, the latter acting as the young man's sponsor. In stratified societies, however, there is a reliance upon the use of voluntary associations for the furtherance of culture. Voluntary associations are prevalent in the United States.

In Samoa, young unmarried and untitled males belong to an association called *Amauga*, which virtually constitutes a communal labor force. Young girls and wives of untitled males belong to the *Aualuma*. The major function of these two associations is ceremonial. Titled males belong to the *Fono*, an association with ritualistic and political functions.

Members of an age-set share mutual rights and obligations throughout their lives. They support and help each other. For example, a group of adolescent boys will form an age-set of warriors. After the boys marry and establish a family, thus becoming responsible members of the community, their specific age-set will function as a political unit, a council of elders serving political ends. Age-sets are prevalent in East African pastoral societies.

Among the general characteristics of a social class, in addition to the fact that status is ranked and that each class has its own subculture, are the possession of a dialect, distinctive housing and clothing, and differing etiquettes. A social class molds an individual's behavior patterns and serves as a reference in judging other people's conduct. Marriage tends to be endogamous (confined to the tribe or social class), membership in a class being inherited. However, membership must be validated. It should be noted that upward social mobility may be rewarded in some societies. But downward mobility never is.

Some societies have a system of pseudo-castes. A *pseudocaste* occupies a restricted place in a society. It is low in the social rank, its members being forced into endogamy and having a limited choice of occupation. An example is the Japanese Eta group, whose members are required to live in segregated areas, slums and suburbs, performing menial and undesirable jobs. Actually, Etas are social outcastes, like the pariahs of India. *Outcaste* means that the members of a group are considered to be outside of the recognized castes of a society—truly beyond the pale of human company, as it were.

The Indian caste system is complicated by the vagueness of the caste structures and the simultaneous specificity of the local subcastes or *jats*. A theoretical totality of the castes does not exist in any concrete form. Therefore, castes are classified as reference groups (like social class). On the other hand, subcastes function as corporate groups (complete with a caste council).

Affiliation in a totemic group may be inherited unilineally. In some parts of Australia, one is a member of a specific totem on the basis of where one's mother was walking at the time she believes conception occurred. Totemic groups are often exogamous (consisting of associations *outside* the tribe or caste) and are associated with some animal, plant, or object believed to possess supernatural powers.

13. The passage supports which of the following statements?
   (A) Members of the same class are unlikely to share similar tastes in clothes.
   (B) No society admires upper-class members who join the lower class.
   (C) A corporation is a group that cannot be based upon kinship.
   (D) Behavior patterns provide little evidence of an individual's social class.
   (E) Individuals who claim membership in a particular class tend to be believed.

14. The content of the passage may be summarized as follows:
   (A) An individual who belongs to one social group is prohibited from joining another.
   (B) From Polynesia to India and Australia, kin groups are the sources of culture.
   (C) Different systems of association prevail across different societies.
   (D) The laws of association that define any society are present in many regions.
   (E) Social groups in every culture are similar to the Indian caste system.

15. The author implies that the members of the same age-set in an East African pastoral society
   (A) tend to model their behavior after the elders in their society
   (B) are not representative of the behavior of age-sets in other parts of the world
   (C) may either accept or reject the social responsibilities for which they are eligible
   (D) are more likely to quarrel with each other than to cooperate
   (E) will serve a series of social and communal functions as they grow older

16. Which of the following does the passage mention as evidence that the members of a pseudo-caste are forced into living only with members of their own kind?
    (A) Samoan Amaugas   (D) East African elders
    (B) Japanese Etas   (E) American fraternities
    (C) Indian pariahs

17. The discussion in the second paragraph of associations that operate in Samoa best supports which of the following statements?
    (A) Every life task in Samoa is connected with a particular association.
    (B) Unmarried males tend to be untitled as well.
    (C) Unmarried males are prohibited from expressing political opinions.
    (D) One of the functions that may be served by an association is sexual segregation.
    (E) There is no association for the daughters and wives of titled males.

18. Which of the following is true of the Indian caste system, according to the passage?
    (A) The subcastes are difficult to define.
    (B) India is the most famous example of a caste society.
    (C) The structure of the castes is neither simple nor clear.
    (D) Upward mobility is impossible.
    (E) Individuals who belong to a subcaste are often outcastes as well.

Money is anything that is in general use in the purchase of goods and services and in the discharge of debts. Money may also be defined as an evidence of debt owed by society. The money supply in the United States consists of currency (paper money), coins, and demand deposits (checking accounts). Currency and coins are government-created money, whereas demand deposits are bank-created money. Of these three components of our money supply, demand deposits are by far the most important. Thus, most of our money supply is invisible, intangible, and abstract.

The two most important inherent attributes that money must possess in a modern credit economy are acceptability and stability. In earlier times in the evolution of money and monetary institutions in the United States, the attributes of divisibility, portability, and visibility were important. The two legal attributes of "legal tender" and "standard money" are not of as much importance today as in the past.

The four functions that money often performs are (1) standard of value, (2) medium of exchange, (3) store of value, and (4) standard of deferred payment. In a modern specialized economy, (2) and, most especially, (1) are the most important of these.

Although it is agreed that the value of money has fallen in the United States over time, there are three in part conflicting theories of value that have been advanced to explain this phenomenon: the commodity, quantity, and income theories. Most economists today espouse either the second or, more typically, the third of these. Any money can retain its value as long as its issuance is limited; it need not have a commodity backing. Inflation or rising prices have been explained by demand and/or supply theories in recent years, although historically the former has been thought to provide the more satisfactory explanation.

Our presently circulating coins are credit money or token money in that the market value of metal in the coin is worth less than the face (or mint) value of the coins. Gresham's Law—that is, bad money tends to drive out good money—explains why coins with a greater market value than mint value cease circulating. Most of the paper money in the United States consists of Federal Reserve notes; the remaining minor types of paper money are called treasury currency. Demand deposits are bank-created money, the supply of which is limited to any single bank by the amount of its total legal reserves. If it lends more than the amount of its excess reserves it would have an adverse clearing balance. Modern fractional reserve banking grew out of the experiences of early goldsmiths who found that 100 percent reserves were not needed. With a reserve requirement ratio of say 20 percent, the banking system as a whole could expand its demand deposits in a 5:1 ratio to its reserves. A monopoly bank could operate as does the entire banking system, since being the only bank it is, in effect, the entire banking system. If some money leaks out of the banking system, its coefficient of credit expansion is reduced from the 5:1 ratio indicated above.

The Federal Reserve, or Fed, is a central bank whose prime function is to monitor and control the nation's money supply and credit through monetary policy in the attempt to stifle inflation, promote economic growth with high employment, and help with the sale of government bonds. It is not clear that the Fed has always understood its powers and purposes. It has had much more success in helping with the sale of government bonds and in performing its service functions than in promoting growth and maintaining stability. The Fed's three main quantitative weapons, in order of importance, are (1) open market operations, (2) discount rate policy, and (3) changes in legal reserve requirements. It has at times had some moderate success in using some qualitative controls as well.

19. From the author's discussion of the importance of *acceptability* and *stability,* we may infer which of the following?
   (A) Over time, the relative importance of certain attributes of money changes.
   (B) The phrase *legal tender* on currency may be disregarded.
   (C) The evolution of money and monetary institutions is drawing to a close.
   (D) Acceptability and stability are important in a modern credit economy.
   (E) The modern money supply is in danger of becoming unstable.

20. One of the author's purposes in this passage is to
   (A) explain the misuse of money that results from misunderstanding the economy
   (B) argue that Gresham's Law needs to be revised
   (C) question whether the national money supply is really related to the actions of the Fed
   (D) compare the modern status of money to its status at earlier times
   (E) survey the definitions of money that were popular with the early goldsmiths

21. In saying that *most of our money supply is invisible, intangible, and abstract,* the author is referring to the fact that
    (A) banks are often reluctant to supply currency and coin in exchange for a check
    (B) checking accounts are not *in general use in the purchase of goods and services*
    (C) information about the balances in checking accounts is not publicly available
    (D) the balance in a checking account is not an actual stack of currency or pile of coins sitting inside a bank
    (E) the balance in an individual's checking account is in a constant state of fluctuation

22. According to the passage, fractional reserve banking is a practice in which
    (A) the metal value of a coin is a fraction of its mint value
    (B) 100 percent reserves are required only in certain federally defined cases
    (C) a fraction of a bank's reserves *leaks out* of the system
    (D) credit expansion reduces tangible reserves to an unacceptable fraction
    (E) the currency and coin a bank has on hand is less than the total of its demand deposits

23. When explaining conflicting theories of value, the author is assuming which of the following?
    (A) Economists are rarely in agreement about fluctuations in money value.
    (B) A change in the prevailing theory affects the value of money.
    (C) Those who espouse the "commodity" theory of value are certainly wrong.
    (D) It is possible to explain fluctuations of money value with economic theories.
    (E) The question of whether the value of money has fallen is a theoretical rather than practical question.

24. The author of this passage might be characterized as a(n)
    (A) disgruntled banker
    (B) argumentative spectator
    (C) interested lay person
    (D) informed analyst
    (E) curious investor

The doctrine of economic determinism may be regarded as the main key to an understanding of the Marxian philosophy. It explains his conception of history and furnishes the ground or basis of his predictions concerning the failures of capitalism and its replacement by socialism of the communistic variety.

Marx proposed that there is a cause for everything that happens and that this is just as true for the changes that take place in society as it is for those events which occur in the fields of the physical and biological sciences. It was Marx's conviction that five epochs of history were brought about through the operation of the inexorable "law of motion," which determines the course of events quite apart from any conscious choice on the part of human beings.

The determinism of the historical process must be distinguished from the kind of mechanical determinism which is illustrated in the natural sciences such as physics and chemistry. The difference lies in the fact that in the mechanical sciences it is possible for persons to choose the conditions that will bring about the results which they desire to obtain. For example, if one wishes to produce a certain quantity of ice, one can arrange the circumstances that will bring it about. This cannot be done in connection with the changes that take place in the social order. Marx held that there is an inner contradiction within the very nature of things and that this is what produces the dialectical movements in history. Every thesis gives rise to its antithesis, and these in turn produce the synthesis which constitutes the next stage in the evolutionary march of history.

It is the material order of things from which all that exists is derived. This includes inorganic matter, plants, animals, human life, society, and consciousness. Matter is not regarded as one specific kind of substance, such as was held by the ancient atomists. It manifests itself in many different ways, one of which is the conscious life of human beings. All mental activity is believed to be a by-product of matter. In the lowest forms of life, mental activity is absent. It developed gradually as the ancestors of the human race learned to use their limbs, to walk erect, and to use tools for the satisfaction of their needs. The contents of the material order which are most responsible for what people think are the factors of production and the social relationships involved in their use and distribution.

The factors of production are the raw materials needed for food, clothing, shelter, and protection from enemies. The gathering of these materials and transforming them into objects which are suitable for human consumption requires the use of tools, the development of skilled workmanship, and the cooperation of individuals who share in the benefits of their labors. Circumstances such as the scarcity of raw materials, the ownership of tools, and different attitudes on the part of individuals involved, create problems of relationship which sooner or later are bound to have an effect on the type of social organization which will prevail.

The most important factor having to do with the social relationships of those engaged in the production and distribution of comsumable goods is the ownership of property. This is evident from a survey of the changing epochs in human history. In primitive communal societies there is no private ownership of property. The resources of nature are available to all, but the ability to make use of them demands successful competition with others. Under the system of slavery the slaveowner had possession of the means of production, including the slave, who did most of the manual labor. In feudalism the serf usually owned the tools used but that was about all. Serfs were forced to sell their services to the landowner for whatever price they could get. In the capitalistic system there is neither slavery nor serfdom, but at least in theory all individuals are free to gain as much for themselves as they are able to do under the circumstances. Each of these systems has contained within itself the needs of its own destruction, and it was on this basis that Marx predicted the failure of the capitalistic system.

The change from one system of social organization to another is not the result of planning or of rational design on the part of the people who are involved. It is due to the contradictions or oppositions that are inherent in the material order. In order to survive, it becomes necssary to develop new and more complicated tools of production. These in turn call for a division of labor and the exercise of different skills, along with an increased amount of organization for carrying on the work of production and of distribution. Ownership and management become more and more powerful, and the lot of the laborers becomes dependent on factors over which they have little or no control.

The class struggle under capitalism is brought about by the division of society into two classes known as the owners and the workers, or what the communists call the bourgeoise and the proletariat. The interests of these two groups or classes are necessarily opposed to each other. This is due to the fact that, while the price of labor is governed by the law of supply and demand, the goods that have been produced by labor can be sold for more than the cost of the labor. Assuming, as Marx did, that the value of any piece of goods is what it costs to produce it, the owners are able to create *surplus value* for themselves. The exploitation of the workers by the owners will continue until the lot of the poor becomes so wretched that they will overthrow the system and create a new order in which they will be in control.

The class struggle, which has been responsible for the different epochs in the historical process, will continue until capitalism is replaced by a socialistic communism. This is the goal of the historical process, but it does not imply any consciousness of the goal on the part of some supernatural power. It is merely the logical development of dialectic inherent in the material order. It will, however, mark the end or cessation of the class conflict because the system of communism will be that of a classless society. Private ownership of property will be abolished, and all individuals will contribute according to their abilities and will receive according to their needs.

25. With which of the following statements about the Marxian philosophy would the author most likely agree?
    (A) The needs of certain individuals should receive priority over the needs of others.
    (B) Religious faith is not at all essential to the movement of history toward classlessness.
    (C) The material order of things is subordinated to the spiritual order of things.
    (D) Marx's conception of a historical movement toward revolution and a classless society is outdated.
    (E) Although private ownership will eventually be abolished, an upper class and a lower class will remain fixtures of society as they have through the ages.

26. According to the passage, a Marxist would probably agree with which of the following explanations of why the capitalist system contains its own *seeds of destruction?*
    (A) Capitalists tend to be more greedy than either slaveowners or feudal landowners.
    (B) As capitalists compete for property, they are likely to destroy one another.
    (C) Owners will eventually eliminate the need for laborers, and production will cease.
    (D) Any individual is free to appropriate a disproportionately large share of property.
    (E) The absence of slavery or serfdom makes capitalism appear to be a fairer system than it is.

27. The *doctrine of economic determinism* may be summarized as follows:
    (A) As human beings evolve, their mental powers change the state of the economy.
    (B) Even if members of the proletariat are determined to prevail, they will not succeed.
    (C) The progress of history is determined by the economic theory most favored by the wealthy.
    (D) The factors that determine changes in the economy are mainly within human control.
    (E) Changes in economic conditions proceed under their own power, without human control.

28. According to the passage, which of the following is a basic problem that results from owners' creation of *surplus value?*
    (A) It is a throwback to the tendency of feudal lords to exploit serfs.
    (B) It does not contribute to the probability of a workers' revolt.
    (C) Labor is compensated with less than the value of their work.
    (D) Owners do not invest the surplus value in labor improvements.
    (E) It is impossible to determine what amount of surplus is most beneficial to the workers.

29. With reference to the *dialectical movement of history*, if the exploitation of workers by capitalists constitutes a *thesis* and the overthrow of the bourgeoise constitutes *antithesis*, the resultant *classless society* may be termed
    (A) socialism   (D) the end
    (B) synthesis   (E) equitable
    (C) communism

30. Which of the following is a possible criticism of the Marxian proposition that a classless society will mark the *end or cessation of the class conflict* that has existed through history?
    (A) The dialectical movement of history will pose a new antithesis to the classless society.
    (B) Property without private owners cannot be managed efficiently.
    (C) A communist system is likely to be overcome by different systems in other countries.
    (D) The material order of things is relatively unimportant to a classless society.
    (E) Other types of conflict unrelated to a class structure will continue to exist.

31. The author proposes which of the following as a Marxian
    definition of human consciousness?
    (A) It did not exist until humans began using tools.
    (B) It is a less specific kind of substance than is matter.
    (C) It is equivalent to matter in the Marxian conception of
        existence.
    (D) It is a result of the existence of matter.
    (E) It aspires to greater awareness of ethical responsibility.

ANSWER KEY FOR READING COMPREHENSION PRACTICE

Brief Passages	Longer Passages Intermediate Difficulty		Longer Passages Challenging
1. B	1. B	21. C	1. C
2. E	2. E	22. C	2. C
3. C	3. C	23. D	3. A
4. E	4. B	24. C	4. C
5. A	5. C	25. A	5. A
6. B	6. A	26. A	6. B
7. D	7. A	27. A	7. C
8. B	8. A	28. E	8. D
9. C	9. C	29. B	9. D
10. E	10. D	30. C	10. D
11. D	11. A	31. B	11. C
12. C	12. C	32. C	12. E
13. E	13. A	33. D	13. B
14. B	14. D	34. B	14. C
15. A	15. A	35. B	15. E
	16. D	36. D	16. B
	17. B	37. A	17. D
	18. E	38. C	18. C
	19. C	39. C	19. A
	20. B		20. D
			21. D
			22. E
			23. D
			24. D
			25. B
			26. D
			27. E
			28. C
			29. B
			30. A
			31. D

ANSWERS TO READING COMPREHENSION PRACTICE

BRIEF PASSAGES

1. (B) The passage states that *persecution ... has considerably decreased in the twentieth century,* which implies that persecution was more widespread previous to this century.

2. (E) Although other choices may be *suggested* by the information in the passage, only choice (E) summarizes the author's overall point.

3. (C) This choice is completely irrelevant to the information in the passage, which discusses *American* families only.

4. (E) Each therapy is associated with some form of self-expression. Choice (C) may be relevant to psychodrama only.

5. (A) By mentioning *reactions they are otherwise forbidden to show,* the author assumes that some children hide their true reactions.

6. (B) All other choices were stated by the passage. The word *all* in choice (B) makes the statement untrue. We cannot assume that brainwashing was practiced on *every* captured soldier.

7. (D) This choice is supported directly by the first sentence of the passage.

8. (B) The passage uses examples from everyday life to illustrate the different sources of frustration. Choices (C) and (D) are not addressed in the passage. Choices (A) and (E) are conclusions not supported by the passage.

9. (C) *Some radical change ... to meet a social norm* implies a more socially acceptable appearance. Choice (D) is contradictory, and the other choices are unsupported conclusions.

10. (E) This statement is implied by the last sentence of the passage.

11. (D) The passage compares the relatively small proportion of Americans voting to *citizens of most European countries.*

12. (C) Each of the other choices generalizes beyond the information actually given in the passage.

13. (E) *Summary* is the key word here. It refers clearly to the essential characteristic of the passage: it surveys, or summarizes, the writing of the Constitution.

14. (B) The author emphasizes that people make facts meaningful: *Facts do not speak; people do.*

15. (A) Because people *want . . . interpretation or evaluation,* they *will require philosophies.* Each of the other choices is clearly irrelevant or contradictory.

LONGER PASSAGES—INTERMEDIATE DIFFICULTY

1. (B) The author states that moral questions *cannot be settled by . . . the natural sciences* or by *observation and experiment.*

2. (E) The passage states that some teach that the application of morality *to particular situations is the work of reason.* Choices (A) and (C) contradict information in the passage, and choices (B) and (D) are statements irrelevant to the question.

3. (C) Choices (A) and (D) are too specific, choice (E) is too general, and choice (B) contradicts the fifth sentence of the passage in that moral philosophy involves an attempt to understand rather than simply to formulate questions.

4. (B) *Intuition is a way of knowing through the feelings,* a type of *direct and immediate experience* that is different from *thinking* or the *work of reason.*

5. (C) Each of the other choices describes a secondary or subordinate purpose of the author, but only choice (C) is comprehensive enough to cover the *primary* purpose.

6. (A) In order to support the statement that *no society is an "island unto itself,"* the author mentions the plight of the North

American Indians. None of the other choices is relevant to the focus of the question.

7. (A) Choices (B), (C), and (E) reach conclusions beyond the scope of the passage, and choice (D) contradicts the final sentence of the second paragraph.

8. (A) A successful change must appear to be *innocent and harmless* (fifth paragraph). The passage contradicts choice (B), and the other choices are not addressed by the passage.

9. (C) The author states that *change is an inescapable, ever-present fact of life* and supports this opinion/attitude repeatedly throughout the passage.

10. (D) This choice is supported by the first paragraph of the passage. Choices (A) and (C) are irrelevant to information in the passage; choices (B) and (E) are contradictory.

11. (A) Each of the other choices requires information beyond the scope of the passage. Choice (A) summarizes the types of revolutionary changes described by the author.

12. (C) The United States Steel Corporation is discussed as an example of the *development of finance capitalism*.

13. (A) Both the third and fourth paragraphs discuss changes in sources of profit, changes that coincided with the effects of the Industrial Revolution. Each of the other choices is irrelevant to the passage.

14. (D) Each of the other choices is either too broad and general or too specific and limited to adequately cover the information in the passage.

15. (A) Dewey believed that *people learn primarily by doing things,* so he would probably agree with this choice, which rejects a type of *passive* learning.

16. (D) The passage associates the *transmissive concept of education* with *many of the ideas and practices that were current in the schools* of Dewey's day.

17. (B) The passage stresses the students' *desire to find out more about the objects with which they have been working* as fundamental to Dewey's concept of education.

18. (E) By devoting a full paragraph to Plato's exploits in Syracuse, the author identifies it as one of the *few major events* proposed to be treated in the passage. None of the other choices is supported by information in the passage. Choice (D) is a possible but weaker choice than (E) because it singles out Plato's tactlessness as the *only* factor in the failure of his experiment.

19. (C) The passage emphasizes Plato's connection with Socrates (*Plato was known as one of his most devoted disciples*) as a reason for his departure from Athens, while also mentioning that *Socrates had been put to death*. These statements support the conclusion stated by choice (C).

20. (B) Each of the other choices proposes that Plato's education or interests were, in one way or another, weak or deficient. The passage does not support a conclusion of this kind—Plato is presented in an entirely positive light.

21. (C) Each of the other choices might apply to a great number of individuals, but choice (C) would not and therefore strengthens our sense of Plato's uniqueness.

22. (C) Because of the French Revolution, *the world would never be the same again.*

23. (D) Napoleon appeared at a *crucial period* and *saved France* from forces that would have checked the Revolution. The Reign of Terror, which occurred before Napoleon's rise, is irrelevant to the question, as are the other choices.

24. (C) Choices (A), (B), and (E) contradict explicit information in the passage, and choice (D) is irrelevant. The passage states that *all of Europe* was allied against the forces of French republicanism.

25. (A) Each of the other choices contradicts explicit information in the passage. The passage states that the *masses challenged the protected interests of the privileged few* and that armies of *common* men defeated professional armies.

26. (A) This choice reflects the author's persistent skepticism about the validity and meaning of history. Each of the other choices contradicts that skepticism.

27. (A) Only choice (A) completely denies any meaningfulness in historical events. Choice (C) might come from someone practicing historical subjectivism.

28. (E) This choice is supported by the final sentence of the passage.

29. (B) The series of questions that comprise nearly half of the passage suggests that this is the obvious choice. Choice (C) is not the best choice because the author raises a series of distinct, substantially different questions rather than reiterating the same one.

30. (C) Although the author does not express violent anger, the characterization of the treatment of the Indians as a *tragedy* and the pronouncement that the whites' behavior was *barbaric* certainly express strong disapproval.

31. (B) Although justice was on the Indians' side (second paragraph), *the Indians were not equal to the firepower of the United States army*. Each of the other choices contradicts information in the passage.

32. (C) This is evidence that the whites killed buffalo for sport rather than for subsistence. The disappearance of the buffalo herd is not, of itself, evidence that the buffalo did not provide subsistence to the whites.

33. (D) The point of comparison is that the Atlantic coast Indians were not fierce warriors like the plains Indians. Thus they did not pose any kind of violent threat.

34. (B) Three of the four paragraphs of the passage are devoted to discussing the abuse of the plains Indians. The "weight" which the author gives to this topic suggests its significance.

35. (B) Choices (A), (C), and (D) are irrelevant to the information provided in the passage, while choice (E) contradicts the identification of demography with sociology in the second sentence.

36. (D) The passage discusses *age-specific* birth rates as a measurement that rectifies the *ambiguities* of crude birth rates.

37. (A) To *rectify* is to *set right* or *correct*.

38. (C) The passage discusses the relationship between population increase and military superiority in the first paragraph. Although choice (E) is a reasonable choice for the nation in question, it is irrelevant to the information in the passage.

39. (C) The passage concludes that *it was not sufficient to construct future population estimates from antecedent trends.*

LONGER PASSAGES—CHALLENGING

1. (C) Only this choice is not mentioned in the passage as a Gnostic dualism. Choice (E) is possible but not as good as choice (C) because the distinction between earthly life and afterlife is discussed in the passage (item 4).

2. (C) Greek philosophy is mentioned in connection with Gnosticism (note the references to Plato and neo-Platonism) as is Persian Zoroastrianism (item 1). Choices (A), (B), and (D) contradict information in the passage, and choice (E) is irrelevant.

3. (A) This example is explicitly connected to disagreement among Gnostics about preparing for salvation (item 6).

4. (C) The creation is explained in terms of emanations, or aeons (item 3). Each of the other choices is contradicted by the passage.

5. (A) This question is answered explicitly and directly in item 2.

6. (B) Each of the other choices receives limited discussion in the passage; however, the concern with salvation is mentioned and discussed repeatedly and highlighted by the author in the third sentence as the Gnostics' *main concern.*

7. (C) Each of the other choices is too specific to cover the general discussion of both people and machines that the passage provides.

8. (D) Reviewing the section on control devices, we may conclude that the unfamiliar placement of the steering wheel is *inconsistent with the* American's *prior training.*

9. (D) The final sentence of the first paragraph supports this choice. Choices (B), (C), and (E) contradict information in the passage, and choice (A) is irrelevant to the discussion of managerial training and skills.

10. (D) The third paragraph states that *sensing* and certain types of data processing are best done by people. Choices (A) and (E) are irrelevant to the question, and choices (B) and (C) contradict information in the passage.

11. (C) The passage is a straightforward survey of a number of different company-related items. Choice (A) is not explicitly supported by the passage. Choices (B), (D), and (E) are irrelevant to the particular content and form of the passage.

12. (E) Noting that the passage is a neutral presentation of information, we must eliminate the other choices because they suggest some strong bias.

13. (B) The fourth paragraph states that no society rewards downward mobility. Choices (C) and (E) are irrelevant to the information in the passage, and each of the other choices is contradictory.

14. (C) In general, the passage addresses systems of association in different cultures.

15. (E) The passage describes the progress of an age-set from warriors to family heads to political elders. Choices (A), (B), and (D) contradict information in the passage, and choice (C) is not addressed and is therefore irrelevant to the passage.

16. (B) Although Indian pariahs are mentioned along with Etas as *outcastes,* the living conditions of the Etas are offered as evidence of the restricted pseudo-caste life.

17. (D) The distinction between the Amauga and the Aualuma supports this choice. Choosing any of the other answers would require generalizing beyond available information in the passage.

18. (C) *The Indian caste system is complicated* and characterized by *vagueness.* However, the subcastes are characterized by *specificity,* so choice (A) is incorrect.

19. (A) By referring to attributes of money that were important in the past, the author implies choice (A). Choice (D) is consistent with the passage, but it is explicit rather than implied information.

20. (D) This purpose is especially evident in the second paragraph. Choices (A) and (E) are irrelevant, and choices (B) and (C) contradict information in the passage.

21. (D) The passage states that currency and coin are *government-created* (minted) money and distinguishes their tangible existence from that of a demand deposit, or checking account.

22. (E) The fifth paragraph explains fractional reserve banking in terms of a 5:1 ratio of demand deposits to reserves.

23. (D) In order to explain theories of value at all, the author must first assume that an economic theory can provide a satisfactory explanation. Although the author seems not to favor the economy theory, it is not stated or implied that it is *certainly* wrong. Therefore, (C) is not the best choice.

24. (D) The author seems, for the most part, both objective and learned in matters of money, credit, and banking. Therefore, (D) is the best choice.

25. (B) The passage states that *the goal of the historical process . . . does not imply any consciousness of the goal on the part of some supernatural power.* The passage emphasizes that Marxian philosophy focuses on the *material* order; this emphasis makes (B) the best choice, while it also eliminates choice (C).

26. (D) This choice is supported in the sixth paragraph with the statement that *all individuals are free to gain as much for themselves as they are able to do.* Choices (A), (B), and (E) are statements irrelevant to the information in the passage, and choice (C) is contradictory.

27. (E) The author emphasizes repeatedly that according to this Marxian doctrine, the *course of events* is determined *quite apart from . . . human beings.*

28. (C) The passage states that *the goods that have been produced by labor can be sold for more than the cost of the labor,* which results in an *exploitation of the workers.*

29. (B) The author explains the dialectical movement as a thesis-antithesis-synthesis series.

30. (A) Extending the Marxian concept of history that is explained in the passage leads to this possible criticism. Although choice (E) may be a reasonable statement, it is not relevant to the question, which focuses on problems of class and class conflict.

31. (D) The passage states that *all mental activity is believed to be a by-product of matter.*